The Hollow Doll
(A Little Box of
Japanese Shocks)

THE

(A LITTLE BOX OF JAPANESE SHOCKS)

AVAILABLE
PRESS

HOLLOW DOLL

WILLIAM BOHNAKER

BALLANTINE BOOKS • NEW YORK

An Available Press Book
Published by Ballantine Books

Grateful acknowledgment is
made to the following for
permission to reprint previously published material:
Bandai Co., Ltd.: photograph of ''God-Jesus,'' 1985.
Nippon Beauty Colour: Aerial photograph of Nagoya.
Shukan Manga Times: Manga cartoon entitled
''Sabaki no machi'' by Setsuo Tanabe, 1988.
S.S. Pharmaceutical Co., Ltd: ''I am king'' photograph.

Special thanks is given to *The Daily Yomiuri*,
an English-language Japanese newspaper
published by *The Yomiuri Shimbun*, for the
newspaper reportage used in this book.
The cooperation of this widely read
and much respected daily was essential
in providing authentic, accurate, and
fair-minded reflections of Japanese society.

Library of Congress
Catalog Card Number: 89-92111

ISBN: 0-345-36440-6

Cover design by James R. Harris
Photography by Ed Tsutsumi
Book design by Alex Jay/Studio J
Manufactured in the United States of America
First Edition: April 1990
10 9 8 7 6 5 4 3 2 1

This book is dedicated to
my wife, Glenna, and
my daughter, Tess,
on whom much of
the hands-on research
was inflicted.

Acknowledgments

The author wishes to thank *The Daily Yomiuri* for their permission to use the newspaper reportage found in this book. The cooperation of this widely read and much respected daily was essential in providing authentic, accurate, and fair-minded reflections of Japanese society.

Sincere thanks also to the following for permission to use material: Bandai Co., Ltd.; Nippon Beauty Colour; Setsuo Tanabe; S. S. Pharmaceutical Co., Ltd.

Much gratitude for the advice and information on the finer points of the Japanese language and culture supplied by the cultural affairs officers of the Japanese Consulate General in Portland, Oregon, by the Japan-American Society of Oregon, and by the Japanese Language Department of Portland State University. Thanks also to friends—*gaijin* and Japanese alike—living in Japan and abroad, for their generous help and cooperation. I am particularly grateful to Bill King, Glenna Bohnaker, A. Cardamon, M. Mast, Ayuko Tahara, Ryoko Hironaga, and Hiromi Mizuno.

A special thanks to those Japanese friends who had the courage to expose their social personas as well as the grace to share themselves. Astute enough to know the difference, they are also kind enough to look past our own particular American brand of social persona: contentious, rationalizing, boastful, self-obsessed, self-justifying, uncompromising, never never wrong, and never ever sorry.

Contents

Caveat

The author has made sincere efforts to accurately ascertain and state the facts that appear in this book. Of necessity many of the facts were to be found in other media sources, the accuracy of which the author has had to rely on. The author apologizes for any errors of fact he has unwittingly passed on.

Though all the portraits that appear in the book as the author's firsthand experience are of actual persons, the reader is cautioned against attributing any portrait to any particular real individual, as the writer has taken care to change the names and circumstances sufficiently to conceal the identities of these persons.

"Everyone Ignored Us Until We Sat Down at the Piano and Began to Play"

When I arrived via train at Narita International Airport outside Tokyo to pick up my wife and daughter, I had, without knowing it, and in the short two weeks I'd been in Japan, already begun to recline into the privileged role of *sensei* there: teacher, professor, admired and cosseted firstborn fountain of truths unchallenged and often unsubstantiated. My wife—at the end of her wits and three flights totaling twenty hours, our two-year-old bleary-eyed daughter canted sharply out from her hip as if their interminable flight into the unknown together had yoked them hopelessly in the terrible equipoise of attraction-repulsion—was already feeling the heft of the packages that would characterize her ordained role in Japan.

I was carrying only my wallet and my newly printed business cards, all I needed: a solid currency and an inflated status. I looked marvelous, the picture of ease and security. My wife looked like she was carrying everything: daughter, diaper bag, purse, luggage hanging all over her like vengeful corpses. To tell the truth, she looked like hell, the picture of harried Mother Hubbard who lived in a shoe.

It was a shoe she was about to live in earnest: literally in our tiny apartment, figuratively within the narrow ambit of the same bundles—child, groceries, laundry, shopping bags, presents—she found herself appointed to, or when she refused, always found someone who thought she should be. And I . . . well, I, of course, found myself anointed to carry the stuffed,

smug wallet and to pass out my embossed business cards—my
town criers, as it were, who strode before me, boasting aloud
of my dizzying station.

In time our roles and their inequity became too glaring
even for me to miss, just as in time I came to see there was
more to be understood not only about Japan but about America, and about myself. Japan would compel me to think about
gender, status, conformity and individualism, masters and serv-
ers, docility and violence, and the ways the magician "culture"
turns these into the demons of our identities.

This book is as much about culture and its demons as it is
about Japan. I was never more content, or at odds, than I was
in Japan, never more at home or at a loss. Japan, because it
seems to the Westerner as familiar as it does alien, served to
magnify for me the dreams and distortions of my own culture
and of the human nature we all share, and thus allowed me to
portray both culture and our nature at once as exotic dress and
recognizable face.

In the interest of such a portrayal, this book was conceived also to be as stylistically interesting as frankly informative. It was meant to be entertaining. However, lest some of its
intended truth fail at times to make it to the surface through
the debris of artistic exuberance, the author hastens to explain
himself:

The vignette structure of the book is modeled after its subject—the heterogeneous Japanese social personality, which itself suggested the book's subtitle as well as a metaphor for the
book's organization: the Japanese box lunch *bento*, a mélange
of diverse exotics that achieve their own unexpected compati-
bility. This vignette approach, then, necessarily makes its connections and sense as much through literary means (such as
motif, juxtaposition, caesura, voice and theme) as through the
usual devices of exposition (such as discursive treatment and
explicit transitions).

Moreover, it's hoped the vignettes actually "conduct"
some of the cultural "shocks" to which the book's subtitle refers that strictly discursive prose would tend to disperse. I also

hoped that such an episodic, associative approach could borrow the capacity some Japanese art has to use spaces and intervals (*ma*) to yield meaningful resonances (*yoin*) among the parts of the composition.

Readers with knowledge of Japan are cautioned against equating *omote* (or *tatemae*), the Japanese term for "appearances" and sometimes "face," with the term the author uses to describe the collective personality society fabricates for its members: "social psyche" (or "social personality"). *Omote* is a Japanese perception of themselves, as is its contrast, *ura* (or *honne*), "the other reality behind appearances," broadly meaning practical human exigencies or private truths. A Western point of view, however, might be that so pervasive are the prescriptions of *omote* that often by the law of simple inversion *omote* indirectly prescribes formulas for *ura*. Being decorous, dutiful *sarari-men* at work by day may present *omote*. Being bibulously liberated party boys at play by night may reveal *ura*. But both are formulas. The one is more formal and proper than the other, but to the Westerner *ura* can seem as ritualized, regimented, and conformist as *omote*. Hence "social psyche"— more Western in perception—is used in this book to describe Japanese behavior and attitude that is formulaic, be it either *omote* or *ura*, or something else.

Moreover, whenever I depict such formulaic behavior or attitude, I am identifying it as a habit of the collective Japanese social psyche that dictates it and not as the actions or thoughts of any individual Japanese. Though it may seem to be the individual who is acting and speaking, it is in fact a double illusion of the ventriloquist; in this case it is the hollow doll who throws *its* voice and pulls the human levers. This is a fact of human existence as true (if less pervasive and developed) in the West as it is in the East. Equally, we Americans can be hoodwinked, baffled, amused, charmed, chagrined, or repulsed by our own mass-made mechanical monster stepping forward autonomously to show our mates, our bosses, our friends and neighbors, our allies and competitors, the most god-awful card tricks of our identity. It is not only the Japanese who get the swell idea to sit down at the piano and show everybody their stuff.

Nor, when I draw a distinction between "formulaic" and "rational" social personalities, do I mean to suggest that the Japanese are inherently less capable of reasoning or that Westerners are intrinsically less susceptible to scripted behavior. These terms are meant only to describe a real distinction between the social personalities Japanese and Americans inherit respectively from their separate cultures.

In fact I believe that neither persona is founded on something innately truer or more real than is the other. I do believe, however, that if culture has little to do with ultimate truth, it has a lot to do with what is simply right and wrong: in human terms, how we treat one another. Yet one's identity is so permeated with one's culture it is often difficult to gain enough perspective on it even to recognize what of it is humane or insensitive, helpful or cruel. It's the aim—clear eyed or quixotic—of all cultural critique to abet that perspective.

There are, of course, those who believe that such a distinction between oneself and one's culture is illusory. They identify themselves indelibly with nation or race, custom or ritual, and are likely to see anything short of praise for these as personal attack. Cultural critique to such people is anathema, and they reflexively denounce it as "bashing" (as in "America-bashing" or "Japan-bashing"), making legitimate criticism out to be mere spleen.

To readers with such a view this book may seem to have nothing but demons. Ever alert to the iconoclasm aimed at culture, they are as likely though to overlook the regard and affection for its individuals, the book's heroes—wry or trusting, obedient or rebellious, trapped or escaped, dumbfounded or catching on—heroes whose heroism is the same as it is for individuals anywhere: part victory, part tragedy, part missed-it-by-miles.

If those are right who believe that culture and the individual are ineluctably fused, we are surely doomed, since much of human history is a chronicle of grief inflicted and justified by

cultural myopias. But if they are wrong, as I think they are—
if the enlightenment sought in Zen but found everywhere by
effort or chance is genuine—we will increasingly discover we
are all much more the same than we are different, however
costumed our national dolls, and will rescue our common
humanity.

As for willingness to examine one's identity and the guts
to transform oneself accordingly, the Japanese may well have
a national surplus in this regard now too. Westerners tempted
to smugness by the portraits in this book need only look within
and around us.

The Hollow Doll
(A Little Box of
Japanese Shocks)

Which Picture Postcard?

There's really no such place as Japan. A lot of people will tell you there is, of course, and will write about it as if they've described it. But don't believe them. Sure, there's the tea ceremony, and bullet trains, but you don't do the tea ceremony or ride the bullet trains in the abstract. You experience a particular tea ceremony, in a particular setting—which may strike you as serene or wildly incongruous—with particular people—who may strike you as civilized and enlightened or as habit-driven obsessive-compulsives—drinking tea that may taste exotic or just bitter. Likewise, you take a particular bullet train, which may go 130 miles per hour or not move at all, from one particular city to another particular city at a particular time of day—which may give you an entire car to yourself or pack you standing like stacked bamboo staffs bathed in an atmosphere of exhaled cigarette smoke and digested seaweed.

What's more, it's not just the events and things that are particular, it's you too. It's *you* who are doing these things (or, more often than not, having them done to you) and not just anybody, or worse, nobody, but you with your pecadilloes and idiosyncrasies, your fastidiously justified but irrational likes and hates, your rotten habits, your cultural prejudices, your childishly insecure terror of the strange, or your ridiculously obstinate romanticism even in the face of the corrupt and the just plain bad—in short, poor, real, mortal, I'm-doing-the-best-I-can-gimme-a-break You.

The resulting effect is a bit like the background-foreground confusion we have looking at those pictures that alternately appear as faces and vases. What Japan is depends on who's looking and what he or she chooses to think is essential foreground and what incidental background. Some visitors will emphasize some things and trivialize others, a general habit in human perception, but still a learned habit, however natural it seems to us, and one that Zen, for that matter, tries to correct. Indeed to use a Zen analogy, it's only more flattering, and not more true, that we deem ourselves thinking creatures who incidentally take nourishment, and not ravaging omnivores who now and again, and rather irrelevantly, have thoughts. Is the head half full, or half empty?

So some readers will not recognize the Japan in this book. Or will not like to acknowledge it. This book is not about castles or geishas or Mount Fuji (actually there are several Mounts Fuji—did you see the right one?). It is not about an abstract or sanitized "Japan," a Japan that doesn't exist. It is about individual, contemporary, urban Japanese (urbanites compromise about 80 percent of the population), expressing personal views and involved in actual events. It is about real Japanese living in a transitional epoch that suspends them between, on the one hand, a traditional but increasingly inappropriate collective persona bequeathed them by their culture and manipulated by social elements, and on the other, a modern, separate personality each seeks to develop out of his or her individual nature. Hence it is a picture whose figures are of necessity diverse and in conflict, a portrait of people who struggle to change and of others who fight to stay the same, images for us by turns hilarious, sober, sympathetic, reprehensible, edifying, unfathomable . . . and always recognizably human.

So the people in this book are not idealized. They are shown in those behaviors many Japan observers often minimize or discount, or—for reasons of politics or self-aggrandizement or romantic blindness, or out of the dubious motive of not wishing to offend—will not mention.

Surrender of the Sexes: Marriage of Inconvenience

Inscrutably, My Dear Watson

Woman Arrested In Murder Case

KAWAGUCHI, Saitama —Police Sunday arrested Nobuko Shinozaki, 60, unemployed, of Amimachi, Ibaraki-ken, on suspicion of strangling her common-law husband Seigoro Asakuma, 43, a blacksmith, at his apartment in Kawaguchi more than a month ago.

Shinozaki phoned police Saturday afternoon saying that she had found a friend strangled at his Kawaguchi apartment.

Police arrived and found Asakuma's body with a necktie around his neck and his feet cut off.

What might that Western prodigy of picayune logic and maddening methodicalness, Sherlock Holmes, snatched from his own island kingdom to another where streets often go without names and houses without number, make of this one-of-a-kind Eastern carve job, the ever-patient Watson at his side, confident of his brainy friend's imminent explanation of this crime and the muddled little puzzles it provides? The magic, for instance, by which old Nobuko would be able to strangle a male nearly twenty years her junior, and a blacksmith to boot. For at sixty a Japanese lady has often brought life to gristle and bone alone and might even be seen bent over an empty baby carriage she pushes not out of nostalgia but so that she won't fall over on her face (diet, paddy work, rheumatism, and endemic obsequiousness have created a generation of such pitiful creatures). Or that troubling niggle of the month it took old Nobuko to notice the corpse in the apartment, or for that matter, Seigoro's absence that same month . . . no wonder she fumbled the identity of Seigoro's composting heap. The tie's a nice touch, though, and who would have thought of the vanishing-feet trick!

Watson's patience notwithstanding, this one might leave Holmes-san—the fine machinery of his mind a nest of soba noodles—eating his opium by the lump, Seigoro an unperturbed stink, and Nobuko as untroubled by Western logic as before.

And what are we, hardly the symbolic epitome of Western reasoning that Holmes is, to make of this grizzly, goofy tableau? Aren't the Japanese renowned for their silent, gritty stoicism, their decorous resolution of dispute by compromise, their civility, their orderliness? Then why is this behavior so bizarre, surrealistic even? All right, kill him if you must, but once you've done it don't add any Halloween flourishes. And having done it, keep a cool head and see it through to the end. Get your story straight, dispose of the body, contrive an alibi, make things, well, *reasonable* at least. Get a hold of yourself, Nobuko. You're way over the top on this one.

Japanese society, and the social psyche it creates for the Japanese, run along entirely different lines than do their Western counterparts. Some of the concepts used to identify these lines for the Westerner are more or less familiar to us: compromise, consensus, indirectness, group identity, conformity, politeness. But what makes consensus so dear to them, conformity endemic, civility seemingly obligatory? Why have the Japanese, who, known personally and privately are among the most sensitive, candid, and humane individuals, seemed so often inaccessible and bizarre as a people?

It's only when we understand the deeper forces driving the Japanese along these lines that we can answer such questions, and maybe fathom the small archipelago people who will increasingly influence our jobs, our finances, our consumption and our commerce, our standard of living and our way of life. Japan is a "formulaic" society, America (and the West in general) a "rational" society, so the collective psyches they respectively contrive for their two peoples are completely different. By examining the differences in these two psyches, we can gain some insight into the crucial forces that make the Japanese not who they are but who they *seem* to be, forces that provoke their slavish routines and their fatal mutinies, their sometimes quiet (and sometimes not, dear Nobuko) desperation.

The Stranger

On any other day you'd think that Japan was a nation of one-parent families, parking-lot, department-store, apartment-house matriarchies. But on Sunday you'd discover your mistake.

They emerge into the brief weekly holiday glare like perverse vampires, fags drooping wearily from mouths, eyes puffed up like alcoholic bee stings, uncommunicative, unrepentant, sand-lot staggerers punched out on last night's serious frivolity, now to do their one-day stand as fathers. They shuffle about the dirt-bed playgrounds seemingly oblivious of each other, and often of their kids. The wives, if they accompany their wasted lords, tack ecstatically at their side and chatter with giddy joy at the rare grace of the royal presence. For this will be a brief audience, they know. If he doesn't blow his lunch all over his end of the teeter-totter, he will either eventually wander away out of sheer indifference or beg off from mounting distaste with this paternal responsibility. Until then his wife's volubility serves only to emphasize his giant sulk.

Japanese *sarari-men* ("salary men" = white-collar employees) see their children for about twenty minutes a day. Their job responsibilities extend into social obligations after work, including often drinking themselves into catatonia with their colleagues and feeling up bar hostesses to lesser or greater levels of satisfaction, or just singing away the evening (and night and morning) at *karaoki* bars, where electronic wizardry produces a redeeming sonic background that makes the smothering forgiveness of Phil Spector's "Wall of Sound" seem like wind chimes. Whatever his fancy, though, the *sarari-man* will regularly not slide into home plate until midnight or 2 A.M. (*sarari-man*'s rush hour runs from about 11 P.M. to midnight), long after the kids have bedded down on the futons.

The Other Stranger

And what about his wife, the mate of this drink-sing-feelie king, this jobaholic-cum-unwindaholic—what will she do when her smashed master falls through the door in the A.M.?

Why, she will be waiting up for him dutifully, with tea and rice, and the guidance he needs to go to bed, not to mention to get up four or five hours later—and do it all over again.

Unless, of course, he missed last Sunday's duty muster in the park with the kids. Or is guilty of a graver delinquency that would cause her to lose faith in him—or worse, face with the neighbors. In which case she very well might rebel volcanically against her unappreciated or unrewarded self-sacrifice and strangle the ungrateful sod with his tie, that symbol of the duty-bound, play-bound *sarari-man*. Feeling her slight keenly enough, she might even cut off the erstwhile wanderer's means of transport to his pleasure caves.

Inscription in "Japlish" (Japanese-English) seen on a sweatshirt:

Volkswagen: My Foot—The World

The Deal

The Japanese marriage, as a formula dictated by their social psyche, is, like most fundamental institutions in Japan, pretty much a straight deal, done according to form. Everybody knows what the deal is: She will bow lower and longer than he, and he will work (and play) longer and later. That is, she will make a home for him, and he will toil like a woodchuck. If that sounds like 1950s America, that's only partly so, for the practical ways this deal is played out are often peculiarly Japanese. At least a third of Japanese marriages are still "arranged" by relatives or other go-betweens, and in most of the rest the relatives still have a persuasive say regarding prospective mates. Nor is everyone even eligible as a mate, however good-looking, rich, or bright; there are racial and other, more elusive considerations (about which more later). And even on the rare occasions when these considerations are most flagrantly ignored, the basic deal is still the same, with romantic love way down on the list of motives.

But even though everyone knows what the deal is, what you see is not what you get. In Japan there is a sharp distinction between young people still free of the responsibilities of parenthood and livelihood and these people when they take on the collective identity and obligations of the *shakaijin* (member of society). This happens for a man when he joins a company, so that when he marries two or three years later he has already undergone his transformation to *shakaijin* (and permanently given up going to movies, for instance). But if a woman can thus see in her fiancé the husband he will become, she is actually ill prepared for how little she will actually see him—that is, for his vanishing act into company and colleagues.

A woman, though she goes through a ritual ceremony at the ward office when she reaches twenty, actually becomes a *shakaijin* only when she marries. But unlike the man, she can undergo a virtual overnight metamorphosis. Since her part of the deal in marriage is to provide a home and not an alluring, interesting companion (as a bar hostess at one end of the scale or a geisha at the other might of an evening), she deliberately adopts a bland and sometimes frumpy appearance, emulating in dress and manner the life of stupefyingly unromantic duties that defines the new her: mothering the children and her husband, keeping the house, shopping, managing the money, and driving the kids on to be paragons in an education system that will make them just like their parents. The husband anticipates and approves of this transformation in his wife, because, after all, that's what the deal is all about. Ask them privately and many will tell you that's the way they both want it to be. They don't want to get to know each other. They don't want much to do with each other. The deal's not about relating or developing a deeper, broader, and maturer psyche through intimacy and personal intercourse. For all intents and purposes there's not going to be any intercourse, of any kind. There's no time, no energy for it. And it's not part of the deal.

And as far as the man is concerned, well, there are other places he's going to be getting his intercourse. Unless of course he gets his feet cut off.

Men in Japan are expected to marry at age twenty-five to twenty-eight, women at twenty-three to twenty-five. So they do. Women who fail to do so are called "Christmas cakes," after the pastry nobody will buy past its season. Men who fail to do so are called men.

Minimum Karma

You are just finishing your morning jog down by the "river," a broad but shallow sewer trickling its treakly way over cans, clothes, assassinated bicycles, all the detritus of the modern industrial sink, twenty feet beneath your running path beside the rim of carefully constructed stone conduit walls meant to contain a mighty torrent. You have jogged this path in each of the four seasons without observing the slightest rise in the water level: a couple inches deep where it staggers over the pebbles, a couple feet deep in rare oily pools harboring escaped and abandoned ornamental fish as huge as the giant snapping turtles swimming with them, and no water at all where it has retreated from the gritty, littered bed. You have seen brave men haul out an improbable carp now and again to take home and proudly poison their families. You thread your way through the solid line of cars bordering the river, out of whose windows ooze men's askew legs, dangling arms, slack-jawed stares, the psychic corpses from last night's pleasure wars. . . . Have they been home yet? Do they have homes? Don't they have to go to work?

At last, transported to psychic realms of synaptic stupor from breathing the pure lead-fed atmosphere of million-car morning rush hour, you flop down at the foot of your thousand-person apartment house—disconcertingly called a "mansion" by the Japanese—to pick the viscous leaves out of the computer-designed tread in your running shoes. Oh, God! That wasn't twigs you trod on. It was one of those mouse-size insects that bedeck themselves with leaves for camouflage . . . too clever for modern city life. You are privately pondering the avowed Japanese reverence for nature and the pus hole made of it here, when, bursting from his cell in the giant cement hive comes Masa, suit coat but sans tie, clutching his guts and grimacing horribly. You glance at your tell-all Sanyo watch: 7:15 A.M. Truly a portent! As a salary man for an insurance company, Masa is usually out with clients and cronies till 2:00 A.M. and not at the office until 9:00 the next morning. He spots you and halts in his tracks, wipes away the mask of torture as though it were a mere fad, bobs his usual ambiguous bow he gives to you as *gaijin* (foreigner), and cheerily names a great Midwestern state in America, *"Ohayo!"* (Good morning). What a trooper, that Masa, never lets the side down. You return his greeting and he runs off backward now, smiling at you and gesturing that his stomach is exploding.

Masa roars off in his *Bluebird* sedan and you walk over to throw your computer-designed joggers into the large refuse bin (the big-bug goo will never come out of the tread). Kyoko, Masa's round, ingenuous wife, utterly candid and human, comes out the same door Masa did, carrying the morning trash and grinning triumphantly. It seems Masa has finally done it to himself: partied and entertained himself into an ulcer. Just as she had warned him. Countless times. Futilely. Now he is rushing off to the hospital to see if the doctors can save him. Kyoko refused to take him. Her small revenge. His own karma, so to speak.

Doctor Grin

Even if that rogue Masa is lucky enough to confine his much worse deserts to this tiny spite measured out by his wife, he is not home free. When he arrives at the hospital for outpatient care, he finds much of the city's population is already ahead of him in line. The halls are jammed with petitioners. It looks like the *chikatetsu* (subway) during rush hour, except that it will take much longer to see the doctor than to get home or to work. Masa could die waiting stoically for his turn.

He could also die having his turn. If Japanese pharmacology is one of the most advanced in the world, Japanese medicine in practice is wildly erratic. In a culture where even some doctors stay out late unwinding like *sarari-men*, where lawsuits are rare, and where personal apologies alone are regularly considered sufficient amends for even fatal behavior, where preventive medicine is at best marginal and hence, too, the knowledge of the body's general health requirements disseminated to the population, some of the important incentives that make for quality health care are just not in the deck.

More troubling, Masa himself knows, is that he could die even if the doctors tell him he's all right. As a rule, Japanese doctors lie to their patients who are, or seem, terminally ill with cancer. The doctors claim they do it to spare their patients' feelings a painful and pointless knowledge. One might suspect they do it also to spare their own feelings. After all, there is a whole bowlful of directness and disharmony (bugbears in Japanese discourse) in telling someone he is going to drop dead soon.

In Masa's case this possibility seems even more vivid and threatening, because just a few months ago one of his friends died of stomach cancer in this very way, unaware of his disease or his impending fate. So, even when Masa is told he simply has an ulcer and better drink less, he is not relieved. In fact his knowledge of his own ignorance in this essential matter, a knowledge and an ignorance in which he is forced to conspire, dooms him to a continual corrosive anxiety, not the best medicine for an ulcer.

Cancer-Obsessed Man Slays Two

KAWASAKI, Kanagawa —A man who thought he had lung cancer and was hospitalized again and again killed his wife and mother-in-law in Kawasaki Sunday morning. The motive was not immediately clear, however.

Kawasaki police were alerted by a phone call from the home of Hatsuki Miyano, 54.

The phone caller, Miyano's son, a 23-year-old office worker, said his father had killed his mother and grandmother.

Police hurried to Miyano's house and found Miyano's wife Yoko, 47, had been strangled.

They also found Murako Imamura, 64, Yoko's mother, stabbed to death with a kitchen knife stuck in her left breast, at her house about 200 meters away from Miyano's.

Police arrested Miyano at his home on charge of murder.

According to police, Miyano was hospitalized in the spring of last year for a pain in the chest but was soon released because no

trouble was detected.

But he was obsessed with the idea that he had lung cancer and complained of insomnia and loss of appetite.

He was hospitalized for a second time on Feb. 14.

This time he said his trouble was depression.

The doctor said the hospital was scheduled to release Miyano shortly because he did not need hospitalization.

Cop Shoots Self

A police officer who thought he had cancer of the stomach committed suicide with his pistol early Sunday at Totsuka Police Station in Tokyo's Shinjuku-ku.

Assistant Police Inspector Hiroshi Kudo, 45, was found lying on the landing between the third and fourth floors of the police station at about 4:23 a.m., with a gunshot wound in his right temple.

He was rushed to a nearby hospital but was dead on arrival.

He had gone on night duty Saturday evening and took a nap from 1 a.m.

When he did not return to duty at 4 a.m., as expected to, his subordinate searched the police station and found him lying on the floor in his uniform.

Kudo had received medical treatment at Tokyo Police Hospital since last August for stomach trouble.

The doctor said Kudo had an ulcer but Kudo thought it was cancer.

He left a note saying he had cancer and was weary of life.

He was survived by his wife, 39, a daughter and a son.

Japanese doctor: I've got some good news and some bad news for you.
Japanese patient: What's the good news?
Japanese doctor: You're fine.
Japanese patient: Then what can be the bad news?
Japanese doctor: You're fine.

A Gentleman

On those mornings when everything goes right—as everything is meant to go in Japan, as everyone is trying his hardest to have it go, as the rest of the world is meant to see it go—Kyoko drags Masa the yen-winner from his death sleep, prepares him a breakfast of miso soup and a hundred bitty minnows in raw-egg dip, which he usually eats in privileged solitude, then harangues him dressed and out the door.

Today you and Masa are both taking the same bus in to Kanayama, traffic hub and commuter bee swarm. Masa is being a good boy of late (at least temporarily), coming home early and joining the regular 7:15 A.M. convoy to work. Kyoko has confided to your wife that she punched Masa in the nose three nights ago when he careened in at midnight, so perhaps it is this shock therapy that has taught him at whose indulgence he rules. What's more, Kyoko has apparently demanded the *Bluebird* today or Masa would be driving to work. Walking beside you to the bus stop, his feet symbolically gone, Masa seems to glance wistfully at all the comfortable cars being dutifully

warmed up by wives to launch their hubbies properly into the
day's economic Jehad. All over Japan this ritual of obeisance
is taking place, Masa must be thinking, while I, poor unhonored
shakaijin, must join the throng of spear carriers. His depression
can only be deepened when you reach the bus stop, since even
for those warriors who fate has decreed must take public transport, there is a respectful send-off. Off to the side of the queue
you join stands a pool of loyal retainers—wives, some children,
even two or three leashed dogs (the latter all of the same short-
haired, stump-legged breed, oddly, as if this morning the dogs
themselves had reached a consensus on national canine homo-
geneity), from which fan club emanates a steady encourage-
ment of growls, bobbing, and mutter. Masa and you board
unsung.

But once aboard the bus Masa has other things to worry
about. Being seen with you, a *gaijin*, is a matter of agonizing
ambivalence to Masa. On the one hand he is proud to swim in
the new direction, *kokusaika*, "internationalism," that is Japan's future. On the other hand it is impolitic to be seen too
much in the company of foreigners, risking as it does the alienation from one's fellow Japanese, an impossible deadly doom.
Worse for Masa, you give up your seat to one of those pitifully
bent *oba-san* scarecrows, a near unheard-of, incomprehensible
squandering of male power and privilege in Japan. Men never
give up their seats to women. Women give up their seats to
children! After all, it's not a matter of doing what's reasonable.
It's a matter of doing what's done. And what will Masa do? You
have put him on the spot, for there is another wizened madame
in the aisle next to his seat. Will he launch himself into the
brave new world of international standards and decorum and
let his side down? Or will he hold tight to the saddle of hereditary bully greed and be one of the boys? Immediately aware of
the profound symbolism of his predicament, Masa clamps his
mouth shut weakly, stares vacantly, and pours sweat, literally,
from his brow. For a moment all of Japan seems to be in that
bus, on the way not to crazy Kanayama but to its future or its

past, everyone breathlessly watching to see where Masa will take them.

You can almost hear the subcutaneous male groans and female sighs as Masa rises and says, *"Dozo"* (please), to the old lady, whose agog stutter of gratitude is actually the only human sound on the bus.

You smile at Masa. His earlier reversals at the hands of the distaff side of gender have obviously played a role in this momentous gesture, but there was still courage in it. You wink at him.

He smiles back.

And from then on Masa makes damn sure he takes a different bus than you.

Feminisuto: revealing how strange still is the idea, and the practice, some Japanese regularly use this adopted word to mean "a man who is kind to women."

Onion and Skin

If the Japanese man gets to be the samurai in this psychodrama, what's left for the Japanese woman? Whatever's left, it seems, and none of it terribly inspiring. By and large her identity is given her by default, according, on the one hand, to what her lord won't or as often can't do and, on the other, to what his nouveau-samurai dream of her is. Consequently her identity is dichotomized into two extreme poles, lackey and ingenue, on an obviously narrow and confining scale. As lackey she is expected to . . . well, to do everything. One is tempted to list her tasks, like cooking and cleaning, raising the children, shopping, getting the wallet to bed at night and up in the morning, but that would be endless and even then wouldn't come as close to conveying the ubiquity of her obligations as does "everything." Certainly "everything" connected with the family's practical and immediate maintenance.

Yet even from the point of view of the Japanese wife herself, these tasks are not just imposed burdens, nor do they collectively acquire the self-image of "lackey" for her. Most Japanese wives, like most Japanese *sarari-men*, do not make a distinction between themselves and their duties. A Westerner, man or woman, usually has a strong sense, illusory or not, of his or her individual so-called "real" self, independent of any particular activity he or she might do or have to do. Westerners tend to look upon their jobs as something they do. Japanese *sarari-men* "are" their jobs. In identifying himself a Japanese *sarari-man* is likely to say, *"Watashi wa Toyota no Sato desu."* ("I am Toyota Company's Mr. Sato.") In other words, it is secondary, if not actually incidental, who Sato is individually; what is primary is that aspect of him that is Toyota. His source of his personal identity is social, not personal.

The same is true of the Japanese wife. She *is* her family obligations, and a hefty portion of her identity is one of "duty," the sweaty, chthonic expression of which is simply "chores." Yet she does not see this as an imposition upon her real self. Her responsibilities might otherwise be associated with any of the numerous Japanese terms for duty *(sekinin, on, giri, gimu, makoto, seii, nimmu)*, yet so synonymous are she and her duty that there is no ideal Japanese word to designate the latter. She *is* her duty to her family.

Try peeling, Zen-like, the layers of skin from this onion, and the onion will not emerge but vanish.

Stop Me Before I Shop Again

If there is a single activity in the diurnal orbit of duty describing the Japanese wife's identity, it is "shopping." The wives all seem to be acquainted with and to use the English word for this activity, suggesting not only its universality but it's special nature and perhaps even the tacky spiritual correlative—not to mention "high"—behind it. The concept includes not only the essential quotidian foraging along the supermarket aisles for provender, but the mindless, endless (and sometimes purchaseless) daily wandering in the forests of tinsel harbored in the great mountain ranges of consumer goods: Maruei, Mitsukoshi, Meitetsu, Matsuzakaya, and their cut-rate analogs, Daiei, Jusco, Uni. It is this second kind of shopping, discretionary shopping, that reveals the genius of the Japanese wife for her willingness to make a virtue of necessity, or at worst to make the best of a bad situation. She has been shrewdly able to exploit the crummy, mandatory task of doing the shopping into the contemporary industrial version of Liberation: "going shopping," a basic formula in the Japanese social psyche.

And go she does. Jamming the buses and subways, the streets and sidewalks, the banks and the magic mechanical money machines, the store aisles, counters, registers, for hours on end, in trips and shifts, through rain and snow, and humidity thick as shellac, trudging on foot or puffing on clumsy balloon-bread-tire bikes.

And shop she does. In fact the economic philosphers of the West who imagine all would be well for their economies—especially the American economy—if the Japanese would just stimulate their domestic spending, might do well actually to go shopping in Japan. While jostled among the consuming swarms of women in any of these *depaatos* (department stores), it is hard to imagine how spending could be any more stimulated, frenetic as it is already, without introducing amphetamine into the Japanese breakfast.

Whoever the culprits, one is not the Japanese consumer who doesn't buy enough; she does almost nothing but buy. But she usually buys only what she can with cash, unlike we dream-driven credit-binge junkies in the West. And what she buys is often socially obligatory and hence usually Japanese made. She can spend tens of thousands of dollars on cumpulsory kimonos for weddings and other ceremonies, thousands more for culturally determined gifts (Japanese seem obliged to give gifts constantly and on the slightest pretext; many of them are never opened, and others simply recycled into the gift melee), and even more on the family auto, made in Japan, naturally—or Germany, snobbishly—though Western goods are vampiricly marked up, with the apparent complaisance of the government.

Not only has the Japanese wife turned the menial task of

shopping to her own advantage by transforming it into an all-day spree, she has also made her duty to do all the shopping into an ironclad justification for holding and managing all the money to do it. Almost universally Japanese husbands turn over every cent of their earnings to their wives, who make the decisions about how and in what proportion it is to be spent, including how much the good ole boy will get to fritter on drink and bar hostesses. His feet can be amputated in more ways than one, though this particular banker must be ever mindful of the uxoricide too stingy a dole has now and again unleashed upon the Japanese wife.

Moreover, the power over the money held by the Japanese wife, as much as it contributes to her legitimate sense of self-worth and as much as it assuages her dissatisfaction with the lopsided fun-divvy, should not be misconstrued as real license. For the Japanese wife is snookered here even in this source of her pride. The areas of expenditure are practically or culturally fixed—food, shelter, clothes, the kids' education, entertainment, gifts, ceremonies, and so on—so in fact her power and privilege turn out often to be merely another responsibility (making the husband's salary stretch) rather than a privilege to spend it any way she wants. Check and mate again.

Generally the urban Japanese wife has been excluded from her husband's routines and circles. Many a husband still eats breakfast lordly and alone. Then he belongs to the office all day, to his colleagues in the evening, and often to the company on wives-not-invited getaways. For centuries women were even forbidden to set foot on Mount Fuji. Such exclusion has tended to give the Japanese wife very few activities (children and shopping) with which to identify. Thus it isn't rare to find such women expressing not the expected Confucian wish to bear a son but the fervent personal desire to have a daughter. As a female Japanese acquaintance once said, so she could have someone to take and teach shopping.

Not to be alone in that Dantean ring of perpetual traipsing and ogling and toting.

Apprentice Japanese Wife

You know what he is thinking, your boss, sitting there, brooding about your wife. It has become known that she is having a difficult time adapting to Japanese life. One proof of this is her belief that for women there is no Japanese life. A second proof is that she has stated this belief. A third is her stating this publicly. There are many more proofs, demonstrated in her agitation, her anger, her loudness, but they are too shameful to speak of, directly. *Gaijin* women seem so demanding, so self-indulgent, so . . . uncalm. As her husband it is your responsibility to calm her. "Be stable!" he exhorts you. Be a unicorn, you tell yourself as futilely. "You must make her understand that now she must live as a Japanese!" There seems to be some confusion about what's the problem and what's the solution, the poison and the antidote—a "cultural conflict," so you don't point it out. You do try to tell him that there is about as much chance of this as there is of Elvis cutting a new song, not even a mathematical one, that your wife doesn't want to become a Japanese wife. Your boss starts back as if slapped. Who would not wish to become a Japanese wife, given the lucky break? his expression seems to ask. You do not suggest that he himself is probably a good guess. You remind him that she was a professional in her own country and that the absence for her here of meaningful employment, its status and rewards, makes her life seem trivial and unfulfilling. *"So desu ka,"* ("I see . . .") he acknowledges thoughtfully.

The next day you are called in again. You walk into the room to discover that all your immediate colleagues, four or five of them, are present. They've obviously taken a meeting on this one. You bow, smiling at everyone (God, you've begun to do it too!) and sit down. Your boss seems especially pleased with himself. A bad sign, you've learned. Pride goeth before . . . , and all that. "Bee-ru-san," he addresses you, "we understand now." You look around at the nodding, sympathetic faces. You set yours to face grim fate. "Your wife-san is unhappy, she is disoriented." So far so good, two for two.

"We understand. She does not know how to shop!"

Oh, well, two out of three ain't bad.

The following morning the wife of a colleague zealously presents herself at the door of your apartment to train the new apprentice. *Gambatte!* (Go for it!)

In the Dust of the Campaign Trail

Though there is one notable exception in Takako Doi, leader of the Japanese Socialist Party (the party in perpetual opposition), there are very few women representatives in the Japanese parliament, the Diet (28 out of 764). The expected role of women in politics is to help their husbands in politics. This is especially the case when the politician husband is off in Tokyo while the Diet is in session, and his local constituency expects her to act in his stead—but only ceremonially, not practically. In these circumstances she will make ceaseless rounds to supporters' homes, deliver ritual greetings at various functions, and attend a funeral every few days. However, she must be careful not actually to speak out on politics or she will be seen as presumptuous, the penalty for which is her husband's rejection by the voters and the family's abrupt affliction with yen-hemophilia. To stave off this grinning specter, campaign wives will submit themselves even to that social formula that ritualizes the wife's subordination to her husband's ambitions, however deluded: She will bow down on all fours—toes-knees-hands-head in the dust—and beg passersby to vote for her man.

The husband of a female politician, on the other hand, is usually not to be caught at this task.

A Japanese wife has been said to have three lords: her father, her husband, her son.

Teen Angel

You've been alerted there's going to be a beauty contest on *terebi* (TV) tonight. You get a can of Asahi beer from the

fridge (a cold box about the size of a footlocker), pull up some
cushions in front of your bilingual, remote control, stereo, on-
screen-display, mat-black Sanyo (seemingly bigger than the
fridge, but with the enigmatic annotation beneath the company
logo: "Intellectual Funny Form—Static Impact In Your Interior"), and you're ready for the cultural cheesecake.

Showtime! Colored strobe lights, frenetic pulse music, fast
camera pans—things look promising. Then, with astonishing
abruptness, the whole world seems to grind to a halt: the cheesy
beat, the rainbow light explosions, the panting camera. Hey.
The five contestants walk demurely onto a low stage without
backdrop and etiolated by plain hot white light, and . . . face
the camera. Without smile, evocative pose, animal élan . . .
without movement even. This could be grim business. Sensing
yourself teetering on the precipice of another cultural disappointment, you glug down your Asahi can of beer just like Mel
Gibson does in the Japanese TV ad, a little pudgy and dull and
wasted in the eyes that gaze blindly out to sea (how many times
did he have to quaff a can before they got a wrap?), and even
wipe the foam from your upper lip with the empty can like your
hero. You know immediately you're going to need all the for-
tifying you can swallow.

The contestants are put through their paces. Or rather
everybody and everything else—the judges, the camera, the
hysterical electronic toteboard—goes through its paces, but the
contestants never move. They stand square front, feet together, hands locked behind or before them, shoulders modestly slumped. In turn they are queried by the judges—all male,
all TV celebrities, one aging goat with dyed hair, one loud braying older goat with undyed hair, one young goat and one popular slob. It soon becomes clear that whatever the avowed
venue, the girls are just cannon fodder for the male celebrities'
wit and antics. The men fabricate clever questions—and the
answers to them—while the girls chirp staccato *hai*'s (yeses) in
continuous subservience. The men—not the girls—are the stars.

And "girls" they are. They couldn't be over fifteen, and

even if they are, it's only a technicality, because they look twelve. Even a generous eye cannot trump up their inchoate, callow forms to the electric realms of glamour. Nor have they even tried for this themselves. Their bathing suits are purposely frumpy, stale affairs, even in the case of the one girl who wears a two-piece. One girl has actually been put into a shapeless cotton sweatshirt for a top. None seems to have considered or been allowed the enhancements of hairdo or makeup.

Perhaps they know the real intent of this charade and felt it was pointless from the outset. In fact they are not intrinsically (or not yet) the beauty-contest type—if something exploitive to begin with can be said to have "standards." While being questioned by the wisecracking male geeks, the girls are scrutinized by a close-up camera panning slowly from feet to face, not failing to leer at crucial spots along the way. Vital stats are superimposed on the screen to mathematically hype the visual rush. This notwithstanding, the contestants' submissive stance makes them appear a bit pigeon-toed, slump-postured, without the support of healthy muscle beneath the amorphous baby fat, except for one girl whose hint of "daikon legs" (a Japanese-devised metaphor after the large, squat Japanese turnip) betrays an ancestral genetic disposition. In other ways they seem identical: 5-feet 1-inch tall, 31-inch bust, 23-inch waist, 33-inch hips—nice, ordinary Japanese schoolgirls, but still jejune in personality and form. Where are all those alluring adult women you see parading daily in the streets by the hundreds now that the nation needs them?

In spite of their intentional ordinariness, their deliberate overt sameness, the contestants are never called upon to differentiate themselves on the basis of individual talents. They are asked only to stand there, and they do.

Mercifully, if tastelessly, the toteboard goes ape for a bit, then settles on a winner. She looks uncomfortably like a wildly popular girl cartoon character seen on TV by the whole nation, children and adults alike, every evening.

Even in victory the lucky girl seems unmoved. Impassively

she accepts her certificate with a murmur . . . then more
strobes, jingle up, dolly camera and fade to you and Mel, both
of you right now looking dull-eyed and soul-shrunken.

Peter Pumpkin Aesthetics

If, by formula, the Japanese wife has virtually all the responsibilities and duties of home foisted on her, she also has
projected on her all the virtues her husband wants her to have
but doesn't want himself. Besides being the servant of his practical needs, she is also the repository for his fantasies of domestic virtue: his batman and his anima in one harried being.
Often addressed by her husband around the house with the
rough English equivalent of "Hey you" *(Oi!)*, the Japanese wife
is still expected to be purer than Caesar's. The more so, probably, since her husband has exhausted all his own purity at
work and celebrated its absence after work. And what a test
of virtue for her, given the almost total lack of sexual activity
going on—for her, at least.

To help her remain on this narrow-gauge track of virtue,
a whole standard of beauty—aesthetics perhaps even—exists:
kawaii. It's easily one of the most used expressions, certainly
by women, and seems to invoke the realm of virtue more predictably inhabited by serious gods such as Duty, Allegiance, and
Stoicism. Perhaps best translated as "cute," "lovely," or "en-
dearing," *kawaii* is better gushed than merely spoken, so as to
match form to content. Children are *kawaii*, as are their toys
and stuffed animals, as are some real animals, such as pandas,
for that matter, as well as the wrapping paper on the ubiquitous presents, women's clothes, and anything else that's cute.
Including women—or the prescribed Japanese male's formula
for the archetypal Japanese woman, an ingenue caricature: a
frail, fawning, self-effacing, undeveloped, peeping creature
giggling behind a shy hand that also often hides disarmingly
vulnerable crooked teeth. You see this beloved stereotype in
the phonebook-size comics, in TV cartoons, in advertisements,

and in the poor legions of real women who acquiesce to bring this callow male fantasy to life.

The raison d'être for all this obliging sappiness, of course, is to protect males from having to face the demands and rights of an equal partner, a mature woman who is fully sexed, autonomous, with equal access to all the options he has. With and in the face of such a real person, the Japanese male would not only have to give up his franchise on fun, he would have to endure the kind of realistic and objective comparisons (as well as honest criticism and rightful demands) true equality permits. In other words he would have to grow up.

But like any child not required to mature, many a Japanese male preserves his ego and his privilege by allying himself with people who won't threaten either, the essential partner in this conspiracy being a wife who is sexless, plain, and obsequious, that is, a little girl . . . even if in fact she is none of these— certainly need not be these, were she not confined to the pumpkin of his fears and personal insecurity.

That she is more the creature of his self-serving imagination than her own woman, as apologists argue by making her the satisfied coequal in this deal, is embarrassingly obvious. All those decked-out beauties one sees in the streets and *depaatos* of Japan can permit themselves such attractiveness only as long as they are single. Their startling overnight abandonment of beauty for frumpdom immediately following the honeymoon can serve only the husband's sense of security and hardly her self-image. Nor can so-called beauty contests, which are in fact not even concerned with superficial glamour, demeaning enough by enlightened standards, but with the patronizing criteria of enforced plainness, much as beggar parents once judged their children not on their comeliness but on their pitifulness.

Robert C. Christopher, in his fine book *The Japanese Mind*, quotes a Japanese government information bulletin; "We may expect many tall, slim beauties among Japanese women in the future. The same physical transformation, however, will make men appear weak and less masculine." One suspects, too, that it is a fear akin to this one, and not the concern for women's well-being, that has seen the Japanese Ministry of Health refuse to make birth-control pills (and the personal autonomy they foster) generally available to women. By default abortion (and maybe deprivation) have become the Japanese woman's main means of birth control.

In fact, for the Japanese male persona, a key feature of this alluring image of "the girl" is passivity. And given the force of cultural prescriptions, Japanese women have naturally tried to accommodate the Japanese male's and the culture's minimalist image of them in this regard. The girl contestants in the "beauty contest" are careful not to move or to speak more than brief squeaks. As could be expected, the social psyche imposes a passive self-image on women that extends into love and sex. On TV it still seems that the two most commonly portrayed types of lovemaking are the purchased, and the forced (often quite simply rape), whose lucky recipients only gradually if ever succumb to the imposed pleasure. Out of bed, of course, many Japanese women are still perpetually skidding around on their knees to feed their husbands and greet male guests, and even learn to effect a special "scurry" (originally acquired via the lovely but constricting kimono), a flat-footed rapid shuffle that announces that they are hurrying to suit not themselves, God forbid, but *him*.

And even institutions that on the surface seem devoted to the interests and betterment of women can upon deeper examination reveal a similar manipulation. Relatively recently, for instance, an extensive system of junior colleges was created in Japan, ostensibly with the purpose of encouraging more women (only about a quarter of Japanese university students are female) to get postsecondary education. Laudable, of course. But not entirely altruistic. After all, university capacity could simply have been increased. However, with Japanese women expected (and vehemently encouraged) to quit work at twenty-five, it is highly advantageous to employers to get women into the workplace as soon as possible (in this case two years sooner) to extract just that much more ill-paid, low-status,

brain-dead work from them. In short, who are employers going
to get who is intelligent, educated, and still willing to pour the
tea, a task that might be a female employee's principal one
regardless of her title and degree. Japan is filled with women
who have degrees in substantial and exotic fields, who have
even studied abroad and speak foreign languages, who are,
through no choice of their own, just wives or tea-pouring
"O.L.'s" (Office Ladies).

Shujin, one of the Japanese words for "husband," means:
"master" or "employer." *Okusan*, one of the Japanese words
for "wife," means: "the inside person."
And there he kept her very well.

More good news: There is a Valentine Day in Japan too.
More bad news: It's just the men who get, and the women
who give.
In fact, on Valentine Day women employees are expected
to give *giri choko* (duty chocolates) to their bosses in thanks.
Don't ask, "Thank's for what?"

Cult of the Girl

The attempt by many a Japanese male to disarm his wife
of any qualities that might threaten him—profession, beauty,
sex, and often knowledge and volition—in effect turns a woman
into a girl. More precisely it prevents a girl from ever fully becoming a women. Nor is it only the wife whose nature is distorted. Along this route prescribed by the social psyche
everybody's development gets arrested or bent. The man, of
course, stays a pampered adolescent, living out the skimpy
character line that is the adolescent's notion of manhood. The
wife, as we've seen, becomes *okasan* ("Mama"), not only to
the children but to the husband, feeding and tucking him in,
managing his money, and scolding him when he transcends even
his normal delinquencies. And with the wife thus unsexed, the
image of the girl becomes ambiguous. No longer only the child

of her father, she is also the Japanese male's collective archetype of a nonthreatening, obliging female and becomes as well
a desirable, if forbidden, sexual object.

Take for instance a recent and very popular contemporary
song in Japan, "Oh, Daddy," a lighter-than-air ditty whispered
in demure sotto voce by one to thirty preadolescent girls of the
same non-beauty-contest ilk. Seen performed on TV—necessary
to register the full effect—the view shifts from the swaying
ingenues to the Oh Daddies in the audience, whose every visage
is the twisted, sobbing mask of a man torn apart on a cross of
paternal affection and carnal desire. Of Japanese female singers in general, the great majority seem to be adolescent.

Occasionally this psychic conflict finds itself inevitably re-
solved in some father-daughter incest at home. Yet since sex,
by cultural injunction, happens so little in the Japanese home
anyway, the usual redemption for the crucified male gets
worked out in the countless cabarets and touch-bars, whose
hostesses dress the theme of the *jogakusei*, the schoolgirl in
uniform: socks and sailor dress. Along these same lines there is
a widespread belief in Japan, part fact and part pure male wish,
that real schoolgirls, in order to pay for clothes or college, take
part-time jobs as schoolgirls in these sex-for-pay clubs. That's
enough twists in identity to satisfy even Jean Genet.

Whatever the truth, in order to keep their larders stocked,
the flesh peddlers can no longer count on impoverished rural
farmers selling them their surplus daughters (farmers, if not
daughters, in Japan are now one of the better protected groups
of voters), and must resort to soliciting new staff actively. One
of the more common ways of doing this is to canvas for recruits
via wallet-sized advertising cards dropped off in public phone
booths. A visitor can generally find several of these cards in
any phone booth in or near a city's entertainment quarter. Why
phone booths in particular is a mystery, but perhaps the pan-
derers believe that any woman driven to make a public phone
call on these streets is desperate enough to blindly obey the
card's instructions.

Speculation aside, these cards tout their purveyors' need

for "models" and "companions," and boast they will even supply successful applicants with pretty clothes. Many of the cards
thoughtfully request potential applicants not to worry if it's
their first time for this kind of "job."

Besides such written assurances and incentives, these
cards often sport colorful sketches of the ideal applicant, cartoons featuring not an alluring body, but a face which is an
anima fantasy of childlike innocence. It is the wide-eyed face
of a little girl.

Yet, as many Western visitors discover, you may never get
admitted to a real Japanese love hotel, cabaret, or touch-bar
(as opposed to the tourist variety) to see those girls. Westerners
are regularly and unceremoniously turned away from their
doors. In part this is simply a way of keeping private from foreigners the unedifying spectacle of Japanese *sarari-men* letting
it all hang out, not to mention preempting what in their view
is competition. (In an enlightening if embarrassing reversal of
the formula dictated by our Western social psyche, the Japanese impute the same superpotency to Caucasian males that the
latter are used to imputing to blacks.) However, at the same
time, Japanese men defend this particular exclusivity by saying
they are protecting their Japanese women from outside eyes.
As we'll later discover, Japanese explanations for their behavior often have a different premise than do Western explanations. In this case, though, such an explanation rings true. For
to the Japanese male persona she is not only a calculating entrepreneur—she is also, psychically, his little girl.

Rori-kon: a special Japlish term used to identify the Japanese
male's obsession with young girls. It's short for *Rorita-
kompurekksu* ("Lolita complex"). Nabokov-san would be
happy.

CHAPTER 2

The Good,
The Bad, And
The Nonexistent:
Irrational
Reasoning and
the Formulaic
Society

Passersby Injured In Drunken Brawl

YOKOHAMA—A group of a dozen youngsters, including high school students, had a drunken brawl on a street in Yokohama with another group of 15 high school boys, and four passersby who attempted to stop the free-for-all were injured, one of them seriously, it was learned Thursday.

Police said that by Wednesday, three of the violent youths had been put into custody at the Yokohama District Public Prosecutors Office for having played principal roles in assaulting the passersby.

The melee took place in the early morning of Nov. 17 after the two groups had a quarrel over a mere trifle as they passed each other on the street of Kami-Ooka, Konan-ku.

The four passersby, all company employees, including Hiroyuki Hori, 22, tried to persuade the fighting boys to end the scuffle, but many members from one of the youth groups beat them up, saying, as quoted by police, "Don't do unwanted things!"

"Don't Do Unwanted Things"

In Japan *everything* is meant to go *right*, that is, according to social formula. The Japanese take endless pains to see that it does. They will tell you that it is absolutely necessary that everything goes right since there are so many of them crowded so close together social life itself can exist only if the right things happen. They perceive their society to be an intricate machine, a fantastic clockwork mannequin, the failure of any single piece of which might bring the entire magic creation to a deathly halt. Each piece knows its task and its place in the whole. Each piece knows it's a part of the whole and that each piece depends upon the other. So *everybody* is very anxious about *anything* going wrong, about *any* part failing to do its job, about *anybody* doing Unwanted Things—even in the midst of other Unwanted Things too late to prevent happening.

The Future of the Nation

Your day at last dribbled to an end, you trudge into the drab huddle of shacks and rain sheds that is Odaka train station and onto the cement platform, the gray winter sky above the tracks scribbled over with a zany web of telephone and electric lines, the vistas in both directions an elementary art lesson in vanishing-point perspective tricked out in marching utility poles and dreary, shrinking apartment facades. As if the scene were not depressing enough, the fates have arranged for you and the local high school to throw the towel in at the same time today, and the platform is packed with boys in their black-crow school uniforms waiting for the same commuter train to Kanayama as you. The air is meat-locker frigid and thick with their smoky breath, yet none of them wears a coat, stoic in their Spartan training for a future of subservience to other—man-made—elements: company and culture. There are only a few girls among them, and you wonder if theirs is one of the basically all-male private high schools, or if the boys have been overzealous in their training and raped and killed the girls, as in the ubiquitous *manga* comics. Maybe the girls are just off in their school uniforms being bar hostesses. Your disillusioned musings are interrupted by a new immigration of jostling boys onto the platform, and you move off to the remotest edge, out from under the platform's protective awning—you, too, a Spartan—to the weather, yes, but not to corporate regimentation like the Japanese. No. To the poignance and pathos of isolated existence in the face of an indifferent cosmos. But already the boys have begun to cast mocking glances your way and a tweaking susurrus of *"Harro! Harro!"* (Hello) ripples your way from them. You realize with a sting that to them you are not a tragic existential hero. Just white foreign freak.

Mythless, you settle down to wait for the dilapidated Meitetsu train to arrive and bear you and your detractors home. A bell clangs dully and a dirty red light flashes over the tracks. But it's just the dilapidated Meitetsu in the opposite direction. It drags in to a halt at the platform on the other side of your tracks. Across the gulf you watch the train's passengers enduring impassively their daily crush. A few of the lucky ones who've managed to get seats by the window cloister themselves in newspapers; the unlucky stand nose-to-nose, or face-to-glass at the exit doors. Few seem to be talking.

Something at the edge of your field of vision catches your eye as it arches past you over the tracks and splats against the train opposite. Chortling among the boys on your platform. Then another experiment in the parabolic physics of trajectory. Splat. Applause, a couple of *Yattas!* ("I did it!"). Right on the window. You squint trying to make out what it is. Oh, no.

Enough of R&D, the boys throw themselves into production. Gleeful, wet death rattles as they plunge up oily ammunition, sucked from head and chest cavities unstintingly. They fill their lungs with explosive winter air, rock their heads back, then abruptly fling themselves forward to launch their viscous hawk at the train. You want to look away but the paralysis of fascination has set in. There must be a hundred and fifty high school boys on the platform, every single one of whom is hysterically hurling lungers at the passenger cars across the tracks. Now, there's consensus and group solidarity for you.

The scene is almost too much to comprehend, much less credit. It seems to have arisen suddenly and from nowhere. One moment it's a group of students leisurely making their way home; the next it's a bedlam's rebellion of revenge spat out on their keepers, society.

Society, meanwhile, in the form of crammed passengers reading their papers and their own thoughts behind the muck-miring window, never blink in this shoot-out. Slime sleets down inches from them, gloss frosting their lens on the world, a pox rain of inside-out toads splatting on their polite, orderly view of life . . . and they don't bat a lash. Even those too late for seats or hand straps, their faces pressed against the door glass, eyeball-to-eyeball with their mockers and the mucous storm, stare, if not serenely at least stoically, back. "The snot is a bit heavier today, don't you think, Kenichi?" you imagine them chatting civilly to one another. Oh, brave sloggers in the face of Unwanted Things!

At last, your gorge on the verge of its own contribution, the train pulls morosely out of the station like an ill-glazed confection on the assembly line.

When your version of the Meitetsu arrives, you, the few other adults, the couple of girls, and the old ladies let the wild ones, the Nation's Future, pile in first. They take all the seats. They light up fags in No Smoking areas. They stare contemptuously at you. You don't say a word. You don't do Unwanted Things. Who wants to get raped and killed?

The Invisible Japan

Many observers have recognized countervailing forces in Japan and have devised dichotomies to explain them: feudal and modern, traditional and pragmatic, industrious and dissipated, regimented and impulsive, civilized and barbaric, public and private, old and new generations, and the most popular,

East and West. These pairs do indeed describe antithetical influences in the Japanese character and culture, but as popular
stereotypes they can be and are used just as effectively to describe other nations and peoples. The Saudis are part feudal
and part modern, the Chinese traditional yet pragmatic, the
Swedes industrious but intemperate, the Koreans regimented
yet volatile, the English public and private, Americans both
civilized and savage, all the East both Eastern and Western
now, and virtually everywhere forever there's young and old.
There is, however, a dichotomy that, if not entirely unique to
Japan, in its pervasive effects and implications makes it so:
Wanted Things and Unwanted Things.

Present-day Japan is in a struggle in which it has often
found itself. On the one hand there is the necessity, and tradition, of holding the social web together, even in the face of
spit in the face. On the other there is the growing sense among
the Japanese themselves that the web either no longer supports
them and their best individual or even communal interests (and
like webs may be more trap than support), or is itself archaic
and impracticable in any event. On the one side, the Japanese
refrain from doing Unwanted Things—even when Unwanted
Things are being done to them. On the other, there are more
and more Japanese doing the Unwanted Things. Yet so adept
are the Japanese at maintaining *kao* (face), it is still the self-
flattering image of the Wanted, tourist-pamphlet Japan that
dominates the imagination of most Westerners.

Indeed, because there is still much of Japan that remains
invisible outside its own islands, this book is chiefly interested
in the Unwanted, the necessary-to-ignore, and the fallout from
its clash with the Japanese notion of what's Wanted. The struggle in some official and some unofficial quarters of Japan to
maintain the Wanted has grown the more determined and ur-
gent the more increasing the encroachment of the Unwanted.
The existence even of the Unwanted must be denied, suppressed, or at least unacknowledged, much as the train passengers whose windows were enslimed by the horde of rebellious
boys remained willfully oblivious to this Unwanted occurrence.

Japan is increasingly disjoined by economic successes and pressures that undermine abiding institutions such as the extended family, where married couples lived with the groom's parents and the mother-in-law ruled the house and the first-born son inherited the land and the responsibility for the entire family. Or such as corporate industry, where, before the soaring yen and increasingly internecine competition (not only international but domestic), lifetime employment and regular promotions were a shoo-in. These and other disjunctures have created a whole new world of Unwanted Things, and thus a whole Invisible Japan for the Japanese social persona to deny.

Social Judo

The Japanese have a saying that exalts the deliberate disregard of Unwanted Things: *noren ni udeoshi*—though the maxim suggests more the virtues of Zen, Judo, or Aikido than the bad habits of denial or suppression. The phrase trades on the image of the short curtain (*noren*) that hangs in the entrance of small stores, bars, and restaurants in Japan, and that, when shoved indifferently aside by patrons, always returns to its original, natural place.

Once Again the Return of the Idea Whose Time Hasn't Come

The Wanted/Unwanted dichotomy itself has a long Japanese pedigree. Under the rule of the Tokugawa clan (1603–1868), the size of houses, of feast meals, even of dolls was prescribed and enforced, as were the clothes one could wear, including underwear. Moreover, contact with the rest of the world was all but cut off. *Gaijin* residing in Japan were kicked out. Japanese living abroad were told to stay there; those who came home, just on a lark, were executed. Christianity, introduced by the Jesuits who came with the Portuguese in 1543 and appealing enough to acquire a half million converts by the early seventeenth century, was all but eradicated by 1638 along with many Japanese who insisted on taking it to heaven with them. The Tokugawas kept the Japanese at home by permitting only dinky coastal ships to be built, and though the clan did permit some minimal contact with Korea and China, of the Europeans only the Dutch were admitted and then only as tightly regulated traders quarantined to a single modest port on a tiny island in Nagasaki harbor.

This thorough exclusion of the Unwanted (in this case the so-called foreign) for over two centuries had the terrifically bracing consequence of Japan's missing out on the advent of modern science and technology, the burgeoning in world trade, and the Industrial Revolution itself—not to mention the development of modern arms, the Japanese lack of which left the Tokugawa boggling and obliging before the Black Ships and weaponry of Commodore Perry's U.S. fleet in 1853, when everything began to unravel for the clan and their Unwanted-Policy.

Soon thereafter, through characteristic Japanese dexterity, virtually everything Unwanted became very much Wanted, a phenomenon we'll examine in a later chapter.

Outcastes

But the Japanese preoccupation with what's Wanted and what's Unwanted is not confined just to the murky, ignorable past. And at least for one aspect of that the Japanese again have the Tokugawa purists to thank. Its existence is one of the most denied of the Unwanted Things in Japan and hence one of the least publicized.

No one knows exactly how the *burakumin* (hamlet folk) class of people originally came to be or to be so sharply distinguished from the rest of the Japanese population. For all their worship of ancestors the Japanese have a long tradition of abhorring anything associated with death (don't give a Japanese a present colored black, you're told), and some commentators think that originally *burakumin* handled the dead or worked in death-related industries such as tanning, leather working,

and weapons making. Others guess that these outcastes were
conquered and enslaved individuals, or simply poor sods with
bad jobs. Whatever the case, originally these people were called
eta (polluted) or *binin* (inhuman), so at least the name *burakumin* is a move in the right direction.

But, a rose by any other name. . . . In fact the Tokugawa,
in their obsession to codify everything so that there would be
no question as to what was Wanted and what was Unwanted,
institutionalized the social hierarchy and thereby not only fixed
the class *burakumin* but in effect made it hereditary. No longer
could you work your way out of the Unwanted Things.

In the early Meiji era, which was the Westernizing-Wanted
binge following the Westernizing-Unwanted binge of the Tokugawa, there were 400,000 outcastes, or about 13 percent of
the population. In 1981 rough estimates put the figure anywhere from 1.5 to 3 million, or maybe 2 percent of the population (though other commentators say this is delusionally low,
since many *burakumin* are "passing" as regular Japanese). The
drop in percentage is encouraging, yet one may still wonder
why in the modern civilization of Japan anyone is considered
burakumin at all.

Legally no one is, of course—a typical way of denying that
the Unwanted Thing exists. The distinction was officially abandoned in 1871. Physically and culturally there is no difference.
Yet in fact and in treatment *burakumin* remain very much a
part of the Unwanted, invisible Japan. One government study
revealed that 70 percent of respondents actually believed that
burakumin were from a different race. Virtually all Japanese
have *koseki*, family registers and scrolls that delineate in detail
their family tree. And though strictly speaking the *koseki* is not
available to just anyone, any prospective in-laws will expect to
see it. As for the rest, a thriving business in bribes and private
investigators make it extremely difficult to conceal one's ge-
nealogy. Secret "black books" exist that list *burakumin* living
districts. As a result, still only about half the *burakumin* are
able to marry non-*burakumin*. And it's not only in marriage
that discrimination against *burakumin* exists. Many companies

and schools as well as individuals have covert policies against hiring *burakumin*, so that as a group they remain in the economically disadvantaged class. Yet outside of Japan hardly anyone knows they exist. And precisely because the rest of Japan has succeeded, at least to that degree, in treating them as if they were invisible.

Koreans or Japanese?

In order to justify the subjugation and annexing of Korea in 1910, the Japanese government decided to promulgate the belief that the despised *burakumin* were descended from Koreans. Apparently this deft equation made it noblesse oblige to exploit Korea, many of whose citizens were forced to emigrate to Japan to survive, as much Korean farmland was confiscated for settling by Japanese, who, incidentally, insisted that Koreans adopt the Japanese language and Japanese names. Most transplanted Koreans ended up on road gangs and in mines, jobs that stigmatized them in the eyes of their Japanese hosts, never renowned anyway for racial tolerance. Then, by the eruption of the even greater War in 1941, the Japanese resorted to press gangs to dragoon the unhappy Koreans into forced labor, so that during the war over a million Koreans had been brought to Japan as virtual slaves.

By the end of the war in 1945 there were nearly 2.5 million Koreans in Japan. Today there are about three-quarter million "Koreans" residing in Japan. The rest returned to Korea, went elsewhere, died, or miraculously escaped being counted along with the remaining "Koreans" there. "Miraculously," one says, because most of these "Koreans" living in Japan were born in Japan, many of them several generations ago, speak Japanese, live like the Japanese, and for all intents and purposes are Japanese. But not to the Japanese. To the Japanese these people are Koreans, will always be Koreans, and as such will always be discriminated against—again, like the *burakumin*, in marriage, education, and employment—and in Japan, that is all there is.

It's those sneaky family registers and scrolls again. If your great-grandfather was expropriated of his land in Korea and had to labor in the Japanese coal mines for the rest of his life, it's going to be more or less there in the records, will always be there, fixing you forever as "Korean." You're never going to be a part of the society in which you live, a society in which there are only two basic categories, us and not-us—*ware ware nihojin* (we Japanese) and the rest of the universe out there.

Japan is not really a nation at all. It is a people, a "race" some say, as the Japanese do themselves. In Japan a few foreigners—and fewer psychologically, like the writer Lafcadio Hearn (aka Yakumo Koizumi)—can become "citizens." But not by long residence, or birthplace, or avowal, or great service can you truly become a citizen of the Japanese. There is really no nation to join. There are just the Japanese, and you already have to be one to become one.

In Japanese the word for "different" (*chigau*) also means "wrong."

See What You Made Me Do?

In 1923 a terrible earthquake destroyed much of Tokyo and killed 130,000 people. Or most of these 130,000 people. At the time many Japanese believed earthquakes were caused by a humongous catfish in the sea who thrashed at the behest of the Sun Goddess when she was unhappy with her imperial descendants. But rather than remove Emperor Taisho (already long since pixilated and sequestered) or his son and regent Hirohito, the government spread a rumor blaming the Tokyo "Koreans," several thousand of whom were tried in ad hoc sidewalk courts by deceived Tokyo "Japanese," convicted of the natural disaster, and then beheaded on the spot.

As victims of discrimination, the "Koreans" in Japan are often laborers or fringe people, forced by default into menial work or crime. Many *pachinko* (Japanese pinball) parlors are said to be owned and run by these "Koreans," just as the "Koreans" are accused of being involved in gambling and prostitution. But besides both our sympathy and our qualms, these "Koreans" deserve our gratitude.

American cars—our Firebirds and TransAms, our Camaros and our Caddies, our Lincoln Continentals? These "Koreans" and some gangsters are pretty much the only "Japanese" who'll buy them from us.

Spending Holidays Abroad

Until the end of World War II a main task of the Japanese Ministry of Education was to promote the official line of the ruling elite as to what was true and not, what Wanted and what Unwanted. After the war the ministry was given the task of eliminating such propaganda from education. Gradually, through the prerogative to approve or disapprove school texts, the ministry subtly regained the power to determine what is true and not, Wanted and Unwanted. Thus Japanese reporters go to extraordinary lengths to get a publisher's original text version and compare it to the emended one finally approved and published. In late 1988 a publisher—saying it was to avoid any "misunderstanding"—revised an already approved high school English text after it was criticized by the far-right Association of Comrades to Discuss the Nation's Basic Issues. The revised version replaced a section on World War II Japanese atrocities (including a Malaysian witness's account of baby-bayoneting) with a passage on *My Fair Lady*. That should clear up any misunderstandings, comrades.

In an earlier flap it was discovered that the ministry had encouraged another textbook publisher to change, among other things, the Japanese "invasion" of China and Korea to the neutral if not downright progressive "advance."

Would that make the "Rape of Nanjing" the "*Dating* of Nanjing" then?

The Emperor Has No Clothes

In Japanese mythology Jimmu, the great-grandson of the
Sun Goddess, founded the imperial dynasty in 660 B.C., and
though General Douglas MacArthur effectively canceled Emperor Hirohito's divine status at the embarrassing end of World
War II, and though the whole question of the emperor's divinity
is no longer much a matter of national belief, it is still often a
source of uninspected racial pride. If divine status is gone, there
is still, at the periphery of consciousness, the comforting notion
of divine ancestry. At the core of this questionable intuition
are events of the sort that took place in 1274 and 1281, when
Kubla Khan, already having conquered Korea and China and
installed himself as the first of the Mongol emperors of China,
launched two invasions of Japan. Bad weather aborted the first,
and the second, along with 150,000 Mongols, was thoroughly
trashed by a typhoon, which the very lucky Japanese dubbed
kamikaze, meaning "wind from the gods." From then on the
myth of Japan's protection by the gods has subtly persisted,
even in spite of that unexplainable divine delinquency at the
end of World War II, when the Japanese were certain the gods
would come to their rescue again, then utterly astonished when
they didn't.

Yet even today, perhaps because immortal ancestry is still
an active tenet in Japanese religious ceremony, the at least sentimental notion of the divinity of royal ancestry persists. It's
one of the Wanted Things, even if only inchoate now.

Hence it was with consternation—and instinctive defense—that the authorities reacted as they did as ever more
information was extrapolated from the tomb mounds being
opened. The burial mounds in Japan, dating from A.D. 250, were
tombs for influential men. So far about 2,200 of them have
been identified, some huge, like Emperor Nintoku's, which is
475 meters long and has three moats around it as well as 20,000
terra-cotta figures in it.

And there's the rub: some of these entombed men had
been emperors of Japan. And the more archaeologists dug

among the artifacts in these tombs, the more troubling their conclusions. Finally, after one such dig, at Kusakabe's Tomb, the Imperial Household Agency stepped in and "covered" it all up again—whether literally or figuratively one doesn't know for sure, because excavation, and with it all information, ceased. Clearly, to some official Japanese minds the struggle of the Wanted and the Unwanted is a matter of national security. This notwithstanding, enough information had already emerged to suggest evidence—Unwanted and hence necessary to ignore—that perhaps the emperors did not descend from heaven at all. Maybe they hailed from Korea. And maybe not just the emperors.

Oh, unkind, mocking Fate.

Japanese Not Japanese Either?

It is also little known outside Japan and little mentioned inside that the Japanese are not the original inhabitants of Japan. The indigenous people are the Ainu, a nomadic hunting and fishing people, Caucasoid in race similar to proto-Europeans and some American Indians. And like the American Indians the Ainu have suffered the fate of a more powerful encroaching race—the Mongoloid "Japanese" in this case—and have been driven off the main island of Honshu to the more inhospitable clime of Hokkaido in the north. Today the Ainu, with their own language and culture, number only about sixteen thousand, and are considered by the other "Japanese" quaintly primitive. Some other Caucasoids, likewise incompatible with Japanese social formulas, are proving harder to ignore:

> NATIVE OPINION: Call me narrow-minded, but I just do not like to see foreign players on Japanese baseball teams. Though some people say that restrictions on foreign players should be lifted, I for one disagree. I care most for Japanese professional baseball. I just cannot feel

*happy when my favorite team wins a
game thanks to the good performance of
its foreign players.*

*When the Yomiuri Giants were
champions for nine straight seasons,
there were no foreign players on the team.
Japanese baseball fans want to see only
Japanese players perform.*

*Is it really necessary to bring in un-
known foreign players to Japan to beef up
a team?*

*Only a small number of these for-
eign players are worth their big annual
salaries. But many capable young Japanese players are sacrificed. Japanese
teams should not hire any more foreigners and just wait till all the others here
now go away. Two years should do it. It
is very stupid to pay valuable Japanese
yen to cheap foreign players who chew
gum during games, spit on infields and
preen themselves like peacocks. (K.S.,
teacher)*

Beef or Bull?

Every culture, every nation, has Wanted Things and Unwanted Things. Yet in Japan this distinction arises from something very special in the way the Japanese social psyche is
organized.

In the West people generally have—beyond mere matters
of taste—"reasons" for designating something wanted or unwanted, for doing something or not. These reasons themselves
are based on an intricate system of principles involving logic,
precedents, and cultural assumptions (such as the beliefs in
progress, in individual franchise, and in the innate validity of
the principles themselves). This system is an historical legacy

of classic Greek philosophy, Roman law, the Renaissance, the Enlightenment, and numerous other forces, and as such it is a system that, if a bit loose, is nevertheless very real. It is not just anything at all and nothing in particular. Not all opinions are equal, or valid, nor is any reason as good as the next. This is something the West has some wide agreement upon—enough agreement even to provide us with principles by which to judge how valid are our "reasons," exalting or demeaning them as explanations, or excuses, or rationalizations, or motives, or causes, or justifications, and so on.

If these distinctions are not quite as clear or obvious in Japanese discourse, as some linguists maintain, for the Japanese social personality these distinctions don't seem even to exist. There are no "principles"—not as the West knows them: no consistent, underlying framework of systematic logic by which to judge the validity of "reasons" for wanting this and not wanting that. Similarly it seems that when a Japanese uses the word *must* or other compulsives, much more often than a Westerner he means that behavior, say, must proceed accordingly not because time and trial have shown this to be the most logical, workable way, but because this is simply the way it's done.

In fact "reasons" sometimes seem to be a relatively recent import into Japan, one that some Japanese have not yet gotten the hang of.

At a 1987 meeting of American agricultural producers, U.S. cattle farmers invited Japanese trade and agriculture officials in the hope of inducing them to import more American beef into Japan. After eating a lot of free steak, which costs up to five times as much in Japan as it does in the United States, the Japanese officials told their hosts that since Japanese intestines are about a foot longer than Western intestines, an increase in beef imports would cause an increase in stomach cancer.

Present company excepted.

The String of Pearls

To the Western psyche things have to make "sense" to be
acceptable. They have to have some recognizable logic, some
tie to common reason if they're not to be dismissed as stupid
or mad or criminal. To the Japanese social psyche it is relatively
unimportant if things make sense. Things don't have to be logical or justifiable, though the apparently even flow of daily life
in Japan would have us believe so. But if things in Japan don't
have to make sense to work, they have to be something at least
as effective, something to assure the relatively harmonious, orderly society for which Japan is notorious.

That something is *consistent*.

And that doesn't mean "logically" consistent either. It
simply means that things must be "predictable," "repeatable,"
the same each time they happen. In the absence of a general
"logic" or rational principles to generate a range of imaginable
behaviors, you must instead simply "know" all the "actual"
behaviors. And know them in all the likely circumstances with
all the probable participants. That is, everybody has to know
specifically what to do and what not to do, as well as when to
and when not to do it, not to mention who does or who doesn't
do it and to whom. Principles don't have anything to do with
it. Nor do "reasons." In fact "reasons" are not much asked for
or given in Japan. It is only important that everybody do what's
Wanted and not do what's Unwanted. You're not supposed to
use "reasons" to devise other ways of doing things. Everybody
already knows the ways things are done, and not done. "Reasons" are too airy, too mercurial, too manipulable—and hence
unreliable. With "reasons," who knows how long Japanese intestines might grow?

Westerners ask "why."
Japanese ask "what."

Die with Your Slippers On

You're slouched down in your chair passing the time with the other sick hundreds in the waiting room (or better, waiting promenade, for your place is at the end of a hundred-yard-long hallway), hoping to see one of the doctors striding purposefully to and from the rooms abutting the hall, flushing timorous patients out of their way like chickens. Something is wrong with your eye. A minuscule decaying piece of the hurtling Meitetsu train has come off the evening before and now you see a waltzing black web overlaying your view of everything. You've been here two hours and have no idea if you're any closer to being seen. Maybe they've mispronounced your name and you didn't understand them. That thought prompts another more likely, more horrible one. They won't know how to pronounce your name, so, to save everybody embarrassment, they just won't call it. They'll just ignore it and you. You'll go away or die—but in either case no one will have to be embarrassed. You slouch further down and practice *akirame*, cutting off all feeling, surrendering to hopelessness.

You're startled back to fear by a horrible moan. Gurgly and downhill through the scales, it's agony as only the Japanese are permitted to liberate it from Japanese decorum. Coming from down at your end of the hall, just around the corner in Reception. You crane your neck to see. It's a scrawny, middle-aged fellow with short hair, wrapped in a blood-spattered sheet, propped up by an older and younger woman holding his arms, dragging him forward, an agonized, ashen expression pulling his features. Nowhere near *akirame*.

You're wondering if he, too, will have to wait in line along with the rest of you, when suddenly the victim lets out a discordant shriek, quite different from the previous moan, a tone of outrage and reproach actually modulating it. The women stop abruptly, guiltily murmuring, *"Ḥai, hai!"* They drag him backward a few paces to the slipper rack, a ceiling-high shelf of slippers where you can exchange your street shoes for clean, inside footwear. Each woman leans down, pulls off one of his shoes, and replaces it with a slipper, while the patient looks on approvingly.

Decorum satisfied, the trio lurches forward again, the patient resuming his terrifying wail. First things first, you suppose. Don't want to die with bad manners.

He's not made to wait, and he vanishes quickly into one of the rooms. You look down at your own feet. Cowboy boots. You forgot to make the obligatory exchange. You're about to sneak off to the slipper rack when a doctor in rimless glasses taps your shoulder, smiling. He's figured a way to save you, it seems, without having to call your name aloud. As the only *gaijin* in the hall you were easy to pick out. Lucky break for you.

After the examination he flicks off the intense light on his ophthalmoscope. Astonishingly he *admits* he doesn't know what that dancing web in your eye is. In English he says, "But it's nothing to worry." Oh, good, the kiss of death.

Everyone Hold Hands

We Westerners sometimes think we discern principles behind the behavior and attitudes of the Japanese, when really we have only projected our Western assumptions, the chief one itself being that rational principles *must* underlie civilized behavior. In fact, though, people can behave just as civilly to one another just because there are no principles to rely on, knowing as they do they have nothing but their reciprocal caution to save them.

For instance, in Japan you can still leave a bag of groceries outside another store while you shop and find it there when you return. Try that in L.A. or London or Paris or almost anywhere else.

But the tacit agreement among the Japanese not to steal the bag is not strictly a matter of "honesty," the usual misinterpretation of Westerners projecting their own cultural values. The Japanese are no more fundamentally honest—or decent, or civilized, as this book reveals—than are Westerners.

In fact the Japanese don't steal the unattended bag of groceries not because they believe in honesty but because no Japanese really believes in or dares rely on that Western phantom. Safer for everybody simply not to do it—by rule, not by "reason."

Of course, for such a view to prevail and society still to hang together, everybody has to behave the same way, not stealing the bag whatever he might privately think or personally need. *Everybody* has to do it, as well as do it *every time*.

This is the real meaning and source of "consensus" in Japan. Consensus in Japan is not a rational principle, wisely deduced from the need to produce cooperative action and deliberately employed to reach decisions. That's an extrapolation typical of the West, not the East. Nor is it an endemic trait of Japanese character shaping events. On the contrary, in Japan consensus is an effect, not a cause. It is just the inevitable consequence of having no common principles—only social necessity—to appeal to for agreement.

An old Japan-hand once noted that the West is based on infrastructure and Japan on surface tension.

The metaphor is apt. For the Western social psyche is held together by a supporting skeleton of reason and principle; the Japanese social psyche is held together by a bubble of agreement supported by nothing but itself.

That Makes Sense

At the time you find yourself living in Japan, you notice that except for the dark limos and official cars used by the modern executive shoguns of government and industry, almost 90 percent of the new Japanese cars on the streets and in the showrooms are white. You ask a Japanese friend why this is so. To check his answer, you ask a colleague as well. They both say the same thing: "White is the color for cars."

Supplanting what in previous, undemocratic epochs were the official instigators of conformity—village coercion, Tokugawan fiat, military edict, and imperial pronouncement—is an industry of publications that compile social statistics and catalog norms. One such book, wildly popular for a while, was *Average*, whose thousands of entries were meant to coalesce alchemically into an homunculus of the perfect middle—describing the average car for the average *sarari-man* of the average age, and so on—and thus serve as mannikin for the Wanted.

Rules of the Game

To maintain social stability in a surface society like Japan, consistency of behavior has to take the place of consistency of principles. And since this kind of consistency by definition has to be nearly universal to work—everybody agreeing to do the same thing—behavior in Japan tends to be according to formulas.

In turn, because the vast majority of Japanese do continue not to let the side down, striving to act in accord with the formulas for what's Wanted, Westerners take these formulas for universal in Japan and thus assume they are principles.

But like consensus, so-called principles such as indirectness, group solidarity, hierarchy, stoicism, civility, and ceremony, are merely abstractions, and not the thing itself—the actual daily behavior of the Japanese. Moreover, being the abstractions they are, they're more Western than Japanese. And it's still more often Westerners rather than the Japanese who go around describing the Japanese this way.

These formulas the West imagines to embody principles are actually something else—akin but not the same. In Japan they are not principles. They are merely practical *strategies*—inevitable, indispensable techniques to hold together a society not held together by any underlying framework of rational principles. The Japanese are not simply by nature given to agreement, circumspection, conformity, order, fatalism, politeness, subservience, or ritual, as their social history plainly shows. More often the display of these "virtues" has been a result of recurring internal political propagandizing. This first took modern form in nineteenth-century state Shintoism, which combined government and religion in the person of a divine emperor, to whom uniform allegiance could be promoted at the expense of democratic and rational "principles," which are always individualistic and socially inharmonious. Subsequent historical events, such as the militarists' imposition of a single national ideology until 1945 (including establishing a Bureau of Thought Control in the thirties), and the final failure of the American occupation to support real political pluralism (rather than conservative orthodoxy and "social stability"), also helped to perpetuate a society of formulas instead of principles and to fabricate a social psyche more conforming than creative.

Whatever the exact historical causes, the individual Japanese—in his personal attitudes and behavior when they aren't tracing out the artificial, mass-produced patterns dictated to him by his social psyche—often thinks and acts in ways quite outside the so-called "principles" of accommodation . . . as we'll see.

At the same time, however, if the Japanese are to maintain the unsupported veneer that is their society, they *must* be considerate instead of willful in their dealings with each other. They *have to be* open to resignation instead of revolt, willing to conform to a uniform plan and not to personal schemes, obedient to authority rather than imagination, devoted to ritual rather than freedom, committed to the group and not the individual, concerned with order rather than spontaneity. Seen thus, such behavior is not a matter of principle but just the social tactics necessary for daily interaction where etiquette has to do the job of principles.

In the West if something goes awry or doesn't conform, if a piece is torn off the exterior, there's always the skeleton beneath it to hold it all together. In Japan, on the other hand, if something goes awry, if people don't do their duty, there's nothing beneath it to save the structure. The whole bubble might burst. The hollow doll that is the Japanese social psyche could shatter, and . . . well, you know what happened to Humpty Dumpty-san.

By the Way . . .

Japanese TV news recently reported a robbery at a store in one of the larger metropolitan areas. The lone clerk on the premises, a young woman, had telephoned her boss at another branch location and told him that a man had entered the store and held her up, taking all the day's receipts. Her boss told her to stay calm, that he would call the police.

When the police arrived they found the clerk by the phone, having bled to death from a stab wound.

She had done her duty in quickly informing her boss of the robbery. She had followed the social formula. As such she knew it was only secondary that she personally had been stabbed, so she had not mentioned it.

A Japanese saying: The nail that sticks out is hammered down.

CHAPTER 3

Owner's Manual: Some ROM Rules for Wa World

A, B, 便

In a culture with an underpinning of rational principles, you have to figure things out. In a culture without these underpinnings—just formulas for behavior—there's nothing to figure out. You have to memorize them. *Wa* (harmony) in the society is achieved not by everyone typing in his own two cents of input but by everyone reading the same instructions from ROM, that portion of the master-memory-chip that cannot be changed or erased, only read. Accordingly, memory plays an almost incomprehensibly dominant role in Japanese life.

Like the male-female Deal sketched out earlier—only one chip in a mosaic that makes up the Japanese social psyche—most social behavior in Japan is still formula, and as formula all of it has to be memorized by the Japanese. Preparing the Japanese for this daunting task from early childhood is what is certainly the central act of memorization: learning *kanji*.

Kanji is the Japanese system of writing. If it looks like Chinese pictographs to you, that's because it is—or was. In another embarrassing blow to the theory of Japanese purity, the Japanese had no system of written language until the sixth century, when they borrowed Chinese characters (and much of Chinese culture wholesale). Because Chinese never really fit the grammar of spoken Japanese, the Japanese have had to create or adopt three other systems of writing as well, all phonetic: the syllabary *hiragana* and *katakana*, and Western *romaji*.

Because speech is the original and basic form of language, and because spoken Japanese has a "rational" grammar, it's too much to say that a system of writing could actually dictate mental organization and social perception. But it is inevitable that something as fundamental as writing, something learned so young and used so often, would influence a way of seeing the world. So the contrast in Japanese and Western writing systems provides a provocative analogy to the contrast between the formulaic, surface society in Japan and the "rational," skeletal society in the West. Phonetic alphabets, of the sort used by Western languages, use a very small number of symbols, which, though themselves meaningless, when combined in various ways produce an almost infinite number of meanings. Pictographs, in contrast, are fixed images, with fixed (if, as in Japanese, multiple) meanings. In English, for example, there are twenty-six letters. In *kanji* there are fifty thousand characters—and many more meanings. You don't sound out *kanji*; you see their pictures. You memorize them.

But, with no beginning letters, how do you look *kanji* up in the dictionary?

Is There No Mercy?

To look up an individual *kanji* in a Japanese dictionary you first have to identify its "radical," the root element considered central to the particular *kanji*. This is not nearly as easy as identifying the first letter of, say, an English word, as there are almost always two to seven radicals in any *kanji*. Once identified, the central radical has to be located in the sequence of radicals. This is not as easy as memorizing, say, the 26 letters in the English alphabet, since there are 214 radicals. If the dictionary has a ranking chart for the radicals, the search time is reduced considerably. Otherwise, it helps a bit that the radicals are arranged from fewest to most strokes, meaning the "brush" strokes required to produce the radicals and *kanji*. (There is also a prescribed sequence of strokes for each *kanji* and a direction for each stroke, but then that is a different Japanese shock.)

To find the particular *kanji*, then, containing the radical just located using the above directions, you count the number of strokes additional to the strokes in its radical, then let your fingers do the walking to the appropriate subsection of that radical's section and begin hunting in earnest.

The English dictionary begins with *a* and ends with *zymurgy*, the chemistry that deals with fermentation, as in wine or beer making.

The Japanese dictionary begins with the one-stroke character *ichi*, meaning "one," and ends with the seventeen-stroke character *yaku*, which denotes an archaic "flute." One might be depressed, though not surprised by now, to note that among the fifty thousand *kanji* in between these two there are some with as many as forty strokes, and one ("dragons moving") with forty-eight.

Perhaps God is impersonal and remote after all.

> *NATIVE OPINION: I believe the Japanese language, Nihongo, is an intangible cultural asset, as precious as a national treasure. In Nihongo we have delicate women's phrases, powerful men's phrases, and various dialects redolent of certain localities.*
>
> *Of course, it is quite natural that expressions should change in keeping with the times. However, the Japanese language is being badly corrupted at present. Male vocabularies are being used by young schoolgirls and various foreign expressions are being coined by the mass communications industry. I understand that foreign expressions can sound good*

to the ears. However, the adoption of such
expressions in everyday language is be-
ing taken too easily.

It is sad that beautiful Japanese
words are gradually becoming dead lan-
guage due to the abuse of foreign words.
We should reconsider the use of our beau-
tiful Japanese language, which provides
many shades of meaning to express our
feelings. (N.N., housewife)

Directions Enclosed

Though we shall later look at the limits to this view, from a certain angle Westerners can't help but believe that the Japanese go places, do things, hold opinions, speak clichés, and enact roles just because that's the way it's done. In Japan there are prescribed ways for picking up chopsticks, folding your newspaper, wrapping gifts, presenting money, bowing to superiors and inferiors, allotting seating by rank, spending your bonus, keeping a mistress (and dumping one), bribing the right god, going on vacation, and killing yourself. In Japan even escapes from formula seem prescribed by formula.

Moreover, where rote memorization of formulas for behavior is an essential modus operandi, there can be some pretty stultifying effects, the typical Western response to which is the one expressed by a character in John Morley's *Pictures from the Water Trade*: that while the Japanese are interesting as a people, as individuals they are boring.

In a traditionally colorful society, many Japanese still try to regiment the colors into formulas. One shopgirl insisted "red" toothbrushes were only for women. Men, usually in Western dress (*yofuku*), wear a lot of black and white, with forays into dark blue and ash gray. Women, especially in native dress (*wafuku*), get a fuller spectrum, but are expected to follow a bewildering algebra of formulas for colors (as well as designs and materials) dependent on age, season, occasion, and formality.

The last avatar for these prescriptions is to be found in special shops for elderly matrons exclusively carrying a line of drear-dress solely in the colors of death: moribund purples, blues, grays. The sartorial menopause promulgated through these mortuary shops underscores the social psyche's strict formulaic distinctions by age.

Not quite so deadly, but still ossifying, is the weird effect a formulaic society can have even on pop singers, society's rebels in the West. No matter how intense the music or passionate the lyrics, every accompanying gesture has plainly been choreographed. This uniform notion of what's Wanted and Unwanted in pop singing gives a contrived, mannered cast to the movements of such singers, making them appear alternately like marionettes or sociopaths pretending to like music.

The worst cases of spirit and life having been embalmed in ritual amber, though, many Japanophiles feel, are those involving some legitimate traditions. *Hanami*, viewing the cherry tree (*sakura*) blossoms, once a spiritual tradition acknowledging the evanescent beauty of life itself, is now mainly a compulsory obeisance, with everybody doing it but hardly anybody really viewing the blossoms. In fact the occasion is now often just a formula for sitting beneath the trees and drinking oneself blind to everything, blossoms included.

A Japanese once remarked that something basic could be learned about Japanese society—its capacity for both beauty and blankness, both serenity and superficiality, both conscious gesture and dead habit, both resplendence and void—by noticing that the cherry trees bear only blossoms, not cherries.

Drunk Teacher Hits Pupil With Light Van

KAWASAKI, Kanagawa— A high school teacher was arrested Wednesday night on hit-and-run charges and drunken driving after hitting a high school boy on a motorcycle, police reported Thursday.

Toshihiko Takizawa, 27, a physical education teacher at Takatsu High School, was arrested as the driver of the vehicle.

According to police, Takizawa's light van hit the motorcycle driven by Mitsuhide Shimazaki, 17, a third-year student at Tokyo Jitsugyo High School, at around 11:20 p.m. Wednesday in Kawasaki.

The impact threw Shimazaki off the motorcycle causing injuries that will require about 10 days to treat.

Takizawa failed to stop after the incident. Shimazaki's friends, who were also riding motorcycles, chased after and caught up with the van about 1 kilometer down the road. Police arrested Takizawa on charges of violating the Traffic Control Law and reckless driving resulting in injury.

Police said Takizawa was on his way home with two of his colleagues after a party under the cherry trees.

Police said that they would also question the other two teachers on suspicion of allowing a drunken person to drive.

Witnesses said Takizawa had shouted at Shimazaki and his four friends when they were stopped at a red light just prior to the incident, saying that their motorcycles were too noisy, police said.

According to Shimazaki's friends, after they stopped Takizawa and his colleagues, the three had gotten out of the van with tennis rackets in hand, saying they hit Shimazaki because he and his friends were being too noisy.

Tea Torture

Chado, the tea ceremony, is certainly still a "tradition" in some spiritual circles, but that Zen-like act of awakened experience shouldn't be confused with the popular practice. As the latter, millions of women in Japan—as part of the training formulas (*o-keikogoto*) by which they achieve the "ideal" of the feminine—enact the tea ceremony, just because that's what women do. This is not the self-renouncing exercise in awareness, meditative concentration, or enlightenment created by the legendary Rikyu, but the multimillion-dollar conglomerate of franchises made in his name. All too often the manner of these mass-produced devotees makes it obvious that theirs is a self-satisfied drill, a habit of gesture without any spiritual ramifications for mind or soul. When foreign dignitaries come to Japan, the females among them are invariably required to get into kimono and do "tea torture," as a friend calls it, and not because one quick run-through is going to make them the wiser but because that's what women should do.

The tea ceremony in its broad and popular dissemination can serve as a metaphor for the formulaic Japanese social psyche, for the very things that make it significant to the popular Japanese mind can make it seem superficial to others. To the former, naturally, the tea ceremony is important first because it is Japanese, and characteristically so just because it and its constituent movements are formulaic. In the tea ceremony there is a Wanted and Unwanted way of executing each of the smallest gestures, of which there are many. And the tea ceremony is satisfying to its million of quotidian practitioners not because it reveals or evokes a deeper self within them but because they know how to execute each gesture. They're "in the know," so to speak, and this itself serves to confirm that the fundamental demarcation for the Japanese social psyche is between correct and incorrect, Wanted and Unwanted, *ware ware nihonjin* (we Japanese) and everybody else. Just the contrary of the experience and attitude Zen would foster, of course.

Like the language, the rituals, and the ubiquitous codifications pervading daily life, the tea ceremony confirms that it is the lovely veneer, the intricacy and nuance of the exterior— the surface itself and not something beneath it—that provides the popular mind with the basis for distinctions. These are the things to know, or sadly fail to know. It is too often self-congratulation that lends motive for giving foreigners quick run-throughs, since you can't memorize the tea ceremony (or any complex pattern) in one go, and your continuing ignorance afterward only validates their faith in the ultimate worth of such surface distinctions as their knowing a ritual, a gesture, a formula . . . and your not.

This is shockingly borne out when a foreigner does in fact learn these patterns: the language, the formulas, the mores. It so defies not only Japanese expectations but their desires, that it unmasks their real intentions to maintain the belief in their uniqueness, and instead of welcoming such an obliging foreigner, many Japanese will actually redouble their efforts to keep him within a safe stereotype, often by speaking English to him, the designated native tongue assigned the generic *gaijin* category, whatever the foreigner's nationality and language. Thus are these Japanese often further vexed by the additional surprise when their auditor doesn't speak English. Such hybrids don't fit into the formula and hence must be unreal, certainly Unwanted, and often necessary to ignore.

A statement of surprise in Japan is usually a statement of displeasure.

It's Not the Size That Counts

To a flabbergasting degree, the Japanese spend time, research, attention, and lots of yen trying to prove their suspicion that they are a unique kind of human. Famous theories have been propounded by them that (1) they have a higher proportion of type-O-blood population, making them better managers; (2) their physical brains are different, giving them special acumen; (3) their bodies contain special enzymes; (4) their language, Nihongo, is fundamentally different than all other languages; (5) their bodies contain a pint less blood, so they die more quickly from wounds; (6) their unique diet and metabolism causes them to get drunk more quickly; (7) they can communicate extensively with one another without words through "gut language," *haragei*; (8) they have lower body temperatures, so they feel cold more; (9) theirs is a pure race; and (10) they possess surplus intestines.

What is at issue is not the truth of these Ripleyesque marvels, but the legitimacy they have within the Japanese social persona and the slavish fidelity that this hollow doll can command in their defense.

Oh No, Not *No*!

Predictably, there are formulas for saying *no* in Japan, elaborate circuitous maps of meandering indirection to give everybody time to act in accord:

Thinking it over now on his way home, Mr. Kondo realizes he has made a horrible mistake. In the laudable effort to better prepare his son for his upcoming examination, he finagled the *gaijin* lady into helping his son with his English. Then, in a moment of rash exuberance over his little victory, he has promised the lady and her husband they could move into the vacant house he owns in Minami ward.

And she has accepted! How could she be so impolite! She should have declined. Or at least demurred. Or told him again and again his offer was too magnanimous, giving him cause to think she did not really want to move there and allowing him to graciously withdraw his offer.

Wait, maybe she's just being polite, in her foreign way, maybe she doesn't want to move in. But she said she did. Ah, maybe her husband doesn't want to move in and she does! Or he does and she doesn't? No, more likely the husband has gone to view the house and seen it to be the shack it is. No heat, mold eating the wood, rats running between the walls, open sewers, a Japanese hole-toilet.

Oh, how embarrassing. They must have thought him ludicrous in the pride of his benevolence. How could he have been so foolish? He has not even an inkling what they feel. They are not open to *haragei*. What was he thinking? He would like to die!

Instead he shall be shamed. For as pitiful as his offer was, he must take it back. The neighbors of the house will not have it. Having *gaijin* living there would cause them constant anxiety . . . as it does him now.

He will just never mention it to her again, and let her perceive his dilemma so that she may withdraw with equal grace. Yes, she has a good heart, he's sure, and will understand. . . .

"Mr. Kondo, how are you today? Is your offer of the house still good?"

Oh, how brazen! ". . . Ahh, you know, here in Japan we have, ahh . . . four seasons. In the winter, ahh . . . it is very cold, ahh . . . then comes spring, yes, a lovely time when the cherry blossoms, ahh . . . but then there is summer, very hot, ahh—"

"You're going back on the deal to let us move into the house, aren't you?"

Eeiiii . . . !

Purei Boru! (Play Ball!)

Many Westerners mistakenly equate formula with tradition. Having few of our own, we often take longevity itself as an earnest of venerableness. But a great deal of formula in Japan has nothing or little to do with tradition. In the larger view, for example, Japan in the eighth century had women rulers, and even earlier (circa A.D. 200) was matriarchal, with female clan leaders like Himiko, the shaman priestess-queen of Yamatai, where men and women lived separately but were generally considered equal—hardly the foundation for the modern Japanese grotesque of patriarchy, now formula, not tradition. Nor obviously is the Japanese national sport of baseball a tradition—but a mania—and it was imported from America over a century ago.

Also called *yakyu* in Japan since World War II, when English words became Unwanted Things, baseball has been disciplined into formula by the Japanese. In America baseball is as much an arena for individual stars as it is for team play. In Japan *besu-boru* is a team sport wherein even renowned players subordinate themselves to the team effort, which is always long on mechanics and short on inventiveness and inspiration. Even the team slugger will bunt with runners on first and third and nobody out to give his team the honor of the first run. Players come early and to every practice, and few of them would think to argue over salary, empty the bench in a free-for-all, rage at an umpire, or stuff cocaine up their noses. Or

punch one another—unless it was to discourage doing Unwanted Things. Robert Whiting, author of *The Chrysanthemum
and the Bat*, elsewhere relates an incident wherein Takashi
Nishimoto, the Yomiuri Giants' ace pitcher, dismissed the in-
struction of his pitching coach, who promptly punched the face
of Nishimoto, who had to pay a five-hundred-dollar fine and
apologize for forcing his coach to punch him.

In fact Japanese baseball and its players are meant to stand
as models to Japanese youth of the honor and worth of the
individual's acquiescence to group rules and goals. So when
things go consistently badly for the team, managers themselves—can you belive it, American fans?—volunteer to resign.

Vote for the Loudest

In the shorter view, too, much of the Wanted and Unwanted in Japan is a matter of formulas that have more to do
with collective opinion than with tradition. For instance, there
are the Japanese manias for souvenir buying and gift giving. If
ever you leave your home town or prefecture, you simply must
buy *o-miyage* (souvenirs) for everyone you know left behind.
You have to plan your packing by leaving enough space to accommodate all the trinkets you're going to haul back. As for
gifts, there is almost no occasion when gifts are not required.
A funeral in Japan reqiuires gifts: gifts for the surviving family,
and return gifts to acknowledge the kindness of those who
brought the gifts. Generosity, in fact, becomes difficult to distinguish from compulsiveness.

Too, some formulas have outlived the traditions that
spawned them—like the degrees of formality and politeness
codified into language and behavior that stem from feudal Japan and its strict hierarchical structure. The Japanese are obsessed with relative status and spend much time and anxiety
over it, peering into each other's obligatory *meishi* (business
cards), trying to divine who is the senior, how deep to bow,
and which honorific to use. These honorifics, *keigo*, prescribe
over one hundred ways alone of saying "I," and though most

are poetic or now obsolete, the remaining ones provide a bewildering variety.

Even modern politicians seem unable or unwilling to ditch
some methods of campaigning first borrowed from itinerant
peddlars but now thought by many observers to be antiquated
and ineffective. Outright and unadorned begging for votes is
one already mentioned. But this is not the only political version
of "functional autonomy." Originally produce peddlers and pan
hawkers would drag their wares through the alleys and coun-
tryside challenging or serenading potential customers. Some few
mobile merchants still employ this method, notably conve-
nience trucks (a sort of motorized 7-Eleven store), who an-
nounce their presence in the neighborhood by playing recorded
music, which, incidentally, is often rather mellow. Less mellow
are the "cardboard cryers," with their interminable amplified
raps on why you should give them your cardboard rather than
their competitors, and on the virtues of the toilet paper they
will give you in exchange.

But entirely bankrupt of mellow are the election cam-
paigners who have adopted and now can't seem to discard this
method of communication with prospective voters, as if the
advent of the mass media, with its potential to reach everyone
everywhere immediately, had bypassed them somehow. During
elections you can hear them all over and from miles away, until
aural meltdown, when you hear nothing at all. Especially elec-
trifying for the nerves are the black loudspeaker trucks on
marching orders from the grim-rememberers in the far-out far-
right. The indifference of their bourgeois countrymen, the
consumer-product omnivores, to cold showers and butch hair-
cuts seems to have driven this radiant-sun bunch to decibel
desperation. Finding yourself in the milieu of their message is
the sonic equivalent of living in liquid brass.

> *NATIVE OPINION:* "Onegai shimasu! One-
> gai shimasu!" *(Please vote for me!) Elec-*
> *tion campaign cars of candidates pass*
> *near my house, appealing to voters to vote*

*for them whenever election time comes.
Can't anything be substituted for them?*

*It might have been all right to hear
the campaign in such a style in the age
when itinerant merchants such as gold
sellers, fish sellers, tofu sellers, baked po-
tato sellers and picture story tellers were
often on streets.*

*In those days, there were no tele-
phones or TV sets, so calling out for votes
on the streets was permissible.*

*There are, however, many ways for
candidates to communicate with voters at
present. Why can't they perform cam-
paigns in a more stylish way? I wonder
whether voters can really support candidates who are old fashioned and pursuing
the traditional way.*

*Even if I am allowed to pick up a
computer as its type becomes out of date,
I don't pick up any because I don't want
any such old-fashioned computer.*

*Likewise, I can't be so noncommittal
as to vote for one candidate at random
because there are no candidates with
whose promises I agree.*

*As I am quite angry about the noise
of these campaign cars, I will not go to
vote in the coming twin election. (K.S.,
company employee)*

Computer Chip Will Miss School Today with a Sore Throat

There is no institution in all of Japan more notorious for
its reliance on rote memorization than the Japanese school system. Westerners who are familiar with Japan's number-one

world ranking in literacy and the superior showing of Japanese
students on achievement tests but who know little of the op-
pression, coercion, and stupefying routine in Japanese schools,
imagine them to be cloisters of intellectual aspiration and curiosity. Actually they are closer to fact-factories, and as we'll
see later, are often violent and suicidal.

Recitation and choral response are the system's two favorite techniques; objective tests its standard means of evalu-
ation. Even in *juku*, private crammer schools giving tutorial
lessons after regular school and on weekends, help is not given
in learning what you haven't learned in the day school but in
memorizing the formulas the national examiners are deemed to
want for answers on their exams.

In Japan these latter exams mean *everything*—no exaggeration. The most important ones are the two that immediately
precede entrance into university, and collectively they make
up *shiken jigoku*, "examination hell." In Japan, kids study
every day all their little lives in preparation for these tests.
Mothers have been known to try to sit with their sons during
the examination (fewer care how the daughters fare, given their
prescribed fate). Testees have been known to set up secret electronic communications with outside helpers surrounded by
books. Kids kill each other and themselves from the pressure.
Mothers are purported to sleep with their sons in order to re-
duce the pressures on both of them. Fathers are said to have
gone run-amok mad at a particularly stupid showing of a son,
a showing that will cost the family millions more yen in entrance bribes and the exorbitant tuitions charged by an inferior
but obliging private university.

"Examination hell" inflicts the most important tests, but
there are others, earlier and throughout a child's education, so
that entry into the right kindergarten can lead, via a route of
entries into the right schools, to the right university, the "right-
est" of them being Todai (Tokyo University), any (male)
graduate of which has it made for life. And to navigate this
route, the main and indispensable instrument one uses is rote
memorization.

Once at university the students, one would think, are in for a quantum leap of book torment. On the contrary, everything grinds to a merciful halt—a progression that's just the opposite of the one for American students, who as a rule do little in high school and are rudely awakened in university. The Japanese students, having killed themselves to get there (or trying to get elsewhere to a better university), abandon their books and themselves to indolence and license. They join the *dokushin kizoku* (the "bachelor aristocrats") in earnest for a four-year respite between the slavery of pupils and the servitude of company stiffs.

Booze Parties Send 66 Youths Into Hospital

Sixty-six young persons suffering acute alcoholism landed in Tokyo hospitals Saturday evening in the wake of parties to welcome freshmen at colleges and new employees at business companies.

Six of them required hospitalization.

The evening's first reported casualty was an 18-year-old college freshman who collapsed on a road at Udagawacho, Shibuya-ku, at 7:20 p.m.

An ambulance carted him off to a nearby hospital.

As the evening wore on, 40 university students including four coeds were rushed to hospitals in ambulances from eating and drinking places in Shibuya and Shinjuku.

Buy Brain, Steal Brain

There are about twenty thousand Japanese studying in American universities, and not even two thousand Americans studying in Japanese universities. And even if the numbers were more nearly equal, the situations would still make the exchange an invidious one, with the Japanese getting by far the better deal.

In America most scientific research, including research of technological value, is done at universities, hence the results are available publicly through publications and student participation. In Japan, on the other hand, most science of technological value is done at companies and hence remains private and proprietary. In effect what this means is that thousands more American science students could attend Japanese universities without the slightest increase in the knowledge of leading-edge technology they might bring back to their eventual employers in American industry. Conversely for Japan, it means that much of what Japanese students learn in American universities can be brought home and exploited by Japanese industry as brand-new technology and state-of-the-art consumer products, which as exports we will buy back from them a billionfold.

Exacerbating this inequity is the ambiguous status of the Japanese "student" in America. In Japan most academics in the sciences have "side jobs" in private companies. As such they are not only "students," or "teachers," or "researchers"; they are employees of Sanyo, Toyota, Mitsubishi, Toshiba, and so on.

In a formulaic society, where individualism is suppressed in the interest of social cohesion and common goals, creativity, in this case in the form of research, is not a natural resource. Creativity generally works against the social formulas, and in such a society everything is dispensable but the formulas. Accordingly Japan has tended to hire foreign expertise and to pay for the use of foreign technology, or simply to "appropriate" the latter through Japanese "students" doing "research" at Western universities. Though this approach is changing as the Japanese outrace Western research and must do their own (as in High-Definition TV and artificial blood), the buy-'n'-take approach still persists in their industrial strategy. The Japanese donate monies, endow chairs, and contract research at U.S. universities to an extent that makes it difficult for the universities not to open their doors to this kind of bargain brain-bazaar: in the $50 million range for 1988.

Because Japan's formulaic society requires everyone to know everyone else's status (so that they'll know exactly how to behave toward one another), Japanese carry *meishi*, business cards that state their name, title, and company. Upon meeting for the first time, Japanese will exchange their *meishi* immediately. A look at the *meishi* of an academic in Japan will often puzzle a Westerner, as it will identify him as a company employee and maybe not as an academic at all. Yet when these same academics go abroad to do research at a foreign university, some will have new *meishi* printed, with their company affiliation deleted, thus concealing their company identity.

Do You Have Enough Provisions?

In Japan many streets still have no names or street signs, and houses no numbers. Because of this it is often impossible to abstract any gridwork by which one could use the logic of cross-vectors to locate an address. Hence when asked directions, a Japanese (even one fluent in English) may well draw you a map of the whole surrounding area first—neat, detailed, and close to scale—then plot out the route you should take. There is nothing for you to figure out, no intersections to compute, no route to determine, no shortcuts to deduce; just a course to memorize—as he has, a schematic for orienting, a formula to follow.

■ ■ ■

Just as "directions" in Japan often require concrete pictures rather than abstract words, so "dining out" seems to demand visual facsimile rather than verbal description.

Before virtually every restaurant in Japan is a glass case in which are displayed *shokuhin sanpuru*, plastic effigies of the food, or at least the specialties, served inside. Usually these culinary replicas appear fairly authentic, though those feigning liquidity, like ramen soup, have a congealed, swamp look to them. Colonel Sanders even has a life-size plastic duplicate of himself before his chicken shacks that would do Madame Tousaud's museum proud.

But one chow the Japanese wax artists—who apprentice for three to nine years in this craft—seem unable to bring to verisimilitude, much less life, is pizza. Perhaps because it is only a recent immigrant to Japan, or perhaps because, if not actually liquid, it nevertheless has a "dynamic" surface of molten cheese and tomato paste, in which swim various bounty—whatever the reason, the real item seems to defy any reasonable facsimile, and in plastic looks uneasily like the violent rejections of the male party-animals along the late-night subway platforms.

Adding to this unsettling effect are the little waxy corn kernels floating incongruously like debris amid the ecology. Yes, corn—a recklessly bold improvisation not usually encountered anywhere else in this dimension, Italy included.

Yet somehow, through some inscrutable process, Japanese makers of pizza (itself perhaps the archetypal *gaijin* meal) have decided that corn is the archetypal *gaijin* vegetable, and therefore belongs on pizza.

Dehydrated cream-of-corn soup is now a standard in the diet of many Japanese, and for a long time cream-of-corn soup was often the only kind of imported Campbell's canned soup you could find at many of the local supermarkets . . . not *gaijin* Campbell's best, if one may venture an opinion. But except for the odd *tomorokoshi* stand selling grilled corn on the cob with soy sauce, most Japanese, as far as you can tell, don't seem all that crazy about whole corn.

When told of their error, the Japanese pizza chefs are surprised, but helpless. It is too late in any case, for corn-covered pizzas cover Japan. Even in Shakey's "-East." *Akirame* (resignation). Everybody's already memorized the formula.

Memory often does the work in Japan that *reasons* do in the West.

Pain by Numbers

You land at Narita International Airport on a flight from Los Angeles that seems to have taken an entire incarnation. Your body is mummified in the fetal position forced upon you by cheapest-one-way-airlines. Your inner tubing is now a petrified forest of extinct but warehoused meals: L.A. barbecue, Hawaiian luau, Japanese sushi *bento*. Your brain has softened and fizzed out the crown chakra from oral overcarbonation. You are a bag of time zones in a tie.

Your new Japanese colleagues meet you at the airport. Four of them. They have all traveled here seven hours from a distant city in order to take you back there. They push you aboard a bus for the two-hour-plus ride to Tokyo. Your colleagues smoke intently the whole way. Just outside the capital city you catch a glimpse of a brilliant distant arcade against the night sky. "Tokyo Disneyland," you say to show off and initiate some camaraderie. "No," one of your companions, Kobayashi, says matter-of-factly, "Queen Elizabeth Two—big love-hotel."

Autopsy over, conversation is reburied for the rest of the trip, which includes a taxi ride, a three-hour business commuter train trip filled with *sarari-men* killing each other softly with their smoke, and another taxi ride. Your lungs, like theirs, are now vestigial organs. You can detect no breath, no pulse either. You are just a ghostly trail of your own ectoplasm.

You are taken to Naka's house, where you will stay for a day until you can get into your hotel room. You say good night. But it is not good night. It is party time, to celebrate your arrival. You can't believe it. You can't do it. Your life hangs by a whisper. Only half-joking, you tell them you are going to die. No one laughs. Die if you must, but there must be a welcoming ceremony, everyone's expression says. If necessary, a burial ceremony can follow directly. You drink beer, eat sweets, sip green tea, crash into the Western bed they show you to. You hope to die. Life as worthwhile in and of itself is obviously a Western illusion.

And so, it turns out, is the desperate hope for sleep. Green tea, *o-cha*, it seems, makes the blackest of Columbian coffee seem like a sleeping potion by comparison. You have all night to ponder the power of formula, as your nerves slowly electrocute in the acid bath of *o-cha*.

Marlboro Mass

In a surface society like Japan, where formulas are the key to imposing uniformity and thus stability, it's inevitable if bizarre that the formulas take precedent over even simple perception and obvious reason. Japanese men know as well as men elsewhere that smoking cigarettes turns your lungs to stucco. Yet it is an essential ingredient in the recipe for *sararimen* and other workers that they smoke cigarettes as often as they've wind to. It is part macho-image, part addiction, part relief in an anxious society—but all formula. And besides, this slow, bad death sails under the smiling flags of *Partner, Peace, Woodstock,* and *Misty Twilight.* Different studies show that anywhere from 67 to 80 percent of Japanese men smoke. Only 13 to 17 percent of women smoke, and you rarely see them do it.

Infants, toddlers, even cradle babies, are given crib toys that are mock cigarette packages identical in appearance to the real thing.

Seen again a few years later as teens, these same kids prove that in Japan even the rebellion of the young is usually to formula. In Tokyo the prescription is for all the teenage "rebels" against Japanese society's uniformity to arrive uniformly

at Yoyogi Park on Sunday afternoon, where they publicly
change out of their social uniforms into their rebellious ones,
and flaunt the collective norms by collectively dancing. The
revolt over, everybody puts back on the clothes Mom bought
them and goes home to eat the dinner she'll cook.

"Bic-Auto"

In Japan there are no old cars on the road. There are
hardly even any not-quite-new cars on the road. In part this is
due to *shaken*, the system of requiring owners periodically to
have their cars checked for safety, drivability, lack of rust, and
so forth. But more than legality, social formula is the cause of
this phenomenon. Even if your car is in great shape, face requires that you trade it in on a new or newer one every few
years. The few "old" cars one does see on the road are called
gaijin-cars, because foreigners are the only ones likely to drive
them, having little face to lose.

Consequently Japanese auto manufacturers were encouraged early on to introduce numerous electronic parts (windows,
locks, mirrors, seats, ignitions, and monitors), as well as lighter-
weight (and thus shorter-life) components into the cars they
built, knowing that the road life of the car was limited to a few
years by the consumers' adherence to the social formula. Cars
with such components would be extremely expensive to maintain longer (especially to Japanese standards), as these components must be replaced rather than simply repaired.

A further unintended consequence has occurred with the
introduction of these cars into the American market and with
the attempt of the American auto manufacturers to produce
comparable kinds of cars. What has always been an American
"tradition"—the resuscitation and maintenance of old cars not
only by collectors but by the less affluent members of American
society—is becoming both too expensive and mechanically impossible with these "disposable" cars.

Yet the conditions that produced the problem have also,
if only marginally, created the solution as well. Americans des-

perately looking for such replacement parts they can still afford
have discovered that many Japanese wrecking yards will give
the parts away free—not being able to find Japanese customers
for the "junk"—just to get rid of them, if the *gaijin* will pay
the shipping costs.

Assembly-Line Sadness

That's it, your *gaijin* wife can't take it anymore, the regimentation, her cut-out paper-doll role, the triviality, the deadly
daily routine, the endless joys of shopping, the lack of career,
of respect, of freedom, of baby-sitters and anarchic friends. She
charges about your tiny rabbit-hutch apartment like Gomen
your caged pet rodent (no pets allowed), a nonsmoker fren-
ziedly smoking one *Mild Seven* after another, tearing her clothes
off in symbolic emancipation, declaring her willingness to throw
you off the balcony of your "mansion" for bringing her to this
"best country in the world to live in" (citing a dubious government study)—a more "reasonable" doom, you note mentally,
than old Nobuko allegedly visited on her blacksmith husband
(citing a reliable giant English-language daily newspaper).

Undoubtedly she is right and you deserve worse, but you
cannot just fold tent and go home now. Failure, shame, anomie,
akirame, not to mention the yen hemorrhage. Instead you call
Maki, the wife of a colleague and the good sport who earlier
tried to introduce your wife to the redemption of shopping.
She'll know what to do.

Maki arrives, marching cheerily into the Hutch of Pain,
looking immune to airborne vibes or immediate reality, a serene
Japanese contrast to the mad-eyed *gaijin* wife, whom she
assures, "We are the same age. . . . I know what you are
feeling!"

The whole stew of grief boiled down to this solid chestnut.
If you got the recipe, you can make the meal.

Your wife bursts out laughing, thanks Maki, and is saved.
An accidental cure—not by peerage—but by futility. *Shoganai*
("That's life").

Center of the Centerfold

All the dark-suit-and-tie boys are huddled around a particular magazine shelf in the huge foreign-language bookstore,
Maruzen, as silently absorbed in their public reading (dubbed
tachiyomi) as they are in their business papers on the morning
mob trip to work. You wander over. Ah, American issues of
Playboy, Penthouse, et al.—you should have known—all men
brothers below the belt if not in blood pints or guts length. Not
one to miss a chance at cultural cooperation, you join them and
pick up the lone copy of *Hustler*. Have all the other copies been
snapped up already, or does Maruzen import only one of the
low-rent reads? In the spirit of pure research you open to the
center. Yes, the inimitable style: glare spotlights, micro close-
ups, no misted lens, no romantic mythology, just anatomical
realism . . . but what's this? Some fiend or misogynist or xe-
nophobe has scratched off this girl's . . . well, her anatomical
realism. In moral outrage you look further. Every page the same
thing, primary sex characteristics scratched out of existence.
You try a *Playboy*, then a *Penthouse*. The same fate. Disgust
turns to frank disappointment.

Somewhere in Japan, tucked away in a darkened ware-
house at a port of entry, must toil a thousand Japanese old
ladies, scuffing away with blades and airbrushes what Time
would erase only at The End, too late for the Japanese censors.
It must be old ladies, don't you think? For who among Japanese
men are pure enough of heart to exact this relentless mutila-
tion? Wouldn't you be tempted to spare one hapless victim now
and again and take her home?

With typical Japanese indifference to rational congruity,
the government allows stag mags to be imported while insist-
ing they show no really naked people. So every single magazine
has to be screened, then scraped of the offending parts—just
the parts.

One would think in a culture like Japan, renowned for its
lack of shame about sexual realities (homosexuality, for instance, seems to leave most of them unperturbed), famous for

the availability and variety of sexual provender, that a little bit of pubic hair, *chimo* ("shameful hair"), might pass muster. The more so given the fare in their ubiquitous dictionary-size comic books, *manga*, the adult versions of which are about nothing if not sex and violence.

But in Japan the formulas for behavior, the recipes for what's Wanted and Unwanted, don't have to have any common logic—and often don't—to reconcile them to one another. Apologists will produce "reasons" if "reasons" are what calm us, but they won't be any more sensical than the formulas, and then we'll need "reasons" for the "reasons" too.

Rikutsu—a word the Japanese use to describe having unreasonable faith in "reason's" ability to know what's reasonable.

A Whale of a Tale

At a recent meeting of the International Whaling Commission the Japanese, following a Scandinavian country with a long tradition in whaling and justifying, announced that in the spirit of objective scientific research they would sail into the Antarctic Ocean south of Western Australia and determine the size of the minke whale population there. To do this, of course, they would have to resume hunting the whales, a long-standing practice they had been argued out of by other countries in 1982, when they agreed to a worldwide moratorium on commercial whaling. For starters they would kill 1,650 whales for science. The whale meat and oil, incidental to science, would be sold to consumers, of course.

They seem to be getting the hang of it—"reasons," that is.

If it's the men in Japan who get to do research in whales and almost-dirty pictures, it's the women who get to be *sukin redisu* (Japlish for "skin ladies") and sell condoms door-to-door.

Bento

The formulas by which the members of a surface society live are invariably fascinating to others for all the reasons that make them so different: their elaborateness, their arbitrariness and irrationality, their impersonality, their compulsiveness, their startling mutability and final insufficiency, and the stunned momentum with which people hang on to them in the face of faithless change and mocking entropy.

That the formulas which conjure the precarious magic holding Japan together have so little logic, and even less congruity, is to be expected. The Japanese social persona itself is a contrivance, a creation, a bit like one of its own creations, the *bento*, its famous box lunch: diverse, aesthetic, exotic, shocking even, utterly aloof from the Western imp of reason, yet still managing to make within its miniature island box a mosaic of completeness.

CHAPTER 4

The Quicksilver Psyche: Authority and the Mutable Japanese Mind

Banzai

In the movie *Merry Christmas, Mr. Lawrence* (adapted from Laurens Van der Post's novel, *The Seed and the Sower*), an English prisoner of war in 1942 Java, Colonel Lawrence, who has lived among the Japanese, knows their language, and understands their society, remarks on the reason the Japanese started a war that now threatens to destroy Japan and its culture: "They were a nation of anxious people, and they could do nothing individually. So they went mad en masse."

Whether or not his view is entirely true historically is less important than the character's insight about the Japanese in general. Often unable to initiate things individually, they are capable of enormous and dramatic shifts in behavior and opinion collectively.

At about the same time the United States was having its Civil War, Japan was having a small one of its own. The result in Japan was the collapse of the Tokugawa, the abolition of the shogunate, and the destruction or co-opting of the samurai caste. In their stead the imperial throne was restored. The emperor who gave his name to this restoration, Meiji, was only a teenager, and the real power and vision came from an elite of business, industry, and government ministers, many of whom were educated about and familiar with the outside world. Their determination was to reject the cultural and economic isolation

enforced by the Tokugawa, a feudalism that had left Japan out
of just about every human advance of the previous two and a
half centuries, and to create an industrial and commercial base
that would enable Japan to compete with the West.

In fact the West became a model during the Meiji Restoration, if not for all its democratic principles, then at least for
its manners and might. As for the former, the Japanese began
to sit on chairs and sleep in beds, wear petticoats and tails . . .
and even try hard to like eating beef. Arinori Mori, a future
Japanese education minister, even proposed dumping Japanese
for English as the national language. One Japanese thinker,
Yoshio Takahashi (according to James McClain in his very bright
and funny essay "Mr. Ito's Dance Party") argued in his book
On Improving the Race that the Japanese were "inferior barbarians" and he espoused a homespun genetic engineering that
required Western women to mate with Japanese men. It is unknown if Takahashi himself got lucky.

As for might, imperial Japan, during the imminence and
dawn of the twentieth century, went on to win spectacular victories over China and Russia, and by the last gasp of
the Great War it had acquired Formosa, part of China, and
every bit of Korea in an empire of raw materials, labor, and
customers.

This wholesale transformation, this collective shift by Japan from quaint backwater to an industrial, political, economic,
military world power took only three to four decades.

After enduring that much longer again, it took only one
more military adventure and half a decade to come completely
apart, seams and cloth.

Son of *Banzai*

The abiding existence of the Japanese social psyche has
meant that much of modern Japanese history, too, has involved
dictating that psyche's constituents and manipulating its direction. As the Japanese militarists and ultranationalists gradually
gained and then held sway in Japan during the 1930s, their

dreams of glory demanded an all-encompassing national unity, which in turn depended on an ever more rigid and orthodox social psyche. National idealogy was mixed inextricably with imperial mythology. From 1936 on ordinary Japanese were no longer allowed to lift eyes to view the emperor. The emperor himself, Hirohito, was not nearly so convinced of his divinity, and as far as the war was concerned, if he did not act to prevent it, he did not want or welcome it as did so many of his generals and bound-for-glory politicians.

Even before Japan attacked Pearl Harbor, she was being strained by a war in China that required rationing at home and that would cost her nearly 190,000 dead. Many important Japanese thought a new war with the West a nutty and disastrous idea. Before the war responsible and courageous Japanese statesmen even spoke out publicly against the military adventurism in China. A number of these men, including prime ministers, were assassinated; others were driven from office or finally into silence. In 1934 a campaign was initiated against everything "un-Japanese," and a new Bureau of Thought Control (as well as a Student Control Office in the Ministry of Education) censored and banned books and magazines, arrested the heretical, forced dissenters from their jobs, and beat them up in the streets. Even new-religion cultists, who at the time numbered well over 100,000, were targets, representing as they did a diluting of the single state-sponsored orthodoxy. After the antagonism with China over Japan's conquest of Manchuria had burst into a real war, the Japanese military used this crisis to take control of industry and the press. By the middle of 1940, political parties in Japan were banned.

By the outset of the war with the West, the ultranationalist forces, including the military, had remade the Japanese social psyche in their own image, and virtually all Japanese, the emperor included, publicly espoused and enacted the new formulas war and its paths-of-glory boys required (including the one about the danger of meat to Japanese superabundant intestines—a dodge to conceal the underabundance of meat in wartime Japan). After the war began there were still important

Japanese opposed to it, like the so-called *Yohansen* group,
whose members came from the aristocracy, the military, business, and bureaucracy, and who believed Japan would lose the
war and undergo a revolution that would destroy the country's
traditional class structure and the privileges of her elite. But
such opponents could operate only surreptitiously, which meant
quietly placing their supporters in key government posts and
waiting till the last months of the war in 1945, when things
were going so badly for the militarists that they could begin,
privately with the emperor, to discuss the options in defeat—
until then a reality completely excluded from the social formulas, however obvious and inevitable.

Even with the desperate conditions, the wartime version
of the social psyche continued to dictate the "truth" irrespective of reality, right up until Hiroshima. Incendiary bombs had
obliterated 2.5 million buildings in twenty-six cities—70 percent
of Tokyo, 90 percent of Nagoya. People ate weeds and bugs,
starved, died of tuberculosis and pneumonia. Thievery, a bug-
bear in the old social formulas, was irrelevant in the new and
became rampant. The military police chief of Osaka suggested
killing all the infirm aged, infants, and the ill (he himself was
healthy and of a safe age) as the nation could not be allowed
to perish because of them. The secret police arrested over four
hundred prominent citizens, judges and diplomats among them,
suspected of favoring peace. A demented functional autonomy
alone seemed to sustain the war formulas. Maniacally the military began planning a final horrific battle in which the Americans would be lured ashore onto the home islands and
gloriously massacred. Two and a half million frontline soldiers
were available for this Götterdämmerung, as were 4 million
military-trained civil servants and 28 million men and women
being trained for civil resistance and ready to be called up during national mobilization. Were the Americans somehow to get
beyond the cities, the Japanese military planned a scorched-
earth guerrilla war from the mountains and forests. A vast re-
doubt, meant to hold the imperial family and ten thousand

military and government leaders, was dug into Mount Minak-
ami, one hundred miles northwest of Tokyo.

The Hiroshima and Nagasaki. The dream died, the com-
pulsive nightmare ended.

For the first occupying American soldiers, many of whom
expected the same fanatical resistance and venom the Japanese
had shown in China and the Bataan death march, in the island
battles and in *kamikaze* air attacks, the civility and friendliness
with which the conquered Japanese greeted the enemy who
had incinerated their cities and their families was incomprehensible. Many Americans had the idea that had they themselves lost the war and been occupied, they would have
continued to resist (as some contemporary movies imagine us
doing in a future, occupied United States). In fact such resistance had been encountered in Europe by many of Hitler's occupying forces. The struggle with Nazism and Fascism was not
just a contest of adversaries for territory, privilege, and glory.
It was a matter of principles, and the principles would not simply vanish with defeat. Churchill's great defiant speech had
said as much. These Americans took the ferocity of the Japanese fighting for a reflection of intensely held principles. Now
for the Japanese to so completely and suddenly change their
behavior and their attitudes seemed to some Americans an inexplicable abandonment of their beliefs.

Of course, there were no "beliefs"—not the principles
these Americans meant—to be abandoned by the Japanese. The
deep and abiding hatred the Americans had inferred from the
cruelty and fierceness of the Japanese soldier had not been
based on irreconcilable differences in principle, and thus as an
ideology did not survive the end of the war. The Japanese all
fought together and unstintingly until that formula was dis-
qualified by the war's end, when everyone in Japan stopped
fighting and the scramble began to see who would establish the
new formula.

■ ■ ■

The Japanese are prisoners of *uniformity*. Westerners are prisoners of their *ideas*.

Change or Die

In a formulaic culture such as Japan's, where the glue that holds society together is everybody agreeing to act together, there is obviously less scope for individual expression or personal preference. But just because such a society requires a uniformity governed by formulas for behavior and opinion, change—dramatic change even—is not thus prevented from taking place. True, there is a self-sustaining momentum in the formulas, but that's true of any social system, even, as de Tocqueville suggested a century and a half ago, in as new and libertarian a country as America. More to the point, in Japan such momentum is a result only of collective agreement and not, as in the West, of underlying principles. Implicitly, or unconsciously, or not, Westerners have agreed to principles; the Japanese have agreed only to agree.

Thus what would seem at face value to make change in Japan more difficult, and great social shifts impossible—that is, the formulas—in fact present very little obstacle to fundamental changes, and just because there is nothing underneath to support them. Or sustain them. If a shift is deemed beneficial or necessary, as it was upon the Meiji Restoration or the end of World War II, then all that's needed is for everybody (whether willing, cowed, or coerced) to turn in that direction and manifest the change. There may well be a struggle among powerful cliques to see who will establish which new formulas to refashion the social psyche, and some souls will have to be led to the altar (there was samurai resistance in the former circumstance and strong leftist opposition in the latter), but for the ordinary Japanese it's not a contest of rational principles. It's not a matter of debating moral arguments, allaying ethical objections, pointing out logical incongruities, or reconciling principle to new behavior. For him the social psyche is a given, a sine qua non, and the question is not whether the social psyche itself should dictate these matters or not, but what face it will assume and what new formulas it will require him to memorize.

For better or worse, for all its vaunted freedom and individualism, the West doesn't have the social flexibility the Japanese social psyche has vouchsafed Japan to make relatively quick and wholesale changes, no matter how practical or beneficial, or maybe even necessary. The fact that our behavior is tied—even intellectually where not actually—to a framework of principles, limits the kinds and extent and speed of changes we might need to make.

In Japan change depends on *unanimity*. In the West it depends on *justification*.

Something equally surprising to Westerners happened in Japan at the end of World War II. When the war's loss tarnished Emperor Hirohito's divinity, and he himself voided it, the Japanese immediately and almost to a person accepted this enormous change of formula. Here was a figure before whom, just days prior, at his distant approach, people had prostrated themselves, hiding their unfit eyes less they be struck blind by his radiance or arrested for their presumption. His was a presence that, if even remotely offended by ignorant foreign governments, would cause some of his young subjects to kill themselves as proof of their umbrage. One minute he was the descendent of the Sun Goddess herself, and the next, just a frail, sheltered little man who would be allowed to go on living in the royal palace for the sake of stability, not theology. In dissent, only a brief, failed attempt by some officers to preempt the emperor's surrender speech, then a few illustrious suicides, before the whole Japanese people turned to fashion a new reality, a different world.

A few never seemed able or willing to, but they were few indeed. Probably the most famous was Yukio Mishima, a preeminent novelist, adventurer, traditionalist, physical culturist, commander of his own private army; a tragic hero with a foot each in the East and the West and the rest of him scattered

about in personal myths and demons. Twenty-five years after
the Japanese did a quick mental change out of uniform into
mufti, leaving imperial divinity and power in a symbolic back-
wash, Mishima put on his military dress-golds and failed utterly
to harangue the garrison at Tokyo Military Headquarters, or the
nation, to return to imperial Japanese tradition. Immediately
after the debacle, Mishima publicly performed his last anachronistic act as a samurai: opening his own belly and having his
spine severed at the neck by the sword of his assistant. But by
1970 this was a formula out-of-date for the Japanese, who responded only with brief fascination, thorough puzzlement, and
dismissing contempt.

If not for Mishima, then for the Japanese as a whole, the
mortalizing of the emperor and the destruction of the social
psyche woven of its radiance was painful but temporary, and
hardly life itself. The bubble had burst, and that's always dis-
orienting, for a while, but still just a bubble. They could always
blow a new one. And they did. The ensuing transformation,
that leap of everybody holding hands, from rubble and ash to
industrial, political, economic, and commercial power has taken
only three to four decades.

Imagine, though, Christians being told that Jesus Christ
was a counterfeit coin but still a pretty good guy, so his effigy
would be allowed to remain on silver crosses and in Xmas
mangers.

What you get is another divinity demoted to emperor:
Santa Claus.

In a surface society, where, by definition, opinion is collective formula rather than personal deduction, basic national
attitudes can shift profoundly and suddenly:

In a recent poll the Japanese were asked, With whom do
the Japanese now see their main friendship and their future
lying? A majority said China, not America.

In another poll the Japanese were asked, If there were to
be a war, who would be Japan's likely adversary? Forty-one

percent of respondents said the Soviet Union; 49 percent said
the United States of America.

Case-by-Case

The flexibility the Japanese can display as a nation they
can also show on the minimalist canvas of daily life. If the social
formulas determine much of the behavior and attitude in Japanese society, it is in the interstices of these fixed social patterns that the Japanese find their liberation. Of course, if a hole
in the formulas is too large—that is, if the situation is so novel
that the formulas cannot identify it or arrange its elements into
familiar relationships and hierarchies—liberty can nova into
chaos. Crevices of light can open into crevasses beneath their
feet and pitch them into bumbling farce, amok mayhem, or cat-
atonic paralysis, as we shall see later.

But in ordinary circumstances it is maneuverability that
the Japanese find amid the chinks that filagree the social formulas. It is here in these familiar spaces that the Japanese locate the freedom necessary to reconcile the competing aims of
their political and commercial tribes (*zoku*), to accommodate
a multitude of separate preferences, and to give expression
to individual natures. It is not the formulas, after all, but
the spaces they leave undiagramed, that make for the more
notorious expressions of Japanese freedom: pragmatism and
opportunism.

Within these spaces of freedom there are obviously dangers as well as virtues—for both the Japanese and their Western
partners, the more so since to the Japanese it is the lack of
rules amid the spaces that makes for the alternatives of opportunity and chaos, while to Westerners it is the lack of *principles* that makes for both.

The Japanese have trouble enough themselves simply
trying to keep track of all the rules, not to mention navigating
the spaces. This trouble is compounded exponentially when the
Japanese are forced to deal with Westerners—partners who not
only can never hope to master the rules, much less negotiate

the spaces, but who imagine it is reasons rather than rules that are missing.

You are both obviously on the verge of going insane. More precisely you are about to drive each other insane. You yourself have just come back to work from the bank, where the automatic teller machine has canceled your anticipated joy. Dispassionately the micro-chip monster has informed you that your spring bonus is 100,000 yen ($700) short of your just and reasonable expectations. Well, if not as much yen, you have passion enough for both you and the machine!

It is not an electronic blunder, you have regrettably been informed by the Japanese colleague who also serves as spokesman for the accounting office and who sits attentively across the table from you now. Deliberately revealing the sulky pain of the once-trusting sucker, you ask him why you have been shortchanged. Politely ignoring the crude directness of your question, he congratulates you in an effort to conspire in the happiness he hopes to infect you with on the grounds of your having received a bonus at all. Letting him see that you cannot allow the issue to be confused even by such a well-meaning con job, you inquire if your colleagues have received their full bonuses. Sucking air through his teeth to confess his poor ignorance of karma's mysterious laws of apportionment, he allows as they did get their full bonuses. Showing the pitiable confusion of the uncomprehending innocent, you wonder aloud why it is you who have been singled out. Generous in his desire to quench your mad thirst for causes, he lurches abruptly toward "reasons" and says you have not been with the company long enough.

Demonstrating for him the famous melancholy nod of the wronged but unduped, you remind him that your predecessor got his full bonus with even less time logged. He subtly reveals his concealed disappointment in your crass appeal to precedent and fetches up his favorite phrase to slay the Western dragon of principle: "Case-by-case," he points out instructively. You bunch your eyebrows to show the bafflement great minds have a right to feel before nonsequiturs, and cut his Gordian knot with a direct reference to the boss's original promise to pay you a full bonus. Nobly he refuses to be forced to count the petty change of logic and makes a vague allusion to your having gratuitously received "much other money."

Your expression lets him know this cheap shot frees you from having to hide your indignation, and you tell him that generosity which is given with one hand and taken away with the other is undone. He shows it is only his delicacy that prevents him from conveying his austere pity for such ignorance of life, which is nothing if not giving and taking back. You show inflated moral amazement at such implied cynicism. His impassive face reveals a condescension before one who seems compelled to display everything he feels. You tighten your eyes and lips to show him that only a man of your strength of character could restrain himself from justifiably strangling such an unprincipled, exploitative . . . His frozen smile proclaims that only a man of his strength of character could continue being civil to this logic-chopping, self-serving barbarian.

"Then, how, would you mind telling me," you ask triumphantly as you drop reason's ace-in-the-hole, "was it decided how *much* bonus I would get?"

"Special case," he explains earnestly.

Outflanked. Overrun. Routed. "This is unjust," you intone apocalyptically.

"Not so. Case-by-case," he insists.

You stare at one another, red-faced, futile, more than an international time zone and an ocean apart. If you don't stop now, you know, one of you must die. Thus do wars begin. To do your part for world peace, you bow and depart.

Shuffling back to your office, you feel the illusion of the place called Japan melting into a palpable paradox in which everything seems rigid formula at the very same time that it seems case-by-case unique. It is as if the laws of men were dissolving and re-forming perpetually.

You begin to appreciate *akirame*, and willingly yield to the urge to nap.

Invisible Ink

Written contracts, *keiyaku*, are not as common in Japan as they are in the West, and even those contracts in Japan that are concluded in writing are not expected to be any more binding because of it. In the West agreements are to be based on and justified by principles, which written contracts attempt to specify and make binding. In Japan agreements, written or not, are based on "agreement," and both parties understand that conditions can change, that shifts might need to occur. So they accommodate themselves for this possibility ahead of time, by investing no great faith in a mere piece of paper.

When a subsidiary company of Toshiba sold technology to the Soviet bloc that eventually went to make quieter and less easily detected Russian submarines, the U.S. government was "justifiably" enraged and slapped a 100 percent tariff on Toshiba imports. The Japanese company, as well as their government, was genuinely embarrassed by their mistake and took full-page ads out in U.S. newspapers profusely apologizing for this cock-up and announcing the resignation of several chairmen, presidents, and board members. Being sincere in their contrition, and having expressed it publicly, the Japanese expected the United States to lift the tariffs. In the West, "sorry" is not enough, and the United States insisted on the "justness" of the punishment. To the Japanese, friends on occasion may rebuke one another for a mistake or a slight, but mistakes do happen in life, and if the offender shows he's really sorry—he can't close the barn door now—it is inexplicable that his friend should want to punish him. Indeed such "unfriendly" treatment shames the Japanese. The Japanese appealed to the Americans' sense of friendship; the Americans appealed to the Japanese sense of justice. The Japanese got angry too.

To the Japanese a *relationship* is what holds agreements together. To the Westerner, *justice* is what binds agreements.

The Boss

Within the interstices of freedom, of course, there are no principles to structure behavior and attitude, so it should not be unexpected to find other forces rushing in to fill the void.

Easily the most important of the forces to jump in where principles fear to tread is "authority," especially in circumstances where decisions are required. Sometimes, where the social formulas can't classify the situation or identify authority, "authority" is simply seized *ad hoc*, or at least fought over, the case when otherwise decorous Japanese contend for a place on the train or position in traffic. Usually, though, authority is officially sanctioned, as it is legally in the government or culturally in the *oyabun* (mentor) or *sensei* (the teacher or the eldest).

The power and status that accrue to authority, of course, may extend to those who have connections to it. This is a fundamental reality in Japan, where *kone* (advantageous connections) is usually a much stronger force than are rational criteria such as capability and creativity, where the avenue to power, influence, and wealth is seen not to be via ability but through association. Status itself in Japan is seen to come not so much from achievement as from the importance of the university or company to which one belongs. In fact some of what the West calls consensus in Japan is often nothing more than the connections of obedient subordinates to some authority.

But regardless of whether it be an individual or a group in which the followers echo the wishes of their superior, it is rare for this "authority" to appeal to principle in order to reach, explain, or justify a decision. The sense for Westerners finding themselves in such a situation is that anything can happen, or at least that there is not much "reason" governing what is happening.

Yoshikawa, the head of the Western History Department, your new employer at the Japanese university, has informed you ceaselessly and in tortuous detours from whatever his current topic—circumnavigations even more surrealistic than Marlin Perkins leaping from alligators to liability insurance—that you will be placed at the "assistant" professor rank and not the higher "associate" professor rank. Having accepted this from the very beginning, you grow puzzled and weary of the odd random intrusion of this theme. He has written you about it before and after your accepting the job offer, called you about it in the middle of the night from across the Pacific Ocean, and now in person, when you have just landed, in the fifteenth round of championship jet lag, it is almost the first thing he says to you, adamantly, almost bullying.

Two days later, your astral body still lagging somewhere in a jet stream, your soul deep-frying in culture shock, Yoshikawa bursts into your office, apparently frying in his own batter of frenzy, and tells you you must hurry. "You are to be invested by the president and the vice-president!" he exclaims. He stares at you in sudden horror. "Where is your tie?"

You look sheepishly down at yourself. Jeans, open striped shirt, cowboy boots. Classes will not begin for another week and you are here today only to hide from Japan, which is everywhere, and in front of you right now. "Back in my hotel. Nobody told me this was going to happen today," you whine. Yoshikawa abruptly reaches forward—good Lord, he's strangling you!—but, no. He's just wrestling the top button of your shirt closed. He stands back, looks aggrieved at your appearance, then resigned—*akirame*, you later learn.

With Yoshikawa pushing you before him, you both enter the university president's sumptuous office. The president, a solid, remote man in his sixties, also a mini-tycoon from the business world, is merely the figurehead here, you've been told. The real power is the man standing beside him—"Kat," for Katayama, to his familiars—a decade younger than the president, a burly, "looser" fellow, some say downright "informal," even "unstable," certainly no longer completely Japanese after all the years he spent in America.

At your side Yoshikawa undergoes a startling transformation before this man, "Kat," his superior and mentor, his

oyabun. Usually commanding, confident, acerbic in his apprais-
als, he seems to have shrunk. His knees and shoulders sag, he
slumps forward, arms hanging impotently, his head bobs inces-
santly up and down as he stammers agreement to everything
the shogun says. He is visibly shaking.

Blissfully ignorant of what specifically to fear, since everything is intimidatingly unfamiliar to you, you content yourself with the safety of the stupid, unable to understand a word
of the ceremony in your honor.

Then, suddenly, one of those little epiphanies that step
out of the shadows of a foreign culture to give you a wink or
an uppercut: Amid the indecipherable you catch the vice president saying the English words Yoshikawa said you'd never
hear: *associate professor*.

Immediately Yoshikawa jerks and emits the teeniest of
squeaks as if an invisible silver bullet has passed through his
mind, which indeed it has. You give him a warm smile. He grins
at you maniacally.

Outside the president's office again, a dazed Yoshikawa,
looking out at you from the rubble of a personal bubble, says
without smile or frown, "You are associate professor now," as
if that's what was always intended.

And you realize, had the vice president instead just pronounced you the pope of the Holy Roman Empire, poor Yoshikawa would be on his knees kissing your college graduation
ring.

Westerners imagine *consensus* in Japan to mean a democratic decision-making process in which individual opinions are
encouraged and given and ideas judged on their merit, with the
best ones winning general agreement from the members of the
group. It's true that in Japanese corporate life attention is paid
to subordinates who are in a position to know the facts, one of
the purposes for the endless train of *kaigi* (meetings) the Japanese call. And given the rigors of international competition
and the new reliance this places on creative innovation, there
is an increasing amount of this kind of decision making in

Japan. Furthermore, with the success and failure of the various innovations, standards and "principles" are newly emerging in Japanese corporate society based more on potential for success or failure than on conformity to a formula or not, to the Wanted or Unwanted.

But in a society where formulas hold the general society together, formulas can't be a matter of individual choice. Nor are the dramatic shifts in these collective formulas open to the ordinary individual's will. In Japan, big decisions, as well as the huge social shifts in attitude and behavior the ordinary Japanese tend so quickly to adopt, still flow from authority downward, and not the reverse. It was only the emperor's decree, after all, that let the Japanese stop fighting and end World War II.

Indeed, that direction, top-to-bottom, is itself a longstanding formula in Japanese society. The Tokugawa formalized, and in many cases legalized, the hierarchy of the classes in Japan, a stratification evolved but persisting firmly in corporate and academic life. Consensus in Japan is not usually everybody getting together and deciding what to do. More often, consensus is everybody else assimilating what the boss has decided and following suit. There are still plenty of modern "shoguns" whose decisions are theirs to make and everyone else's to follow, be they arbitrary, undemocratic, or even eccentric.

He Can't Talk Now

In one Japanese university a high-ranking administrator, like many such officials, held other "side jobs" in corporations and other universities. One of his "side jobs" took him often to other cities and countries even, so that he was more away from his university than present. To suit the demands of his idiosyncratic schedule, he created a change in the formula for being absent and being present. He was absent when the door to his office was shut. He was present when the door was slightly ajar and the radio was on.

Whether he was "really" in his office or not was no longer

the formula, and hence no longer the test for fact. If a crack of light and broadcast sound seeped from his office, people acted as if he was there . . . even when he was in Paris.

When You Awake,
You Will Remember Everything

Another general faculty meeting has been called. Normally you simply receive a pale lavender mimeographed memo slipped under your office door announcing the fact in impenetrable (but by-now recognizable) *kanji* characters. Since the date and time are always indicated in Western arabic numbers and the place is invariably the same, you manage at least in this situation to function well as a tricky illiterate. This time, however, someone has undertaken an interlinear partial translation, obviously for your benefit. In handwritten red ink it reads, "Important. We must all come. We will decide who gets allocation." That last word is no doubt a dictionary discovery.

Next day, draped funereally in your best dark coffin-coat and -tie, you take your seat along with the two-hundred-odd other faculty members in the low-ceilinged, dining-hall-size room. Your place as lumpen is at the end of the table farthest from the luminaries at the front of the room. You sit next to Jun, your self-appointed interpreter at these affairs, and a marginal figure himself in the sordid food chain of the university faculty. He is young, still in his twenties, wears a loose, even lumpy sportcoat of tiny gray-and-black checkerboard material over a casual V-neck sweater, and must perpetually brush his twice-too-long hair out of his easy, open face. He is the most relaxed Japanese you have ever met, his manner always a casual promenade in some internal eternal spring. You speculate he has an open-refill prescription for ludes.

Only the long table at which the *daimyo* (lords) sit, leagues away at the front, faces directly out onto the diminishing ranks of retainers, the humblest of whom are the likes of you and Jun. You and the rest of the rest sit at tables at right angles to those of the administration at the head, often staring at each

other while the latter strafe you perpendicularly with a rain
of policy.

Your university has an exclusively male faculty. There is
a rumor that one woman actually teaches here, but you have
never once laid eyes on her and suspect she is a paper-fiction
wrought to satisfy some new directive from one of the minis-
tries. The half-dozen women in the room are uniformed office
staff press-ganged into tea-pourer service.

Once begun, this particular meeting quickly shows itself
to be a polite competition between two factions, which remain
unidentifiable to you until Jun explains it is the humanities and
science schools debating the proportions of the annual fundings
for each department. Yet it is an odd sort of "debate," as neither side actually dares rebut the arguments of the other,
addressing their "points" instead abstractly, indirectly, ambiguously, even poetically at times, apparently to some hypothet-
ical, impersonal being powerless to respond or decide.

Such airy speculations go on for about an hour, during
which time the only progress has been in the collective effort
to create an entirely new atmosphere of pure cigarette smoke.
Then an odd, articulate growling sound commences from the
front. "Kat," the executive VP, harangues the same invisible
auditor for twenty minutes, invoking *giri* (duty) several times.
His voice sounds like that of a bear who has discovered language at the same time he is eating live salmon whole.

Then as abruptly as he began, he stops.

There is a pause in which nobody says anything.

The pause stretches out into bona fide Silence. The Silence
is complete and seems to sink shafts into your unconscious,
threatening to suck you nauseously down into its morbid ed-
dies. It has endured for minutes and hints of no end. You look
around frantically. Everyone seems to be staring into the
opaque surface of the tabletop before him. Even Jun is awash
in the macro–mind currents of *haragei*, the electrochemical
conversation twinkling in the visceral wiring.

Your hair is literally standing on end, and you feel on the
irrepressible edge of leaping up and bellowing out the chorus

of "God Bless America," when someone mumbles vaguely, is echoed remotely by a couple others, and the group stirs to individual life—and adjournment.

Jun, who is in sociology, looks up at you and makes a fatalistic gesture. "Vice president says science should get most money," he allows, then wanders away.

In the silent void of self, each person has been internalizing the new formula voiced by "Kat," the boss. Each alone memorizing the new configuration in which they'll all be holding hands together, when they wake and speak again. Thus are truths made. Worlds created.

Though it has begun to change in the last decades, so endemic has been the *oyabun-kobun* (mentor-protégé) system that it pervaded even medicine. Consequently many Japanese physicians continued to employ antiquated techniques and theories introduced as far back as the nineteenth century, techniques and theories passed faithfully on from generation to generation by *oyabun* to their loyal *kobun*, the latter of whom owed their position to the former. Truth—certainly health—often took second place to loyalty.

Itadakimasu! (Let's Eat!)

There is a Japanese saying, *"Tsuru no hitokoe"* ("the crane's voice"), which is a synonym for the emperor, but which also colloquially means, "The boss's word is law."

Sometimes you wonder what might have happened to you had "Kat" pronounced you not "associate professor" but "tasty crab."

Father Knows Best

One inevitable consequence of a formulaic society in which almost everybody is preoccupied with following formulas and only a few with determining them is a common, implicit faith by the many in the "wisdom" of the few. And even where there's more skepticism, there's still a general surrender to the "authority" of the few. This paternalistic system had its feudal version in a strict hierarchy of classes, where, at least philosophically, there were as many obligations on the part of the superior to the inferior as the inferior had to his superior.

The Japanese words *amae* and *on* both convey this special relationship in which the subordinate, child, or protégé looks to his boss, mother, or mentor for privileged treatment. This treatment can include unqualified love, protection, jobs, promotion, forgiveness, advice, presents, and on occasion rebuke. Moreover this unique Japanese doting seems to have little to do intrinsically with the merit or worth of the recipient, who accepts it all as his due, a narcissism first acquired at his mother's indulgent knee—or she on her knees, in this case.

What the inferior is expected to give in return for this largess, though, is his allegiance, his credence (or at least the show of it), and at times his trembling dread.

NATIVE OPINION: Mrs. Nakasone invited some foreign first ladies, who came to Tokyo with their husbands for the summit, to a theater to see the kabuki play kanjincho, *in which Togashi, barrier keeper of Ataka, reveals his samurai's sympathy for Yoritomo, whom Togashi has been ordered to capture but lets go.*

Ronald Reagan was far from samurai Togashi in sympathy. The U.S. president and the other leaders of industrialized countries rigorously represented the interests of each of their countries, not the interests of Japan.

Prime Minister Nakasone had earlier flown to Washington to win Mr. Reagan's special favor, and thus let the president play the role of Togashi, in a metaphorical sense. But Ron refused. To conclude, Mr. Nakasone turned out to be a complete failure, while Mr. Reagan, allied with Mrs. Thatcher and other leaders, were successful in paying attention to their issues of the rising yen and terrorism.

Psychoanalytically speaking, Mr. Nakasone seems to be excessively inclined to depend on some sort of help from others. I would not say that this is his peculiar psyche. Juniors' dependence on seniors for generous help based on mutual trust has been nurtured by the Japanese collective unconscious for the past 100 years.

However, such an iemoto [head family] type relationship is not applicable to an international counterpart, particularly when the Japanese are negotiating on political and economic problems with Europeans (the majority of Canadians and Americans are of European origin).

Theoretically knowing there is a psychic difference between East and West, Mr. Nakasone still could not suppress the eruption of dependence from his unconscious into his conscious. (Y.A., of Toyko)

The Japanese will tell you that while there are all kinds of ways for the Japanese language to suggest the passive, dependent aspects of "being loved," it's not really possible in the Japanese language to say "I love you" and express the same assertive, active meaning these words convey in a Western language like English. Accordingly the Japanese will often use the word *rabu* (Japlish for "love") to convey this meaning. Complicating the matter, though, is that they also use *rabu* to mean sex. Politics can provide an example:

Since 1955 only one political party has held power in Japan: the Liberal Democratic Party (LDP), which is in fact conservative and, at least in its perpetual tenure, apparently hereditary. To some, that's *rabu*. To others, that's getting *rabued*.

Hutch Sweet Hutch

More than anything else, what the subordinate must give is faith in the rightness of things as they are. As in any paternalistic relationship the deal is a straight trade of responsibility for security. The boss gets to make the big decisions, but if they don't pan out he also gets the flak, full force, which in Japan means resignation, and still, at times, honorable suicide. The subordinate, on the other side, is spared the agony of big decisions and their failure, but he is cheated of the autonomy of adulthood—Milton would have said even of a "soul."

Human nature being what it is, having faith others will do what's best for you is little different than believing your interests and those of the cosmos are identical: you won't recognize when you've ceased being a diner and started being a meal.

The exorbitant prices for almost everything in Japan—even before the apotheosis of the yen—are notorious. Land in Tokyo goes for about ten thousand dollars a square foot, and tiny apartments can sell for millions of dollars. The ordinary Japanese themselves are boggled by such hysterical costs, which are inflated results of rotund trade surpluses and financial earnings that still go regularly into industrial modernization and real estate speculation, or abroad for more investment earnings, rather than toward an amelioration of the miserable housing situation. Such earnings account for the ten largest banks in the world being Japanese. And on paper, even simple urban householders are often millionaires; yet if they sold their land for the money, they would have to turn around and spend it on something smaller still just to have a place to live.

A typical recent fallout from such land-price inflation is the creation of three-feet-wide, eight-feet-long, one-room

apartments renting for about $225 a month. More startling is
the fact that these subcompact models of the traditionally bemoaned "rabbit-hutch" apartments are going like hot noodles.
The ordinary Japanese are still paying up, implicitly trusting
that this is just "the way things are." In fact, of course, things
are this way because in a society where the parent-child relationship serves as the model for obedient citizenship as well as
collective social change, it profits other Japanese to have it so.

With no sentimental value included, the land alone in the
emperor's Tokyo palace grounds is reportedly worth more than
all the land in California. L.A. included.

You May Kick This Picture of the Tires

When Americans decide to buy a new car, they will invariably peruse the newspaper ads, call dealers, and trudge
around to various car lots comparison shopping.
If a Japanese wishes to buy a new *Silvia*, say, she (it's
more often the woman who will make the final decision on this
item) doesn't go shopping at all, much less comparison shopping. She will probably have two or three new-car dealerships
in her immediate neighborhood, but you'll probably never see
her, her husband, or any of her neighbors there. The dealerships serve simply as bases from which salesmen sally forth for
days of handing out car literature and gently wheedling local
residents—sometimes for years, implacably and often futilely.
(You think you're tired of the encyclopedia peddler?)
What's more, once the Sato family, say, has been ground
into acquiescence by years of polite, corrosive pestering, they
would never think of disputing whatever price it is the salesman quotes or of looking elsewhere. The salesman is in effect
the authority on the price of cars. The price he shows them
from his list is what cars cost. And the Satos pay it, no questions asked.

Made in Japan . . . Almost

It's now cheaper to buy a Japanese car in America than it is in Japan. In fact it's now cheaper to manufacture a Japanese car in America. Some Japanese auto makers, such as Honda, are doing just that, then sending them back to Japan to sell to the obliging Japanese customer for even greater profit. Koichiro Yoshizawa, a Honda vice president, was reported announcing that the sticker price for the two-door Honda Accord (tricked out in a bit of leather and pumped-up stereo) will be $21,000 in Tokyo, or $6,000 more than for the comparable model in the United States.

During the international economic summit in Tokyo in 1986 journalists from around the world were stunned to discover the immediate economic costs simply to be there to cover the story. One reporter from Düssseldorf used up some of his precious time on Japanese television to say he would have to wait till he got back to West Germany (notoriously expensive itself) to afford to buy the Japanese-made Brother typewriter he had come to Japan to buy.

Thank You

Pricing in Japan is a result of several factors, including the infamous byzantine Japanese distribution system of numberless middlemen, but virtually all factors depend upon and exploit the willingness of Japanese consumers to adhere to social formulas and trust the authority behind them. Because of the cultural mystique rice has for the Japanese, and the power of a small lobby of farmers, high-quality American rice is kept off the Japanese grocery shelves, leaving Japanese rice costing up to five times as much as the American equivalent.

A small beer at a coffee shop costs $4, a cup of coffee $3. In grocery stores imported cherries sell for well over a dollar apiece and are packaged only five or six to a pretty paper cup. Imported strawberries are twice as expensive. A canteloupe or a honeydew melon will come boxed singly in a hand-built wooden cage or its own high-tech, multicolor, print-photo carton: at about $50-$135, it is product, not produce. No sane or ordinary person buys steak—not at a restaurant, nor even at a market, where it can easily cost $50 a pound.

It costs $500 to get your telephone hooked up (Nippon Telegraph & Telephone is worth more than AT&T, IBM, GE, and GM combined). Another $1,000 or so "thank-you" money to your landlord for his generosity in renting you the apartment. Thank you.

Gorufu (golf) is the participatory sport of passion among the Japanese, 10 percent of whom play the game (though millions more, quixotically, own clubs). Many courses restrict women in some way, such as barring them on weekends, but compensate by allowing them to be the only gender permitted to caddy. Wishing to join in the spirit of things, you go to the nearby golf course to sign up. You go away and never come back when you are told membership costs $75,000. Later a friend tells you that was a steal. Membership at Koganei Club outside Tokyo is over $2 million.

The formulaic Japanese notion of community and shared identity has a profound effect on their market system. Merchants are not free to make economically rational decisions, but must abide by the wishes of rival neighborhood merchants in respect to price and advertising. Consumers, in turn, buy long-established brands from merchants they consider part of their immediate community (formerly the village), meaning the shops in their neighborhood. These, after all, are the people they know, live among, and, from our point of view here, depend upon for mutual adherence to the social formulas. Given the indispensibility of these formulas in Japan to hold things together, trust takes precedent over lowest-price as the chief virtue. Given such a priority, it's easy to understand the Japanese tendency to exclude outside (especially foreign) manufacturers and merchants who suddenly try to enter the community commercially, even when they do so with lower prices and products of comparable quality. It's also easy to see how this results in an opportunity for existing local merchants to charge exorbitant prices.

Airline fares are an example. In the mid 1980s you could buy a ticket in L.A. and fly to Tokyo for less than half what it would cost you to buy a ticket in Japan and fly back to L.A. on the same airline, in the same season, in the same seat. Yet scarcely any Japanese consumers were aware of this discrepancy.

In fact this kind of predatory pricing aimed at its own consumers—while at the same time exporting at a loss just to keep foreign-market share—is prevalent in Japan. It continues to exist in part because many Japanese consumers are willing to be skinned to keep Japanese companies—and hence their jobs and the nation itself—strong and secure. It also persists, though, because most Japanese consumers aren't aware of the gouging or at least of its extent. Their ignorance is sometimes due to a surreptitious government hand in the sting that makes it hard for the consumer to detect. For example, since Japan has maintained strict quotas on foreign beef, including restricting which cuts can be sold and which stores can sell them, the inferior cuts allowed into Japan from America, say, often mislead the Japanese consumer into thinking *all* American beef is inferior.

Statistics, too, can hoodwink the Japanese consumer—as well as mislead an admiring Western public. In 1987 Japan was reported to have a per-person GNP of $19,200, as compared with America's $18,200. Japan, the Japanese were told, had become the richest industrial nation. However, in 1988 the Organization for Economic Cooperation, in adjusting for the real cost of goods and services in each country, came out with recomputed GNP's in which Japan lost almost a full third of its previous "nominal" per-person wealth, dropping to $13,000. The United States, because it had served as the original basis for comparison, remained at $18,200. Even not buying $50 steaks and $100 melons, the Japanese consumer spends twice

the portion of his income (24 percent) on food as does the
American on his.

In a paternalistic system in which the consumers play the
trusting and uninformed children, they remain largely ignorant
of how the system works, and when it exploits them.

But, as we shall see in our next chapter, the Japanese
consumer is catching on.

Midnight Genius

You are awakened in the middle of the night with a light-
ning bolt of entrepreneurial insight. It is a sound business premise in Japan that if ten thousand Japanese consumers will buy
a new product, it's quite possible ten million will succumb, so
contagious is the fever of social formula, even at the trivial
level of fads.

If you could just market mini-pics of hair, self-stick merkin
stamps, as it were, that the Japanese buyers of American *Playboy* and *Penthouse* could use to replace the deleted originals
. . . why, let's see, at 500 yen a swatch . . . my God, you'd
almost be able to afford to play nine holes of *gorufu*!

CHAPTER 5

Glitches in the Program: Dissatisfactions and Defections

Are We Having Fun Yet?

The results of a recent government study supposedly designed to compare relative quality of life in various countries around the world was announced on Japanese television. As it turned out, so the government claimed, Japan was the greatest place on earth to live. Yet even the announcer himself (usually not given to such emendations) felt it necessary to admit that there was considerable public exception taken to the authority of these findings, not least on the grounds of the Japanese' small, crowded, expensive living quarters.

Depending on one's point of view, this study was ill or aptly timed, coming as it did hard on the heels of a survey conducted by the Japan Broadcasting Corporation, nearly four-fifths of whose respondents said they felt they were living in a second-class country.

> NATIVE OPINION: My family sometimes socializes with foreigners, and when foreigners become acquainted with others, they invite them to their houses. I have often wanted to invite our foreign friends to our home, but when I think of the rabbit hutch we live in, I feel uncomfortable doing so.

A few days ago, however, I made the big decision to invite our foreign friends over to our house. They seemed to be pleased in a way, but didn't seem to know what to say about our small and shabby home. These people usually compliment others on their homes.

Our house is old and less than sixty square meters. But still, it seems to be the largest among the families in my son's nursery school.

At the same time, though, I see many foreigners in Minato-ku and Chiyoda-ku, which are first-class districts. The deluxe condominiums there are filled with foreigners!

Even though Japan is the richest country in the world, these condominiums are much too expensive, costing hundreds of millions of yen! I want to know why ordinary Japanese people like us can't have such residences in our own city. (S.K., housewife)

Chemical Peacefare

You are staring torpidly out the window of your classroom, sweat dripping into your eyes on a glaring, tropical July day. To the edge of the world you can see only the tile roofs and industrial stacks and scaffolding that cover this entire region of the megalopolis like a bed of broken bottles. Your fifty students are taking their midterm exams, symbiotically it sounds like, from the loud hum of *sotto* chatter behind you. You don't want to turn and look at them for fear of what you know you'll see: general if quiet discussion of probable answers. The notion of cheating seems to be different here.

You sigh. *Akirame.* Then you blink. Peer closer. A couple

hundred yards away a great yellow ball of a cloud has lifted
suddenly from a smokestack at about the same level as your
second-floor classroom. It's about the size of a house and so
thick as to be opaque. Your nervous system screams it doesn't
want to die.

"Shut the windows!" you shout at your students. "Shut
the windows," some of them mutter back, speculating it might
be just one more language drill. "No!" you yell, "We're going
to be poisoned!" They look at one another, casually puzzled—
the usual frame of mind in the classroom, you've learned—and
try to find out what you've said from their neighbor.

"Gas!" you point outside, and dash down the last row
slamming windows. Only the students in the window row crane
up to look outside; the others, though they may cheat like pi-
rates, are obedient to the rules and remain at their desks.
"Gasu," says one of the craners mildly. More mumbling.

You watch in horror as the noxious yellow cloud quickly
drifts toward you and the students playing tennis below. They
stop their game and look up at it. It bathes over them, and in
a moment, though they are only twenty yards from you, they
have vanished within the cloud. You gasp, thinking of the
mustard-gas deaths of World War I.

When the yellow cloud moves on, there are no corpses
strewn upon the wire. Just kids poinking the little lime-green
balls back and forth. You turn to your students, diligently at
their task. Suzuki in the third row has capitalized on the minor
distraction of imminent chemical death to copy Ito's paper,
you see.

In the cities air pollution is virtually toxic at certain times
during the day. In some spots traffic cops have had to go back
to their station every hour or so for bottled oxygen. In spite of
the availability of lead-free gas in Japan, during rush hours the
dead smell of cooked metal-poisons inebriates the brain and
embalms the vitals.

One honorable solution to this problem adopted by millions of Japanese is the deliberate regular renunciation of in-

ternal combustion for pedal-power. The nation's air, as well as the inner organs of its people, would be saved by the bicycle. Almost immediately another kind of pollution has arisen. Abandoned bicycles clog the rivers and jam the underparks of the elevated walks. Municipal governments now have regular daily details who sally forth to dredge the water- and walk-ways for this discarded machinery.

And even the undiscarded bicycles, the millions of them used daily by the obliging *sarari-men* and their wives, fill whole blocks of sidewalks, are scratched and dented and torn up by late pilers-on. Until even civic-minded pedestrians and local residents have begun to rebel.

NATIVE OPINION: Bicycle pollution is now a social problem in Japan. Many bicycles are left at random on a street near my station since there is not enough space to park the bicycles at the free parking lot nearby. A toll parking lot for bicycles was built, but not many people wanted to use it even though it is only a few minutes from the station. They still tried to park their bicycles in the smaller free parking lot, and often used force to put their bicycles into the little space available.

On the other hand, new people keep moving into my less crowded area from the big city because of the housing problem. This means more bicycles. Most people don't want to pay to park their bicycles, so they try to use the free parking lot. Then some of them began to leave their bicycles in other places. They didn't care about pedestrians being bothered by bicycles, and left them in front of shops near the station. This made some people angry.

So some people got together to decide how to get rid of those bicycles. First of all, they put up posters to let people who leave their bicycles without permission know that the road is not a parking lot. These posters were useless. So the group took a firmer line. They moved all the bicycles by truck to the free parking lot at the next station each morning.

Now there are no bicycles on the road. Some people began using the new toll parking lot, while others still use the free lot even though their bicycles are sometimes damaged.

The removal of the bicycles was a good idea. But after a while people will forget what happened before and begin to park on the road again.

I hope people stop moving into our area here. I can see no solution to the bicycle pollution. Maybe I will have to leave this bicycle hell town. (K.J., of Tokyo)

Obligation

Partly because of a general Western unfamiliarity with Japanese daily life, and partly because the Japanese are so adept at acknowledging and advertising only the Wanted aspects of their society, Westerners often remain unaware of the dissatisfaction of many Japanese with their society, overestimating the unanimity and harmony among the Japanese. For though most behavior and attitudes are still codified in Japan, actual behavior and opinion are diverging ever more sharply from formulas. The Japanese, in reality, dislike much in their lives and, no less than Westerners, can resort to violence and other Unwanted Things—increasingly so these days—as we'll see in ensuing chapters. And even where they aren't violent,

many Japanese complain regularly about various aspects of
their lives. Lawsuits about the noise the bullet trains made as
they blasted through cities lasted ten years, during which time
a number of the litigants died, committed suicide, or went mad.
In the end, of course, they won minor concessions and lost everything else.

That most Japanese still display Wanted behavior to the
great extent they do, in fact, is not always so much a matter of
their personal agreement with the status quo as it is the per-
ceived mutual necessity to preserve their general skin:

During your first two weeks in Japan, a Japanese colleague indentures himself to your service, helping you get
around, rent a flat, buy furniture and groceries, get phone service, (you sure he said $500?), open a bank account, and act as
general translator. Moved by his goodwill and unstinting effort,
you thank him often and warmly for his self-sacrifice. Each
time he says with remote pleasantness, "No need to thank me.
I *have* to do it."

Betrayal

Since the yen began its precipitous rise in late 1985 and
early 1986, it has become increasingly clear to many Japanese
themselves that they are not all in this together, that the commercial segment of the economy is simply exploiting the ordinary Japanese' allegiance to social formula and trust in
authority in order to price-gouge. As the yen rose in value
against other currencies, foreign goods became cheaper for im-
porters, yet somewhere in the daisy chain of distribution the
price of many of these goods actually continued to rise. The
Japanese consumer became baffled, then upset. The government, usually hand-in-glove with business, seemed at first to
try to explain the unexplainable, vacillated, mused, mumbled
ambiguously, then even offered some criticism itself. The media were filled with stories of this discrepancy between costs
and prices, and of the lame hooters offered as "reasons" to
explain it away.

Prices Still Increasing, Despite Weak $

Consumer prices of commodities in Japan are still rising, in spite of the weak dollar and cheap oil, while those in West Germany, also benifitting from the weak dollar and cheap oil, have already dropped considerably.

Consumer prices in Japan increased by 0.9 percent in April, compared to the same month in 1985. The F~ ic Planning ᴀ~ hi~'

According to the agency's calculations, although electricity and gas fees were lowered in June as a way of passing on windfall profits from the strong yen to consumers, it was only enough to lower the rate of incre~~ consumer pric~~' only ᴖ ᴖ

prices of commodities pushed down other consumer prices by as much as 1.6 percent. If energy fees had not declined, consumer pri~~ April would ~ ~ mi~~ ~~ ~uld ~ ~in~~ ~~~ ~

Price Surge Noticed Despite Cost Decline

Nearly 70 percent of Japanese people feel that commodity prices have increased in the past year despite the fact that the yen has sharply appreciated against the U.S. dollar and crude oil prices have dropped during the period, an opinion survey by The Yomiuri Shimbun revealed Monday.

Who Is Pocketing The Profit On Chocolates?

In defense against all this bad press (not to mention the consciousness of Japanese consumers this press was raising) the Japanese produce industry, a strong lobby and one of the native producers most protected by the Japanese government, made a good old WW-II-style propaganda movie suggesting that American fruit was so full of chemicals and pesticides it could cause birth defects.

The film got zero stars from critics and audience alike, who saw it for a badly camouflaged appeal to keep prices, and their profits, bloated. People began to recall how most of the pollinating bees had been killed off in Japan by pesticides and how just a couple of years ago a whole flock of birds had dropped marble-eyed dead just from pecking the skin of some oranges in a local Japanese orchard.

The big-budget bomb was withdrawn from distribution.

Consumer Satori

Since the end of World War II the Japanese have been carried forward as a body not only by the momentum of formulas and the will of authority but by their manifest predicament, obvious to every Japanese. At first there was the utter devastation of the war, which the only hope of overcoming was a Herculean collective effort toward a single national goal: economic recovery. Then unremittingly there is the virtual dearth of raw materials in Japan, a cause for deep insecurity among the Japanese, and one that helped lead them into World War II. For instance, 99.6 percent of the oil they use must be imported. Only a total national effort, they have felt, can offset this ineradicable disadvantage.

Then with recovery itself, the fact that almost everyone benefited from the prosperity became a practical incentive to follow the formulas and the authority behind them, to maintain the unanimity and the system it supported. In economic terms this has meant stable employment, modest consumer spending with a corresponding high rate of personal savings, low consumer borrowing, a good standard of living, an export-based economy, and gargantuan trade surpluses—and, again, all this in the absence of raw materials, colonies for markets, or a world military presence. Rather, their success is the product alone of their own spiritual resources: enterprise, hard work, opportunism, and collective effort.

But with recovery have come all the modern demons and their familiars. Urbanization has caused hideous overcrowding, loosened the cohesive power of the village and the extended family, and abandoned original rural virtues. Prosperity for its part has created sharp divisions of wealth, opened new opportunities to pursue individualistic aims, and shifted values from community to consumption. Internationalism has imported foreign attitudes and values especially attractive to the young, but influential among women and the educated middle class as well.

And now world trade has made the domestic Japanese economy more subject to disjunctures via the rising yen and competition with emerging commercial powers like Korea and Taiwan, as well as provoked demands by the other nations that Japan awake from its now anachronistic "little island" dream of itself to acknowledge its reality and responsibilities as a world economic power.

Japan, both before and since the war, has had remarkable disparities of wealth, just as it has had abundant internal social conflict—notwithstanding the image of universal harmony, *wa*, promulgated so successfully by the Japan National Tourist Office. In fact, when we speak of unanimity and uniformity within the group, we often mean "group*s*," for the wider general allegiance to national goals and authority hasn't prevented the intense factionalism and competition within Japanese politics, industry, and commerce. Mitsubishi and Toshiba may both be Japanese companies, but they compete fiercely with one another.

Historically there was intense labor conflict before and after the war, and the sixties were just as volatile in Japan as in America and Europe, with pitched battles between students and police, universities and faculty held captive, bombings and torchings, some of which is continued to this day by underground leftist groups, such as Chukakuha, who oppose Japan's political system, the monarchy, U.S. bases, and Narita International Airport. In 1986 they burned train stations, bombed tracks, and launched (ineptly) rockets (ineffective) into the imperial grounds. During Hirohito's 1989 funeral they caused a harmless dirt slide along the procession route. Yet often these disruptive or violent antisocial acts have been depreciated by the Japanese at large as either well-intentioned overexuberance of youth or the nutty inscrutability of the tiny fringe. The key, in fact, to such disaffection remaining isolated from the general citizenry has been the economic well-being of the large Japanese middle class.

Yet now and increasingly for the ordinary individual Japanese these social and economic changes have more and more come to threaten those advantages and rewards that were his and her stake in the system.

A society in which formulas and not principles account for continuity, one in which paternalistic authority rather than democratic temperament makes the real decisions, one in which naive trust takes the place of individual awareness and initiative—such a society can survive as it is, only so long as its members continue to believe in everyone's mutual commitment and reciprocal advantage. Without a "framework" to fall back on, there is just the integrity of the veneer vouchsafed by everyone's agreement to keep it intact. So when members start abandoning these agreements, letting go hands, the whole edifice is in danger.

This is the situation now in Japan. Even Japanese who have always trusted implicitly in the rightness and beneficence of "the way things are" are beginning to doubt the good faith of authority to act in their best interests. The rise in the yen and the accompanying contraction in the Japanese economy (causing reduced overtime, diminishing bonuses, layoffs, unemployment), the spectacularly unfolding Recruit scandal involving government influence-peddling (more about which later), the imposition of a 3-percent consumption tax, even a simple legislative change that now allows for the distribution of an inheritance equally among siblings—all these make it increasingly difficult for a growing number of individuals to discern their personal advantage in the system. As some let go hands, there is real danger of more and more letting go.

You can be sure that those in power and privilege fear this danger more even than do the ordinary Japanese.

NATIVE OPINION: I really regret having been born as the first son in my family.

*My two younger sisters married after
our parents put them through college. My
sisters are now living in comfort and
affluence.*

*On the other hand, just because I
happened to be the first-born son, my wife
and I must take care of my bed-ridden old
mother, even though we inherited no
property.*

*Ironically, the person who is actu-
ally taking care of my aged mother is my
wife, who has been treated badly by her
mother-in-law for over thirty years.*

*In principle, all brothers and sisters
are equal and therefore should share the
responsibility of taking care of their aged
parents. Actually, however, there are
many cases similar to the situation in my
family. Younger brothers and sisters
think only of having a good time and fob
off the burden of looking after their aged
parents on the eldest son.*

*Such a system may be rational if the
eldest son inherits all the property for
looking after his aged parents, as in the
old days. But it is unbearable when the
eldest son has to take care of the parents
without inheriting any property. I think
it is unfair. (S.A., teacher)*

Ms.

Even rebellions that have been going on quietly and min-
imally have escalated as individuals less and less identify their
personal welfare with the group's—be it the nation's, the company's, or the family's. Japanese women, long the obliging victims of a socially imposed stereotype the size of a miniature

locket, a self-effacing smile framed in the window of her small cage, are now catching on in ever-growing numbers to the demeaning roles and no-win situations their society and their men have conned them into. Hitherto willing repositories of the male notion of feminine beauty and self-effacing decorum, they can't help but notice that many of the images of sexual desirability in their society are entirely different than the images the males have imposed upon them, their wives. Advertising is full of *gaijin* women representing the ideal of sexual attractiveness, as are the promotional pictures outside many hostess bars, cabarets, and sex shows.

With this in mind, the reader might recall the "girls-wanted" card-ads described at the end of chapter one. The fantasy faces they depict are not only deliberately childlike, they are ambiguously Western and sport any color hair but the Japanese' universal black.

> *NATIVE OPINION: Hawaii is no good. I went to Hawaii for my honeymoon. I had been longing to go there for my honeymoon. Until I arrived.*
>
> *What should I have done there for four days in a bikini, a short-legged, flat-breasted cosmetic-case beauty? Honestly speaking, it was a mistake to go to Hawaii.*
>
> *The man who had just become my husband sharing our honeymoon, and was supposed to take a fancy to me, was attracted to a blond beauty instead.*
>
> *We divorced shortly after coming back from the honeymoon. Of course.*
> *(Restaurant owner, Tokyo)*

What's more, the traditional image of the Japanese woman as passive and shy has always had a counterpoint in Japanese folklore and popular mythology. Both Freud and Jung pointed out that whatever is repressed or unacknowledged in the human psyche is likely to insist upon its reality with a terrifying revenge. The Japanese woman, imprisoned by the male's dream of her as domestic for his pumpkin-home fantasy, is quite capable of exploding the claustrophobic boundaries of the social identity he has imagined for her.

Increasingly this maniacal female mutiny is finding vivid expression on TV and in comics, both useful indicies in Japan of popular attitudes. In one popular program the main protagonist is a heroine with a difference: she transforms from a shy *jogakusei* (schoolgirl) into a vengeful karate expert who kicks boys' teeth out. A new popular sitcom features a boy and girl whose souls have magically switched, leaving the boy simpering and shrinking and the girl loud and pugnacious. In general-audience TV cartoons as well as in the comics, the Japanese female is ever more openly portrayed as a gas-under-pressure, liable to explode terrifyingly under the incessant pinpricks of her duties and dearths. A recurrent image in cartoons is of a demure, doting, tweeting mama suddenly transmogrifying into a screaming virago, her face vividly distorted into a grotesque of erupting rage filling the TV screen, while her usual tormentors, her family, now miniaturized themselves, huddle in shivering, tear-sprinkler, pants-peeing dread while the former anima destroys their home and psyches.

Then, too, startling numbers of Japanese wives have simply begun to jump ship. Many just vanish, moving to other cities, where it is difficult to trace them if they escape registering at their new ward office. Others are simply not pursued by their husbands, who are either dumbfounded by such flaunting of formula or indifferent—he can always give the kids to his mother to raise.

And there's the rub. For the woman who can't abide her pumpkin-shell life, for whom hysteria and rage offer insufficient counterpoint or relief—abandoning her husband still often means renouncing her children. Even though judges are awarding custody to the mother more frequently now than a decade ago, given the way society and career are set up in Japan the fleeing wife can scarcely imagine what she might suddenly do to support a family. So a husband often ends up with the kids— if he wants them.

Thus many women are putting the renowned Japanese virtue of patience (though not stoicism) to new uses. Utilizing the time their husbands lavish at the desk of duty and the trough of pleasure, they attend counseling sessions (some public and graphically personal on TV, called *minoue sodan*), visit lawyers, advise one another over lavish lunches, bide their time . . . then, when the kids enter or graduate from university, bid a legal *sayonara* to a usually thunderstruck husband, who for the life of him cannot figure out why she would want to do that.

Aiding her in this understandable scheming is her privilege (duty) to hold and manage the household finances. Years of planning and patience spent skimming off money from the household budget in order to accumulate the private stash (*hesokuri*) all Japanese women seem to have can yield a secure, if modest, retirement. Recently, though there are very few women in the Japanese Diet (parliament) indeed, the emerging determination of women not to leave their future in the trust of their husbands has seen the passage of a law ensuring women a legal right to a share of their husband's pension.

A Japanese saying: "A good husband is healthy and absent."

Too, for the women who decide to stay in their marriage, there is the growing determination just not to take it anymore. More common in younger marriages, and still hardly the rule, the wife who is educated and more informed about the rights and expectations of her Western counterpart won't brook her husband's disclaiming of paternal duties or his tippling and philandering, however "professional" he avows them to be.

In a show of female strength not so long ago, what had been a celebration exclusively of maleness since the seventeenth century, Boys' Day, and the flying of the carp streamers, *koinobori*—those colorful fish "kites" we Westerners dangle unawares from our porches—was officially changed to Children's Day, and many sonless families with daughters, hitherto left out, began defiantly to fly *koinobori* too.

Dairy Dreams

In those marriages where she can't or doesn't care to strike a new deal with her absentee lord, the Japanese wife has some other options. While males have always had establishments to which to retreat for the extramarital company of the opposite sex, it is something brand-new for women. At clubs like *Caesar* and *Hercules*, male employees dressed like cowboys or sailors, or "gods" with names like Thor, Apollo, and Jupiter (attesting to the Japanese haziness on the lineage of Western classical divinities), court the female clientele's whims and desires. Here self-liberating wives, office ladies, and women managers can now browse the delights their compatriot males have had a franchise on for centuries.

For the wives who haven't the money or opportunity or cheek for such public frolicking in touch-bars, there is the standard love affair, pretty much patterned on the same universal model, though in Japan often consummated during a quick trip to a love-hotel. This old standby, however, might involve sleeping with your husband's friends (what other males are you going to meet?). So, Japanese enterprisers, known to be ever ready to fill a commercial vacuum, have created another option for neglected, taken-for-granted wives: telephone "love" clubs. Such clubs, like the one designating itself "Milky Call,"* drop "invitation" cards en masse into mailslots throughout the city— during the day when the husband won't see them—appealing to the lonely Japanese wife to make a call and sign up with Mr. Dairy's stable. "Milky" deliveries to follow.

There are obviously going to be some tragic consequences to these desperate escapes from the prison of social formulas.

---

*In Japan, "Milky" refers to an exceptionally sweet kind of candy.

One of the more common and depressing occurs because of a coincidence of two distinctive features of Japanese society.

First, day care in Japan is either exorbitant (up to $500 a month), restrictive (excluding infants), inadequate (closing before mothers get off work), or downright dangerous (as are some of the privately-run daycare centers called "baby hotels"). Traditionally a woman's main duty is to her children, whose care is not to be entrusted to strangers, and until recently there has been an extended family present from which to draw alternate child care. Now, with ever more urban, nuclear families, the mother often has no one else to spell her or spare her sanity.

Second, in Japan, as we've noted, there is a unique notion of the group as an integral, and not incidental, part of the individual. In the West, of course, the closest we are ever to come to experiencing this is for the individual to become an integral part of a group, just the reverse. In Japan one word that conveys this feeling is *uchi*. It can mean or suggest "home," "family," the familiar "workplace" or "colleagues," or even the very personal "my." Regardless, it connotes a warm, exclusive sense of belonging. As opposed to things outside, everything that is *uchi* is beloved, familiar, safe.

Hence, to escape their unrelieved maternal duties, Japanese mothers will sometimes leave infants and toddlers alone, asleep, in their apartments and houses in order to shop, go to lunch, or even step out on the town at night with their husbands, given that miraculous opportunity. They may lock the doors when they leave, feeling that this is the only precaution necessary because of the intrinsic security of *uchi*.

Sad to say, these mothers are too often tragically proved wrong. The close juxtaposition of much Japanese housing, its highly flammable composition—plus the widespread use of kerosene heaters in the winter—all make for fatal fires and gas asphyxiations.

Eight to Five

Japanese men, on the other hand, have always had what looks to outsiders like plentiful, regular, and sanctioned relief from the rigid formulas of the company (*kaisha*) and of society. But we have to realize that, as infinitely preferable as his lot is to his wife's, much of his "relief" is itself formula and thus obligatory. He *must* go out with his colleagues after work, the assumption being that teamwork is enhanced by buddy-dom. To beg off from such quasi-obligations has customarily meant career suicide in Japan, and often means that still today.

This notwithstanding, some *sarari-men*, usually younger ones, are forsaking the afterwork male bonding for domestic pleasures, believe it or not. Seeing it as a clear-cut choice of career or family, these men have opted to know their children and wives before they drop dead of company spirit. Regarded as incomprehensible and anathema by their bosses, their attitude is derisively termed "my-home-ism."

Another cause for a growing "my-home-ism" is the TDU system (or *tanshin funin*) created and used by many Japanese companies. Because a *sarari-man*'s soul is by formula, if not by law, company property, his company can do with him as it will, the most feared "doing" being to be placed on TDU: Temporary Dispatch—Unaccompanied. Japanese companies feel free to move their employees where they will, often abroad, regardless of the latter's situation or the other social formulas such a move will conflict with. Japanese wives and mothers, ushering their kids through the gauntlet of Japanese education, are loathe to remove them from their grueling routine of private lessons, cramming and public schools, and are downright unyielding about taking them abroad to foreign schools, where they will both learn Unwanted Things and *not* learn the facts and fodder they need to pass "examination hell." Moreover, in some cases the company simply tells the employee he is going alone. There are reportedly well over 200,000 TDU Japanese employees now.

TDU can last as little as a few weeks, but just as often it can last a year or more. What the *sarari-man* uncoupled from family faces, of course, is not just absence from his loved ones (whom he might rarely catch sight of even "living" at home), but the daunting task of taking care of himself—a task for which he is no longer prepared. TDU is supposedly one not inconsiderable cause for the billionfold consumption of *insutanto ramen* (dehydrated cup-of-noodles) among the Japanese.

One recent case of TDU involved a *sarari-man* who had been sent by his company, sans family, to Korea a decade previously. He begged to be transferred back to Japan, but apparently he was too valuable in Korea. Rather than a direct no, the company speculated, "Soon . . . maybe soon."

And for those for whom neither home nor *kaisha* can quench their thirst for individual anarchic liberation, there is the night:

Midnight Metal Samurai

A remote, insistent buzz nags at the edges of your sleep. You groggily take a vague swipe at it from amid your futons and quilts, and the irritating sound seems to veer evasively to a lower frequency. You sail lazily down toward the deep currents of sleep again, when—that insect noise yanks you abruptly to the surface.

You crack your eyes in the dark, hoping against luck to spot the mosquito against the moonlit paper window so that you can burst the minuscule intruder between two hands clapping. The noise takes another crazy dip, then begins to climb eerily up the scale, increasing in volume as it goes. A horrible suspicion begins to inveigle your judgment, but you resist irrationally. No, it can't be, you simply will not have it, it is not going to happen.

The hell it's not. With an abrupt quantum leap in volume, the presumed mosquito haughtily casts off its insect disguise and swells to menacing human proportion. Your eyelids snap to incredulous attention and your muscles tighten around you in a paroxism of panic. Oh, no, please, you beg your own deity and all the company of little gods inhabiting the islands of Japan, please let it be anything but that.

No chance. It's still some blocks distant, but it's on its way as sure as fate itself, heaping up the decibels as it comes. Futilely you tell yourself that maybe they're just on a parallel street, that you won't get the full weight of it this time. In fact maybe this is as loud as it's going to get tonight. You can bear this, you tell God, trying to cut a deal.

No deal. On they come, rolling up the paving behind them, and all the houses, and all the apartments and all the people, vacuuming them all up in mounting sonic cataclysm (Surely it can't get louder?) until it crescendoes into a single perpetual roar that obliterates the boundaries of your room, your mind, your dreams and values, your memories, and your will, snuffs out time-and-space itself—Gape and despair, mere mortals—the Midnight Metal Samurai!

For all its veneer of lacquered harmony and professed contentment, Japanese society is a tough chew for the individual, demanding an obedience to collective values that enables them to harness group energies and minimize the impediments conflict causes. In the light of day the streets belong to the complex of social and work obligations that is Japanese society, but at night these metropolitan straightaways are the transient kingdoms of urban bands of Honda, Suzuki, and Kawasaki muscle bikes, liberating their riders from their hidebound company roles and incinerating their normal social considerations (not to mention the hearing and sanity of everyone within earshot) in an orgy of internal combustion.

The Japanese, whose *gaman* (endurance) prevents them from complaining, generally suffer these night riders in silent rage; but occasionally a thwarted sleeper is driven over the edge. TV news recently reported such a man, who leaped from bed and killed one of the metal warriors with a board by knocking him off his Honda on the rider's fourth pass of the night. The tormented insomniac said he was very sorry and would not do it again.

Phantom Biker Hurts 3 Women

ICHIHARA, Chiba—Three young women were attacked and injured Friday night by a motorbike rider who swooped on the girls and hit them on the head with a blunt weapon, police reported.

The first attack occurred around 7:30 p.m. when a 15-year-old high school girl bicycling home was struck on the back of her head by a motorcyclist who then roared away. The weapon appeared to be a metal bar.

Around an hour later while police were investigating this attack, two other women were similarly attacked about two kilometers from the scene of the first assault. The victims were a 17-year-old office worker and a 19-year-old college student, both of whom were also riding bicycles.

All three women suffered skull injuries requiring about 10 days of medical treatment.

Police believe all three attacks were committed by the same culprit because the method of assault was identical. An alert was issued for the attacker.

Blessed Surcease

Even for those men who allow themselves no respite from the daily grind, there is the imposed respite of collapse.

For four decades the fortunes of the Japanese economy and the samurai-salary men who drove it on were straight, upward lines on the profits chart. Hard work invariably paid off and became the chief criterion for success. Then the yen rose dramatically in value. It became harder to sell Japanese products abroad, profit margins shrank or vanished, competition

among the Japanese companies themselves grew necessarily
fierce. Tough decisions, often at odds with customary business
practices, such as steady (often unmerited) promotions and lifetime employment (even for the "by-the-window bunch," dead-
wood who are given no work to do) became unavoidable.
Promotions were fewer, people had to be laid off. Harmony,
group spirit, and personal serenity were taking a shellacking.

The typical response of the Japanese *sarari-man* and
manager has been to do more of the same: Try harder! (the
same command with which Tojo in 1945 wanted the emperor
to inspire his exhausted people to fight on). But there is a limit
to the efficacy of this virtue, too, and some market forces—like
war realities—have nothing to do in the first place with hard
work. Especially in Japan, though, as we've seen, formula often takes the place of reason, and momentum of insight.

So the *sarari-man* worked harder. And harder. And earlier, and later, and through lunch, and through weekends and
holidays and vacation, until one morning he could not get up
off the futon. That was the first and universal symptom of a malady that is now a well-known and pervasive syndrome in Japan.
No matter how much his wife tugged him, hectored him, cursed
and threatened him, warned him, beat him with brooms, cajoled
and flattered him, begged him on hands and knees to remember
her and their children—he would not get up and go to work.

There are now a growing number of small sanatoriums in
Japan catering to the multiplying victims of this urban occu-
pational funk. The patients lie immobile on their backs in plush
beds, forced by minimal space to be close and at odd angles to
one another, staring at invisible red ink and diving sales lines
delusionally projected onto the ceiling. Psychiatrists in white
clinical coats slipper softly among them, whispering, comforting, trying to hush the clangor of the bullet train to nowhere.

Sarari-men have a saying in Japan: *Mi o ko ni suru*, which
translates "to work hard." But literally it means "to grind oneself to *powder*."

Even the contemporary warriors at play on the summer diamond, the models for Japanese youth of the worth of training, obedience, stoicism, and "fighting spirit"—the professional baseball players—seem not entirely convinced of the worth of these virtues. If group unity and team spirit were so vital, they reasoned, then how come these itinerant *ronin* American teammates were getting so much more money than were the Japanese players, who were also confined to one-year contracts and forbidden to have agents?

In early 1986 the newly formed Japan Professional Baseball Players Association—a full-fledged union—met to draft demands for more equitable pay. And though only twenty representatives of the forty-six invited showed up, with most of those absolutely unwilling to advocate "free agency" or the right to have an agent, their simply being there was a social revolution—much as if the Boy Scouts were to demand baksheesh money from old ladies they helped across the street.

Well, Then, Just Draw a Picture of It

If memory is the common glue in a society like Japan, held together by formulas for thought and deed, that glue is made the thinner by changing attitudes of the young (*shinjinrui*, meaning "new species of human") to that center pole of memory, *kanji*, the original writing system. Each year the elders wring their hands over the young, who often manage to memorize even fewer of the 50,000 *kanji* than the measly 1,850 they are asked to know and turn ever more to the phonetic *hiragana*. If they won't use the fixed ideograms, might they not leap out of the *bento box* entirely?

CHAPTER 6

The Blind Eye: Insensitivity Outside the Formulas

Dosoku de Fumikomu (Entering the House with Your Shoes Still On)

The Indian mystic Bodhidharma founded in sixth-century China what later became Zen in Japan. Called Daruma by the Japanese, he was so determined to achieve enlightenment that he sat for nearly a decade looking into nothingness while his legs atrophied and vanished. Perhaps acknowledging the role determination plays even in so elusive a matter as chance, the Japanese have made Bodhidharma a talisman of luck. Politicians, merchants, anyone undertaking an enterprise that entails risk and vicissitude, buys a squat Daruma doll and paints a pupil in one of his cloud-white eyes. If he is successful by the end of the year, he paints in the other eye.

Outside the social formulas in Japan, it seems that spiritually one eye gets stuck shut sometimes.

If the Japanese personality has its public (*tatemae*) and private (*honne*) faces, the venues for these two faces don't seem to distinguish themselves accordingly—at least to the Westerner, who expects the Japanese social psyche to have a strong "public" (civic) element to it. But to the Japanese the real distinction may be between what's mine (or "ours," the group's) and what's nobody's.

If the private household or the workplace are abodes to be meticulously kempt by the Japanese, the "out-there" (the streets, parks, even Mount Fuji) is everybody's nowhere. You are no more likely to find a public park looking like a manicured garden than you are to find it a littered, Agent-Orange dust bowl (or kept from being one only by paying a legion of caretakers to clean it up). An urban river might well be an elephant's graveyard of discarded consumer goods and pestilent effusion. And if the longing for what is green and alive conquers the lack of "public" identification and a park or urban river is spared, one's "sensibilities" in public are not.

In "public," shunned bicycles mine pedestrian ways the same way people mine one another's hope for serenity. Famous for perpetually considering how their behavior might affect others within their group (family, village, *kaisha*, apartment house, etc.), the Japanese thus are permitted a corresponding disregard for those outside the group. Queue lines are honored more in the breach than in the lines, and the Japanese driver, though by miraculous injustice statistically safer than his U.S. counterpart, often seems to have slipped not only the bonds of social reserve but a straightjacket too.

Public transport, especially the *chikatetsu* (subway) and the local commuter trains, have apparently been tacitly designated unposted ground for bad behavior. It stands to reason that if everywhere you go you must be selfless, the saving recompense of selfishness must be snatched from the intervals of being nowhere: going and coming. Gloved platform attendants do indeed stuff the crumbs of commuters into trains already stuffed, by any standards of physics, much less of civility, doing so with apparent relish, as if the best job in Japan outside of *oyabun* is getting to punish your fellows for there being so many of them. "All right, if we're all in this together, then you're all going to have to fit in there together!"

Once layer-caked into the train, voluntarily or not you are drafted into a guerrilla war that is as grim as it is futile. Especially if you have no seat. As if there were space or breath to be won, the passengers torment one another with subtle heels ground into the bridge of feet, inconspicuous knees into groins, invisible elbows into ribs, knuckles into spines, and if you're a real pro, even fingers into eyes, though this requires considerable practice in the subterfuge of feigned pointing at passing landmarks and should not be tried by amateurs at home (New York, for example). And all of it usually in preternatural silence and accompanied by smiles. Unless, of course, you all find yourself abruptly invaded by the high school boys. Then, as we've seen, everyone is suddenly and equally taken prisoner of war.

Yet these little, daily wars of attrition are naught compared with the psychic no-man's-land made of public transport after the witching hour:

The last Meitetsu train of the night is carting you home from a command performance thrown by some businessmen who have been pretending for some weeks to learn English from you. Scholastically they have been a disappointment to you. Tonight you were a social disappointment to them. You drank only enough to kill a monkey and failed completely to take your pants off, as did Akiyuki-san, who insisted on demonstrating how Japanese men used to be able to ride the trains thus unencumbered—until all the foreigners arrived. Silence after this remark, then Akiyuki is gently chided by Chitoshi-san, a slightly older man, for his tactlessness, causing Akiyuki to beg your forgiveness on all fours, demanding to be allowed to take you to "pretty girls" to wipe away the shame. You tell Akiyuki-san that that is unnecessary, that there is no shame, but he relents only after you beg him to on all fours, telling him your *gaijin* wife would divorce or even kill you for that indiscretion. Much astonishment all around. Then indulgent mockery for you, the minion to *kaka*, petticoat rule.

But now, wearily on the way home to life under *kaka*, having failed to descend the evolutionary ladder yourself, it seems you are about to get an object lesson in same. Sitting across from you, or rather "heaped" across from you, is the master who will teach you. At the moment he is in a meditative state, wrapped in the redolent aura of Suntory whiskey, his blood-mapped eyes open but sightless. Inhabiting a body in its late twenties or early thirties, he seems only to occupy his disheveled business suit, a temporary corporeal guise of the master, no doubt. His tie has come completely undone in the incarnation process, it seems.

Abruptly he returns from whatever other world, and his eyes come to focus. On you. He can't believe it. He laughs aloud. You look around, but nobody else—the few riding the late train—takes notice. He rummages in his pockets, perhaps for a token from another dimension, but only comes up with his fags, called *Sometime*. They are all broken in half. More casualties of time travel. He throws them down happily and leans forward to get a closer look at you. His smile is utterly different than that of his daylight counterparts; he is completely enchanted by you, or by your appearance. He asks you a question you can't make out. He seems crestfallen by your failure to comprehend. Nothing more defeating than a bon mot misheard. He mutters sullenly, then stands up to show the world he can do it. He sways about on sea legs and says something belligerent to you. It sounds like more *kaka*, but when he repeats it you recognize it as *baka* ("ass!").

You ignore him, as you're supposed to. Everyone in Japan loves a drunk—the much appreciated, even respected *yopparai*. Drunks are forgiven almost anything in Japan, quite literally murder now and then. After all, when would you get to be a jerk in Japan if not when you're drunk?

He staggers the step it takes him to stand over you. He points at you in disdain for the benefit of the other passengers, one of whom helpfully suggests he sit down. He's astonished, then amused at the impertinence. He is in the process of un-buckling his pants for whatever arcane display (could this guy be the avenging astral projection of the maligned Akiyuki-san?), when the train slides to a halt, dropping him backward into his seat. The doors open, no takers, and close.

Then, just as the train is pulling out, a Hollywood miracle happens. A woman dashes onto the platform and up to your train. She halts right next to your window, her arms stiff at her sides, fists clenched, and casts a withering, wide-eyed laser-death look at your tormentor. She doesn't move a muscle, make a sound, but she manages still to paint a Medusa of white rage. The train picks up speed, the woman's eyes immolating the of-fender even as he is borne away.

You look at him. He is on his feet, gaping back at the window that last framed what could only be his wife. He gestures guilt-ily, tardily toward the next train stop, wearing now the obse-quious smile of the daylight, already bent in the semicrouch of contrition. *"Sumimasen* (Sorry)" he mumbles vaguely. Seems like there's a lot of *kaka* going around these days.

Just before the train hauls to a stop, your guru of glut turns suddenly red and sweaty, tries to grin at you, and just makes it out the door before he liberates his dinner and drinks all over the Kanayama platform.

Some *baka* about, too, maybe.

Deadlines

Shigeo Nagano was the best. Everybody liked him. Every-body trusted him. He cheated everybody—or at least four thou-sand investors (mostly housewives and pensioners)—out of $1.5 billion with his "Pure Gold Family" gold-contracts scam. As in the Miura murder case (more of which later), reporters camped outside the suspect's apartment—in this case in Osaka—waiting for his arrest.

Instead two men in street clothes pushed their way through the crowd of some forty reporters and announced quietly that they had been asked to kill Nagano. Two private security guards said they should not do that, but ignored the two men as the latter broke in through a small window, dragging in behind them a short sword. The crowded representatives of the media tussled for the best vantage.

The videotape made that night's TV news and the top of the charts. One of the avengers held Nagano in a wrestler's headlock while the other skewered him with the sword. Fatalistic, Nagano put up scant resistance and made little sound. Spiffy, he wore his sunglasses through it all. *Akirame.*

But if the witnesses at the scene seemed paralyzed by *akirame*, some other Japanese watching it on TV were not, and they called TV stations to express outrage. Outraged, too, were some in the media itself. The *Yomiuri Shimbun* (newspaper) questioned not only the society's nonviolent myth but its social values.

If what is "public" in Japan is really just "out there"— that is, nowhere and nobody's—it is understandable that in "public" few of the usual provisions have been made for etiquette to take up the slack in principles. True, Japanese pedestrians will all stop for a red light, yet if just one of them decides to walk against the light, they might all walk against it. And driving in traffic can feel like joining a cattle-call audition for the next Road Warrior movie. Nor is anyone spared. That otherwise holy shiboleth of group solidarity, *ware ware nihonjin* (we Japanese), becomes a mere slogan, and the Japanese who count on it might well wish things were a little less "case-by-case." In "public," where circumstances often lack a clear authority otherwise prescribed by social formula, many Japanese tend either to vault wildly to brazenness, as in driving, or to freeze into mother-may-I statues.

On July 23, 1988, a Japanese Maritime Self-Defense Forces submarine, the *Nadashio*, and a civilian sport-fishing boat, the *Fuji Maru No. 1*, ran into each other in Tokyo Bay. It was no fender bender. The *Fuji Maru* sank immediately. The submarine, which was running on the surface, suffered little damage.

At the moment of collision about twenty people were thrown off the *Fuji Maru* and into the water next to the submarine. Witnesses, including some from the fishing boat itself, reported that the submarine crew members who were on deck simply gaped at the people thrashing about and screaming in the water before them.

One survivor from the *Fuji Maru*, who was later rescued by another boat, expressed his astonishment at the gawking inertia of the submarine crew watching him, and said he even began to assume that it must be an American submarine and changed his shouts for help from Japanese to English.

Though the submarine was easily the vessel closest to the flailing passengers, it was other boats coming to help that saved seventeen survivors from the water. The submarine pulled two people to safety.

Maybe that's what "*Self*-Defense" means.

The Second Coming
(Batteries Not Included)

Japan is jammed full of gods and ghosts and spirits and demons—good ones, bad ones, helpful and malicious, eternal and evanescent. One—with the power to flabbergast, if nothing else—the pilgrim seeks not in the magical formulas of the Shinto shrine, nor in the solemn effigies of the Buddhist temple, nor in the animistic woods and mists of the mountain forests. Rather the devotee must search out his deity in the motley, mechanical hectic of *TOY-RAND*.

At first glance *TOY-RAND* (Toyland) seems only another familiar retail avatar for gaudy and amazing relics in the child's universal religion of play. There are dolls and balls, monsters and models, play-house/play-war paraphernalia, trikes and kites and puzzles and games. But *TOY-RAND* is more. More than a monument to the child's hallucination of ritual home-ec, athletic glory, and military invincibility. For here, squatting amid

his oblivious, trivial court of fun-for-sale bozos, is . . . God-
Jesus.

God-Jesus (his first name being pronounced "god-oh" in
Japanese) is about half a foot tall, smaller than your average
powerless teddy bear. Much smaller than his namesake, we de-
voutly hope. Nor does he have long hair or blue eyes. In fact,
he doesn't have any hair at all, an omission that downright
discourages human identification—probably a true but none-
theless depressing feature of gods. He does, however, have
white skin—preternaturally white—and blue trim, if that's any
consolation. But what really sets him apart as a god, gives him
his cachet, so to speak, are his red eyes. Big red eyes. Big sightless, pupilless eyes that light up like radioactive hell. He's a lot
scarier than his Renaissance pictures.

God-Jesus is a very squat, blind, hairless, plastic toy robot.
He looks, in fact, like any other toy robot: a featureless, stiff-
jointed, sexless, unclothed machine.

Indeed, only two things distinguish this deity from his
mere-mortal peer robots on the shelf. First, he has his name
modestly printed in tastefully small black letters across his
overweight waist: "God-Jesus" on the left side of his circuit-
board buckle, and "Fortuneteller Robo" on his right. Much as
any good-ole-boy or cowpoke would have tooled on his leather
belt "Billy-Bob." You c'n jes call me God-Jesus.

But the wonder that really sets God-Jesus apart from his
plebeian fellows (as the boast on his belt suggests) are his powers of divination—a magic much prized in Japan. You can ask
God-Jesus any question about anything in the universe or beyond and he will answer you as long as it is a yes/no question.
To accomplish this wizardry, God-Jesus calls upon the aid of a
minimicrochip in his stomach, which sets him nodding and
shaking his head to your questions. What makes him nod rather
than shake? . . . well, God only knows. The hearts on the box
in which he comes suggests that God-Jesus is especially suited
to questions about love. After all, God-Jesus has always loved
this topic best. Though in this case there seems to be some cultural confusion between "romantic" and "universal" love.

There is also a TV program, a comedy, that has as a regular feature a man in a loincloth and long hair hanging from a cross on the wall, apparently asleep or dead, before whom anxious, tittering audience members beg their case for prayed-for prizes and favors. If it's convincing testimony (rare), a bell rings and they're rewarded. On the other hand, if they can offer up only routine sorry mumblings (frequent), the crucified god's eyes open scampishly and the beseecher is doused with a bucket of water from high above—much like (another cultural confusion, you wonder?) the heroine in the movie *Flash Dance*.

There is now a board game on the same theme with the same character. God-o sure works in mysterious ways, doesn't he?

If that's not mysterious enough, there's a fast-food restaurant in Japan called GOD Hamburgers. That God-Jesus is a real card.

Nobuko's Thesis on Blaise Pascal

Many Westerners mistake the Japanese preoccupation with ritual and ceremony for evidence of a deep spiritual nature. Actually, in so-called spiritual matters the Japanese are very pragmatic, as opposed to mystical. In religion many of them seem much more concerned with the paraphernalia and gestures than with the numen of belief. In fact, religion in Japan is more cultural than religious.

Unless it's just the lure of the impossible challenge that drives them, this difference seems to have escaped Christian missionaries, who abound in Japan to this very day. Indeed there are more missionaries in Japan now than before the Tokugawa pogroms; and yet, for all the manpower, zeal, and earnestness, there are proportionally many fewer Christians in Japan today than in the first, preexclusionary years of the Tokugawa era. And in many cases even the few conversions they manage are misunderstood by the missionaries—or overlooked to avoid a sense of futility. Conversion in Japan does not at all mean a profound "spiritual" shift. It is not that uncommon in Japan for a person to practice several religions simultaneously: to be born Shinto, married Christian, and buried a Buddhist.

In survey after survey similar results emerge: Eighty percent of Japanese claim to be Shintoist, 77 percent Buddhist, 1 percent Christian, and another 1 percent other. Then, too, 80 percent say they don't care about religion. Add those up and you have 239 percent of the population pragmatists.

No wonder there's overcrowding.

Such pragmatism, when tuned to religion and mated with Japanese fastidiousness, can appear to Westerners as indistinguishable from superstition, "spiritual formulas," if you will, for which the Japanese have a notorious penchant. One well-educated, urban Japanese couple found themselves in an exhausting, if not unusual, predicament while trying to adhere to such a formula. They had acquired a new apartment and moved

their belongings in, only to find out that it would be unlucky
to live there before the New Year, three months away. With a
tour de force in logic, they decided it wouldn't exactly amount
to "living" there if they went somewhere else to sleep each
night. So, every night after dinner, these harried vampires
would slip out while darkness fell and dash off to the house of
the groom's parents.

And our Nobuko, the alleged murderess of the blacksmith,
the pair who opened our book? Is it possible that she hoped to
slow down, at least, the man's malevolent wandering spirit,
come back for retribution, by lopping off his feet? Under the
circumstances it certainly stands to reason. No use taking
chances.

Victims

No one can gainsay the suffering of the Japanese people
in the months closing and those following the end of the Pacific
War, their special status as sole victims of the nuclear bomb,
nor their general active commitment to peace. With diligence
and purpose—yet virtually without bitterness—they keep alive
a memory of an act humankind must never repeat, if for no
other reason than human survival.

Nor does it diminish the truth of their suffering or commitment to point out that, at least in the popular imagination,
the Japanese memory of the war is almost completely one-sided.
Their commemoration of Japan as ground-zero for a horrific
military experiment is virtually unbalanced by a memorializing
of Japan's behavior and responsibility in the war that only
ended with the A-bomb. The Bataan death march; the Burma-
Siam "railroad of death"; the sack of Manila; the "731 Unit"
germ-warfare experiments on Allied prisoners; the atrocities
against civilians in China, Malaysia, Indonesia, and elsewhere
in Asia; not to mention the obvious impetus that was Pearl Harbor—these unpalatable and unexonerating memories occupy

only marginal space in the social psyche of the Japanese, as well as in the institutions that might make that psyche more whole and honest.

Most foreigners who visit Japan to participate in the various "Peace Days" bring with them some healthy guilt and spiritual pain; to them the commemoration is a universal commitment to awareness, a matter of grief and resolve for all of humanity, not just a memorial to a single people. Yet the "Peace Days" are in fact more simply national and local than these visitors would care to know. For each of the "Peace Days" has been set to coincide with a date of a major Allied bombing (conventional as well as atomic) on a Japanese city.

In 1955, through the efforts of Norman Cousins, two dozen "A-bomb maidens," young women who were severely scarred by the nuclear explosions in Hiroshima and Nagasaki, were brought to New York for lengthy treatment at Mount Sinai Hospital. It was important that these "maidens" receive plastic surgery to minimize their disfigurement, not only for their psychological well-being but for their social rehabilitation. Japanese society, as we have noted, can be especially harsh on the foreigner, the outsider, the "different." With their disfigurement, these young girls suddenly established and entered an entirely new category of "different" and thereby suffered some of the same ostracism as did other "aliens." And victims of the A-bombs in general—even those with relatively unnoticeable physical injuries—often came to be seen as being from a different category than "normal" Japanese. Sometimes they were simply orphans, who, being without the context of family, now had only an amorphous identity and hence diminished connection to Japanese society.

Another legacy of the war and of the continuing garrisoning of American armed forces in Japan are the children of mixed-race parentage. Derogatorily called "halfs" by "whole" Japanese, they represent a tragic case where half a loaf is not better than none. Neither Japanese nor American—nor *even*

Korean—they correspond to none of the formulas for identifying who one is or isn't. And if the Japanese in art love nuance and the merely suggested, and in conversation the indirect and implied, in social identity they abhor the ambiguous. Many Japanese, just in order to have some category to put them in, for the sake of orderliness, think of them as American. Yet they are not American, and the great majority of "halfs" are relegated to marginal employment, narrow marriage opportunities, and association with their own kind—a species of very few indeed.

The best fate "halfs" can generally hope for is to make good fortune of their bad (as a woman once suggested and later became a saint proving how difficult that is), exploiting the uniqueness of their caste and the exoticism of their beauty—both acknowledged in Japan—by becoming entertainers and models. In Japan, especially, those whose lives are measured out in the social recipes need desperately the vicarious vision of those whose lives are not.

Better Dead Than In-the-Red

In July 1988 a leader of the ruling LDP party, Michio Watanabe, who in Japan is known to be a plain-speaking sort of guy and who at the time still hoped one day to become prime minister, opened his mouth and garrulously expelled enough hot air to make room for his foot. Watanabe, in a speech before his fellow party members, ruminated aloud on the difference between Japanese and American attitudes toward debt. Americans, he allowed, have no savings and use credit cards a lot. The Japanese, he went on to boast, are so shamed by bankruptcy that they flee into the night or commit family suicide. Then, drawing a scandalous contrast to these two edifying Japanese solutions, Watanabe voiced the opinion that in America there are many blacks, and so on, who casually go bankrupt using credit cards whose charges they know they can't pay. In the ensuing storm of amazement and disgust (from both U.S.

and Japanese quarters), Watanabe apologized for "misleading remarks."

To many Westerners, Watanabe's remarks were astonishing, the more so since they reprised an earlier tacky skit by another Japanese politician. On September 22, 1986, the then prime minister, Yasuhiro Nakasone, discussing national literacy and intelligence levels at a meeting of his Liberal Democratic Party, announced, "In America, because all those blacks, Puerto Ricans, and Mexicans are included, they're far and away lower."

Westerners had been universally shocked at the blatant racism in Nakasone's remarks, especially coming as they did from a man who had made his reputation as one of those rare Japanese with skills in international diplomacy and intercultural communication. Some Western observers even took his remarks as a deliberate rejoinder to Western Japan-bashing, itself a result of the growing trade imbalance between Japan and the West. Yet there is a simpler and more likely explanation for Nakasone's remarks.

It is important to note first that Nakasone seemed and probably was legitimately surprised at the hostile reaction in the West to his remarks. He later apologized, no small concession from a country's head of state, especially when compared with, say, recent American presidents, who seem never able to say they're sorry, even coming as they do from a country where "face" is supposedly of much less significance. Be that as it may, the original unguardedness with which Nakasone made his remark, and the subsequent contrition he showed for it afterward, suggests he thought he was only repeating a harmless truism. It is very likely that his Japanese audience felt so, too, since Nakasone's remarks only echo what is a commonly held notion in Japan. After all, "Little Black Sambo" dolls and books abound in Japan and echo its racial condescension. It is not implausible to imagine even that Nakasone had anticipated ritual approval for his comments in the West as well. Was he not, in his mind, offering a mitigation for the poor showing of American as opposed to Japanese children on intelligence tests?

In a society like Japan's, which is held together by formulas rather than by a framework of moral and intellectual principles, the ideas people hold tend themselves to be formulas: more collective opinion than individual deductions, more memorized recipe than personally discerned fact. There is little empiricism involved in these social notions, and they become the more indistinguishable from truth the more they are uttered as legal intellectual tender and, worse, accepted as such. Within the group these notions play to standing room only; outside the group they are incomprehensible or even vile. And their utterers are quite dismayed at the reaction they reap from outside.

For all their renown for sensitivity to detail and nuance—well earned—the Japanese oddly also have a reputation for insensitivity. Foreigners identify it in a variety of ways: as "insincerity," "amorality," "crudeness," "rudeness," or "superficiality." Again, such epithets are seldom applied to individual Japanese (those who have both developed an individual self different from the collective one and who are willing to reveal it to Western friends) but are frequently applied to Japanese acting out of that social psyche that is always at hand for them as off-the-rack persona, the psyche that is the subject of this book. It seems that once outside the detailed prescriptions of formula, it is *terra incognita* for many Japanese, who find nothing there by which to distinguish the appropriate from the inappropriate, or to elicit empathy, or, as we'll see again later, to prevent some truly incomprehensible, no-holds-barred, psychic-meltdown behavior.

In the case of Watanabe's and Nakasone's remarks, it is not so much a matter of their being "insensitive" (which they are, of course, from a Western point of view), but of their being mere social incantation, a platitudinous jawing utterly remote from fact, truth, or even the men's real feelings or personal experience.

Austrian Corporal's Echo

On an equally discouraging note, an echo from World War II
has begun to sound in modern Japan. Books have begun to appear whose subject is "the Jews." While this is a fair enough
topic when dealt with from a historical, religious, or ethnic perspective, most of these books seem mad for finance. A few of
them look like bad acid-flashes of the phrenological economics
of the thirties and early forties; most are obviously contempo-
raneously hatched craziness, whipped up to delirium tremens
of fancy in which, among other things, byzantine connections
"reveal" the Jews to be behind the Chernobyl nuclear disaster
in 1985. Together these kinds of books number sufficiently to
rate their own special shelves in general-trade bookstores.

In mid-1987 one of these books screamed its shrill way
onto the best-seller lists in Japan, selling over half a million
copies: the prolixly and monophobicly titled *If You Understand
the Jews, You Can Comprehend the World*. As if that weren't
enough in both body and soul, the author added an explanatory
subtitle: *1990 Scenario for the Final Economic War*. Updated
title to follow, no doubt. Other popular books on this apparently unkillable theme capture the spirit of their message on
their jackets: menacing Stars of David, conspiring orthodox elders, a putative "Jew" gripping a moneybag.

Paradoxically the thinking that launches these aimed but
unguided missiles is maddenly recognizable at the same time
that it is flabbergastingly original. We're all familiar with the
canard about "world Jewry" controlling international banking.
The new corollary to this thesis is that these plotting invisible
hands have manipulated the yen to inflated values that over-
price Japanese goods abroad and cause unemployment at home.
These are social formulas imported from 1930s Germany, familiar if reprehensible to us. But that these same elusive Jewish
bankers are backing South Korea's commercial challenge to Japan (Why was Seoul chosen over Nagoya for the 1988 Summer
Olympics?), or that they are secretly behind the dramatic increase among Japanese youth's passion for comic books, rock

music, and *terebi* (TV), thus undermining their work ethic—are revelations to most of us.

There are fewer than a thousand Jews in Japan, and they are in no danger. Such sentiments as these books espouse, if loathesome, are not truly anti-Semitic. They are often as admiring as complaining, and not real thought or actual belief in any case. They are pure formula, and almost exclusively a faddish literary version at that. As such they go a millimeter deep and hardly serve as a motive for behavior. The Japanese themselves know, for that matter, that they have the ten largest banks in the world—that is, that they themselves are the invisible hands, the "Jewish bankers." Yet, however shallow or ephemeral this xenophobia, it betrays the very parochial awareness and formulaic "reasoning" that has made Japan a commercial and financial world power, yet kept her from a world view.

The Chef

Chef Yamada is famous for his cuisine. Locally if not internationally. His manner shows it. Confident, direct, unhesitating, garrulous, sure-handed—but ever personal and amicable. He even has his own TV show. One secret of his success—and the success of all fine Japanese chefs—is the freshness of his ingredients. Today Chef Yamada is going to make a seafood stew. Yummy.

He points affectionately at some finger fish squirming on a plate. He explains, queries, speculates, chides, ruminates. The fish wiggle. Yamada seems to have digressed. Like all fishermen, you suppose. But still . . . you wish he would dispatch the fish; they're not going gently into that good night. Eyes popping, bodies suffocating on cement-air. Your own lungs begin to tingle.

At last Yamada looks down, seems suddenly to remember his finny friends, registers surprise. One fish springs a desperate centimeter into the air. Yamada must take this as a sign, because he produces a long stainless-steel skewer and carefully impales the tragic hero through the mouth. Involuntarily you bite your tongue. Well, anyway, that should put an end to his misery.

No, it shouldn't. The fish flaps hideously on his inedible steel meal, his eyes pools of black nightmare. Yamada's eyes twinkle. He fills the skewer up with the remaining fish. The prong fairly dances with panicking life. Yamada explains an intricate step, his expression turning serious, shaking the living antenna in his hand imperiously.

Lesson taught, without further ado Yamada slaps the crucified fish onto an electric hibachi, where they twitch and crisp. You release your tongue, and scrounge around for that old theory that fish don't really feel pain.

But you've hardly had the overture. A now purposeful Yamada hauls a live lobster out of a bucket and slices it in two. No ceremony, no banter . . . just division. But Death himself must be comatose, so slowly comes his kiss. Yamada has turned his full attention to the meaty buckling tail, pointing out its plump juiciness, while the severed front torso clambers off, aerials winding, legs jitterbugging to last adrenaline dreams of escape.

Your body is mapping out its own adrenaline grid. You watch Yamada drop the lobster's tail into a Dantean wok-fry inferno, while the hallucinating head walks off the edge of the table. Good, you scream silently, end it, dash yourself on the linoleum below!

Yamada doesn't notice the defection. He is in a cook's race with time. A quick glance at the fish griddle—eyes melting nicely—then it's on to a real delicacy, octopus. Yamada dredges the violet creature from another bucket and plops it down, legs a splayed star beneath it, onto the center of the table. With one hand he grabs the octopus by the top of its bulbous head and with the other picks up a kitchen sword and severs the head where it narrows to meet the body. The animal's innards, a voluminous live cell-pudding, literally rush from the cavity, erupting out the top. You feel you're about to slip into anaphylactic shock and, checking your pulse, you miss seeing which part—the skin or the visceral cream—Yamada's put into the stew. Are there no vegetables in this recipe, you want to protest.

It doesn't matter. A maniacal Yamada is holding a turtle in his hands pointing resentfully at its shell. No, too much . . . you recall your childhood pet, the soft-shelled Shelly from Woolworth's five-and-dime. Yamada turns Shelly on her back, you beg off, flee, ready now for corn-on-the-pizza.

As to callousness, there is a perverse strain—some would say an aristocratic strain too—some individual Japanese direct at themselves, in a tenor not exactly like any in the West, but partaking a bit each of epicureanism, heroism, tragedy, and even nihilism. The closest thing we have may be Russian roulette, which hasn't any of the classiness of the Japanese custom: eating *fugu*.

There are four species of *fugu* the Japanese epicures pursue, paying up to $300 per meal. Usually served as *sashimi* (raw), the blowfish is sliced into paper-thin, translucent petals of pearl and arranged into lovely rosettes and delicate portraits of crane, the bird in Japan symbolizing long life, ironically. What's special about *fugu* isn't really its taste—like chicken when cooked, like fish when not—but its presumption to Fate itself. Eating it can kill you.

Fugu can be eaten with any safety at all only in certain seasons, late fall through winter usually, and because parts of the fish (such as the intestines, liver, ovaries, and skin) are poisonous in any season, it must be prepared by a licensed chef who has apprenticed for years and passed a written qualifying exam. This is indispensable, since *fugu* contains tetrodotoxin, 160,000 times more powerful than cocaine and about 270 times deadlier than cyanide. The major challenge for the chef, obviously, is to engender an effect upon the diner that is closer to cocaine than to cyanide.

This is a tricky business, since it takes only a single milligram (a pencil point) to turn your eyes the same chill emerald glass as those of the dead fish you're eating. Mistakes, or delib-

erate if masked suicides, do happen; about twenty people a
year in Japan die in this gustatory lotto, though it's claimed
that millions partake. Even at those odds things go wrong often
enough to account for much published, perhaps revered, lists
of ordinary—but more often illustrious—martyrs to courage or
craziness. Shortly after New Year's in 1975, for example, the
famous Kabuki actor Mitsugoro Bando VIII (an officially designated "living national treasure") sat down to a *fugu* meal. As
a renowned Kabuki master, Bando VIII was as capable of te-
merity, flamboyance, and spectacle as is his three-centuries-old
theatrical art. He demanded of his chef a special dish of *fugu*
liver, which was and is legally prohibited by Japanese law, so
toxic is this particular part of the fish. Undaunted, Bando demanded another helping. By now the playful tingle and exu-
berant warmth the *fugu's* drug bestows must have bathed his
judgment in euphoria, for Bando called for another plate.

One can but imagine and take pity on his poor chef. How
do you tell the greatest living Kabuki actor, a man with a name
like Bando the VIII, to quit eating? How do you tell Elvis no
more peanut butter & speed?

Bando had that and a fourth helping before toxic paralysis
stilled his reach and froze his lungs. Tetrodotoxin is a nerve
poison that spares the mind: the angel is witness to its own
breath become cold statuary. *Itadakimasu.*

Even humble sushi is not without its danger, incidentally.
If prepared or stored, or originally selected by a rank amateur
unable to distinguish the healthy from the unhealthy, the raw
fish (*sashimi*) you are eating out of chic might well give you
"lung flukes" (*Anisakis* roundworms, actually). This miniature
bowel-fiend is a rather nasty parasite that digs into your stomach wall with its boring-tooth and sometimes crawls up your
throat, causing you to cough a lot. Lozenge, anyone?

Wan-Wan!

The eighteenth-century Japanese priest who founded the Jo-i sect (anti-foreign party), preached that the Japanese had descended from gods and the rest of humanity from cats and dogs. This view, and the meager Japanese tradition of wildlife conservation, reflect an uninspired attitude among many urban Japanese to keeping pets. It couldn't have helped this attitude that in the closing months of World War II they had to eat all the dogs and cats just to stay alive. As for cats now, one often gets the impression that many of them seem to have suffered a fall from the affiliated "private" domain to that "public" ring of hell: nowhere. In that lonely purgatory only the sturdiest survive, though the sturdiest look downright emaciated and scrofulous from disease and neglect. They're a discordant sight, macabre, appearing suddenly, with a stiff, somnambulist gait and hair punked out on street grease, an indifferent, starving specter.

Dogs are a different matter. The more they catch on in the affections of city dwellers, the deeper they, too, enter the maze of urban delirium. Usually not permitted in the "mansions" and gigantic apartment blocs, they are nevertheless secreted there by desperately fond owners, who find it safe only in the wee hours of pitch night to take them for walks and relief.

"Legal" dogs, the ones that live in houses, are spared the claustrophobic vampire existence of their illegal fellows, but given the crowded state of housing in the city, they often have virtually no space in which to move about, much less run. When they do run, its only on the lead end of a short leash, a mad, rasping haul of their owners off to the "public" park, where their proud, puffing masters watch them defecate on the grass— which rare material in urban Japan seems reserved for this canine activity. If there is no grass to be found—as on the moonscape of playgrounds—their owners will guide them into the children's sandboxes, where the dogs can leave presents for the kids to play with.

Dog food seems more the exception than the rule. Given

the high cost of food in Japan, many owners are unable even
to imagine why anybody would spend good money on special
victuals for a dog, when there's always some leftover rice at
the end of the day. Many dogs are as visibly unelated by this
diet as you would expect them to be, culture notwithstanding.
You see them stare at the glutinous white mush in their bowls
and then up at their masters as if to say, "Hey, this is rice!"

But the real nightmare for dogs in Japan must be a sojourn
in the "kennel." Given the exorbitant cost of baby-sitting "human" babies—on the miraculous occasions when such service
can be found—seven to twenty dollars an hour—one can only
quake at what space and care for "doggies" must cost. "Ken-
nels" often consist of nothing more than the narrow driveway
next to the pet store, where twenty or more dogs might find
themselves in an area no bigger than a sushi bar, each short-
tethered next to, behind, and in front of the other, stepping
into and skipping gingerly out of their own accumulating, musky
mounds of former rice . . . and all of them locked in a Skinner-
box chain of round-robin barking.

It's the barking you can't stand anymore. It rises in random, rasping explosions from behind the wall bordering a house
next to your apartment building and drops its shrapnel in your
ears. You can't work anymore, or read, or sleep, because either
the dog is barking or you are neurotically waiting for him to
begin barking. One day, in a fit of ill-considered desperation,
you wait on your balcony for the owner to appear, a middle-
aged successful *sarari-man* at National (Panasonic), and harangue him like Mussolini above the piazza, only in dictionary
Japanese, shouting things like *wan-wan!* (bow-wow!) and *ben-
goshi!* (lawyer!). To no good end, of course, for anger publicly
displayed is the same as madness in Japan, and anyway there
is a Japanese saying to the effect that he who gets angry first
has already lost the argument. He waves cheerily and drives
away in his plush *Debonair Executive*.

In despair you turn to Kyoko, the gentle, helpful soul
whose sympathy and wise counsel have always stood you in

good stead in this strange land. What does one do in Japan in such a dilemma, you whine to her?

Kyoko's gentle brown eyes look candidly into your crazed, sleepless green ones. "Japanese endure," she says simply. "Until they can't and they kill the keeper." She makes a thrust-and-twist motion with her hand, gripping a knife from her imagination.

Several midnights later, lying awake listening to the hoarse hysteria of the neighbor's dog, wishing some *deus ex machina* would winch down from another dimension and murder the cur, you are startled by a single, sudden, horrible *crack*, as if a thirty-six-inch Louisville (Yokohama?) Slugger has just hit an official Spalding out of the park. Almost simultaneously there is one short canine shriek. Then silence.

From behind the neighbor's wall, no doggy sounds ever lift again.

Man, 39, Held Over Death Threat

ODAWARA, Kanagawa— A 39-year-old man, who had been arrested for abusing his former employer's dog, was rearrested for allegedly threatening the former employer's life it was learned Tuesday.

Police identified the man as Isao Mizoguchi, unemployed, of Odawara, Kanagawa-ken.

Before Mizoguchi was recently fired, he had been working for Ikuo Iwamoto, 50, a construction company owner, of Odawara. Furious with his dismissal, Mizoguchi kidnapped Iwamoto's pet "Chibi," a one-year-old female dog, Friday morning. Mizoguchi tied it to an elec-

tric pole and hit its head and front paws with a 90-centimeter-long iron bar, police reported.

Mizoguchi was arrested for hurting the dog and released Monday morning after paying a fine of ¥20,000.

Mizoguchi then went to Iwamoto's house at around 10:20 p.m. Monday and threatened Iwamoto's life.

"You asked the police to arrest me just for hurting a dog," Mizoguchi allegedly told Iwamoto. "I can kill a human. I will destroy your company," police quoted him as saying.

He was rearrested after Iwamoto called the police.

CHAPTER 7

Meltdown
of Manners:
Out of Bounds
and
Over the Edge

Typical happy ending in an adult *manga* comic book.

"Gift" Scandals?

Just because a society has no underlying set of rational principles doesn't mean it is "unprincipled." On the whole Japanese society functions remarkably well and is astonishingly successful and relatively sane. Its rate for violent crime is still among the lowest in the world, a statistic that translates into a personal feeling of security in the city streets, even at night. Yet Japan is a first-world, cosmopolitan nation, and as such has all the conditions that make for crime in Japan as they do elsewhere—but with a characteristic Japanese flavor. In general there are two kinds of crimes in Japan: those that are part of the social formulas or that exploit them, and those that result when the formulas fail.

Japan is a culture where personal relationships regularly hold more sway than individual merit, and where position is often the real principle. *Oyabun* often demand promotions for their protégé *kobun*, irrespective of the latters' ability or incompetence. In such a system there is bound to be ambiguity about what is simply privilege and what is criminal. Moreover, since relationships often provide the opportunity that logic and legality might provide elsewhere, and because gift giving is the epidemic means in Japan of initiating, furthering, and mending relationships, it's not always easy to distinguish a present from a bribe. Graft is a staple of Japanese news (as in the recent, quaint "Yarn Twisters Bribery Scandal,") replete with official protests about mere gifts and loyal contributions.

Certainly Kakuei Tanaka, a former prime minister, had trouble distinguishing the nature of the 500 million yen given him to influence aircraft purchases in the Lockheed scandal, for which he was convicted six years later in 1983 and seven years after his resignation over a previous scandal. But if he had lost a bit of face, Tanaka lost no power, eventually seeing his protégé Nakasone become prime minister. Tanaka served none of his four-year sentence, and it was only a stroke that finally dissolved his power and extended his legal appeal *in perpetuum.*

In mid-1988 this gift/bribe ambiguity emerged spectacularly in "Recruitgate," Japan's latest influence-peddling scandal. At the center of this scandal was one Hiromasa Ezoe,
a daring entrepreneur after the familiar Japanese archetype,
who took his small magazine-publishing business, Recruit, and
engineered it into a multibillion-dollar conglomerate dealing
in real estate, financing, computers, information services,
and publishing. Indeed, his company's growth was spectacular. Too spectacular. Healthy growth careened into the meta-
stasis of cancer that at last count was gobbling up 170
politicians, bureaucrats, and tycoons. Nippon Telegraph and
Telephone (NTT) executives, including the august board chair-
man Hisashi Shinto, were arrested, as were vice-ministers of
labor and education.

It seems that Ezoe, in his yen to promote his interests in
computer leasing and in the job- and graduate-hiring-informa-
tion market, had been selling stock in Recruit Cosmos, the
real-estate arm of his empire, to Japan's influential and
mighty—actually preselling the company's as yet unlisted stock,
a ploy that is illegal in the United States but in Japan is just
another sleazy instance of *kozo oshoku* (institutionalized cor-
ruption) and the advantage in *kone* (connections). To the mighty
who found themselves strapped for cash, another of Ezoe's
companies (the financial arm) would supply low-cost loans for
the stock purchases. In 1986, when Recruit Cosmos went public, these privileged stockholders were able to sell and make a
killing—at the expense, of course, of ordinary, unprivileged
stockholders.

The temptation of easy profits is especially alluring to Japanese politicians, each of whom must spend over $1 million a
year just to maintain his seat and an estimated $2 million to $3
million to wage an election campaign. It's no surprise that over
half of Japan's post-WW-II prime ministers have found themselves under investigation for graft. And easy profits are even
harder to come by in the post-Tanaka era of Japanese politics,
since the 1976 Political Fund Law has limited an organization's
campaign contributions to 1.5 million yen (about $11,000).

Fund-raising secretaries are now pressed to conjure novel
schemes to garner the necessary funds, a circumstance on which
Ezoe seems to have capitalized.

The scandal itself has unfolded like some bad burlesque.
Only a few weeks after the seamy story begins to leak in the
press, Hiroshi Matsubara, Recruit Cosmos presidential secretar-
iat, is caught by a hidden camera trying in vain to hand over a
five-million-yen "gift" to opposition Diet member Yanosuke
Narazaki, who with others is pursuing the investigation of Recruit. Leaders of the ruling Liberal Democrats—among them
past, present, and likely future prime ministers such as Nakasone, Takeshita, Abe, and Miyazawa—are reported to be recipients of Recruit largess. They in turn blame it on their
secretaries. Miyazawa, after having been caught changing his
story, swears he will resign as Finance Minister if he has to
change his story again. He does and resigns on December 9,
1988. Opposition parties, claiming complete virginity in the affair and sensing their first real opportunity to wrest power from
the Liberal Democrats in three decades, howl righteously for
their skins. The howling is adulterated a bit by moans as the
opposition is revealed to have their own Recruit stock profi-
teers. The Japan Socialist Party, even the extravagantly self-
named Clean Government Party (Komeito), all suffer hasty
resignations due to "misunderstood" funds. To everyone's embarrassment only the scorned Japan Communist Party seems to
have kept its virtue intact.

To stem the rising muck-tide, Prime Minister Noboru
Takeshita in the last days of 1988 appoints (according to headlines) "Cabinet Untainted by Stock Scandal!" The press points
out that, disclaimers notwithstanding, three of the cabinet ministers have received money from Recruit, including Keizo
Obuchi, the Chief Cabinet Secretary, who was asked by Takeshita to look into possible ties between new cabinet ministers and
Recruit. Then, three days later, the newly appointed Justice
Minister, Hasegawa Takashi, the man who would be leading the
investigation of Recruit, is reported to have received thirteen
years of "donations" from Recruit. He apologizes. He resigns.

In the first few months of 1989 it's a glum Liberal Democratic Party—ruling or not. It loses what should be a cinch election in Fukuoka, where more than 150 LDP luminaries, including Prime Minister Takeshita himself, come to rally support for their local candidate. In mid-April Takeshita himself sees his popularity slip to 28 percent. In defense he swears that all of the Recruit donations he has received are legal. The very next day the emerging truth forces him to change his own dismal tale: Some of his Recruit bounty is illegal. His popularity sinks to 3.9 percent, the lowest of any postwar prime minister. Fearing perhaps that he may literally vanish when his popularity reaches zero, he finally resigns. But effective later. After all, there seem to be no chickens in the fox coop to replace him.

If politicians occupy an orthodox niche in society but an increasingly dubious one in their constituents' trust, *yakuza*, Japan's strange version of organized crime, are often described as exactly the reverse: as pariahs to the establishment but heroes in the hearts of the little people. How retouched is this portrait of the *yakuza* is not easily judged by Westerners, for whom *yakuza* are best known for their body tattoos (*irezumi*) and for executing their fingers to apologize for mistakes. They began under various names in the Tokugawa period (1603–1868) as either bully bands or the self-protection organizations formed to oppose them. Their feudal hierarchy, reactionary values, and strict codes of "honor" and allegiance have made them into a proletarian version of the *samurai*. The word *yakuza* is of uncertain origin but may refer to a losing hand in *hanafuda*, a Japanese card game, suggesting its class origins and allegiance as well as the brutishness and the romance of being at the bottom. But their actual social status defies the categories prescribed by Western logic. They admit to being involved in gambling, protection, and debt collection (others add prostitution, pornography, drugs, and gunrunning), and one leader—recalling earlier epochs—openly vowed in a 1988 televised interview to assassinate the prime minister if the ruling elite

got too rich. Instead of being jailed, such a vocal advocate of
unreasonable means is accepted as just another odd shape belonging in the mosaic. In fact *yakuza* have public headquarters
established in various cities much as any respectable organization would, and for all their proletarian ideals and membership,
and their outspoken hostility to established authority, they are
believed by most Japan watchers to have enough *kone* in the
economic and political establishment—supplying it with muscle
and money—to be counted a part of it, however incongruous
this mix is to Western reason. *Yakuza* are said to number over
100,000, in many hundreds of associated groups, some of which
are already in the United States.

Ian Buruma, in *Behind the Mask*, his masterful analysis of
how Japanese movies and other cultural imagery reveal Japanese attitudes, shows how the *yakuza* movie, a popular
subgenre in Japan, portrays them as tragically doomed, often
solitary defenders of tradition and the common man against the
heartless, rootless forces of modern pragmatism, the latter per-
sonified by the "scheming entrepreneur" and the "corrupt politician." Not surprisingly, these characters are occasionally
associated with that great destroyer of old-Japan harmony and
happy, universal compliance with social formula: America.
Yakuza movies tap into a more general Japanese longing, *ako-
gare*, in this case for a perfect past which in fact never existed.
Most of those who dream of returning to those grand old days
would not, of course, have been the samurai they fantasize but
the peasants the samurai dismembered (legally) for a slight or
for *tsuji giri* (testing the edge of a new sword). This notwithstanding, the fantasy is alive as a brilliant tattoo on the collective social skin.

Your Money or Your Serenity

If there is any crime in Japan uniquely transformed to suit
the Japanese psyche, though, it is extortion. With "gifts" and
"donations" endemic in the system, it is easy to understand

extortion in Japan as only a demand for bribes *after the fact*.
Mistresses about to be dropped by their patrons traditionally
demand exorbitant *isha ryo*, "consolation money," forcing the
trapped philanderer into choosing to continue the affair or set
his ex-girlfriend up so that she can start a business or one of
the numberless *kissaten* (coffeehouses) forever grand-opening
and going bankrupt in Japan. Jack Seward, one of the most
knowledgeable of Japan-hands and author of a revealing insider's book, *The Japanese*, tells a hilarious tale of a Japanese
friend whose spurned mistress burst into her lover's home during his wife's dinner party and lay down supine, refusing to
leave until he took her home. It is not even unheard of for a
man to demand money of a woman if she wishes to end their
affair and she is wealthier than he is "principled." Rarer but
similar is the demand for "satisfaction money" by a party from
someone whom he knows or imagines to have insulted or
shamed him. This latter is often nothing more than an excuse
to extort some needed cash.

Such motives are behind a uniquely Japanese brand of extortion, *sokaiya*. An individual, or a small group of individuals,
will purchase an inconsequential amount of stock in a company, giving them no real leverage for decision making but allowing them to attend the stockholders' meeting. Once at the
meeting they may make so much commotion that no business
can be conducted or, alternatively, such a mortifying spectacle
of themselves as to bring everlasting shame on the company.
They may even threaten to reveal company secrets (whether
they posses them or not) or reveal private-life transgressions of
company officials.

So distasteful is disruption, or the mere prospect of it, to
the Japanese sense of decorum and group harmony, not to mention the rank fear of their wives having to endure and revenge
the public shame of their husbands' amorous indiscretions (remember Nobuko?), that companies gladly pay off such extortionists to stay home. In a utilitarian twist, some companies
have paid such bully-boys actually to *come* to the meetings in

order to help decorously manipulate the stock in a favorable direction.

By sheer logical, or more often "illogical," extension, even ordinary if inspired Japanese have seen the light as far as blackmail is concerned:

Girl Blackmailer Wanted Money For Beauty Treatment

KAWASAKI, Kanagawa —Police Friday arrested a 17-year-old girl of Saiwai-ku, Kawasaki, after she sent a threatening letter to a company president, demanding ¥6 million, part of which she planned to use for an operation to remove excess body fat, according to her confession.

The girl was charged with attempted blackmail for sending the threat to the 47-year-old president of a company dealing in adiabatic materials in Kawasaki-ku.

Her letter gave a totally fictitious story that the president's wife and a male accomplice had tried to kill her and she wanted satisfaction.

She ordered the businessman to bring ¥6 million to Kawasaki Station on the Japanese National Railways. Waiting police arrested her when she came to pick up the money.

The girl reportedly told police that she wanted ¥3 million for beauty treatments to slim down, and she also wanted money to publish a magazine.

Brand-New Flavor!

It seems it is ever more fashionable in Japan, if you're short of the jingle, to threaten the routine of someone who's got some of both. It's almost impossible to convey the depth of security formulas provide for the people who live in a formulaic society, or the pitch of anxiety when the formulas are disrupted. And who knows this better than the Japanese themselves, so who more fit to prey on other Japanese by exploiting this cultural susceptibility.

It is astonishing to the Westerner to see this kind of extortion succeed, based as it is on assumptions entirely alien to us, yet succeed it does. Cases have eventually come to light in which some simple yet audacious bloke had years ago wandered into a bank, asked to see the manger, told him to give him money or he would come back and blow up the bank and its employees, and as a result had been getting paid off ever since. Though this unsophisticated ploy fails sometimes, it also continues to work often enough to give it a kind of informal cultural aegis. And when it does work, it does so because the manager or president is simply tormented witless by the whole situation and may even find the prospect of bringing in the police just one more added disruption he'd rather dispense with in favor of merely dealing with the extortionist.

Of course such accommodations to extortionists, as even Western presidents have found, tend to make extortionists into careerists rather than dilettantes and in Japan can create some unique criminal careers, themselves producing headlines absolutely aromatic with local atmosphere:

Noodle Poisoner Linked To Real Estate Swindle

The Metropolitan Police Department has learned that a noodle poisoner who threatened two major noodle producers had tried to sell the house and land of former singer Mariko Kurata without authorization in spring 1984, the MPD said Wednesday.

Indeed, poisoning the food product of a company from which you hope to extort your fortune has become a bit of the rage in Japan of late. Perhaps taking its cue from the Tylenol poisoning cases a few years back in the United States, these lone entrepreneurs seem to show an almost hypoglycemic obsession with the junk-food market, often targeting candy and soft drinks. For a long time party or parties unknown were preying on the soda-pop machines, of which there are an infinite number in Japan, somewhere on every urban street, sometimes a half dozen in a row, each containing up to twenty different bottles and cans, including cold coffee beverages, mysterious health elixirs, and indefinable milky swill, besides of course the usual fizzy sugar fixes.

One such case, long running and apparently still unsolved, had the murderer buying a can of pop from a machine, drilling a tiny hole in the can's bottom, through which he injected some really cruel industrial chemical, soldering the hole back up, and placing the can back into the dispensing bin into which the cans fall after you deposit your coins. Thus, when a patron later reached in to get his drink and discovered the extra can, often a different variety, he thought a technological miracle had chosen him for special benefaction.

What was really miraculous, darkly so, was that even months after this poisoning spree had begun, when the media were full of news and warnings about the crime and its method, people would still pick up the second can too, convinced that fortune had singled them out for this *omake*, a free "extra" (as in a way it had), and gulp down death on the spot.

Such is our human need of miracles. Perhaps the more so in the land of floating formulas.

This Is Not the Real Me

Japanese urban society lives and dies by tension. To operate, even *exist*, it extols the conventional and regiments the individual. To motivate, it offers the self-satisfactions of imagined uniqueness, and pride in the virtues of obedience and stoicism. To survive, it resorts wholesale to cigarettes, sex, and shopping. When none of that works, it leaps out of its skin.

Routines, social formulas, rituals are fine for telling you what you are, where you belong, which is your place, and what to do. But how do you come alive, how do you become whole? Inside the lines the Japanese are the best there are. Across the line they're way out of bounds and all over the wall. It seems that once beyond the thoroughly mapped social geography and the comfort and guidance that the formulas provide, the individual Japanese has little to fall back on within himself except extraordinary but exhaustible endurance. With the goal of social stability, Japanese society goes to infinite lengths to fashion a conforming social persona in its subjects. Of necessity it does so at the expense of the individual personality, which it has regularly seen as a hindrance and upon which it has spent little nurturance or intellectual commitment. All too often it seems that when he runs out of rules, and the individual Japanese must reach elsewhere inside, many find not a personal reservoir of "self" upon which to draw but a void that can sound only its silence or hatch the original brute demons of our species.

Middle-Aged Man Beats Errant Wife To Death

KYOTO—Police Monday arrested a middle-aged man for allegedly beating his wife to death in a fit of anger because she stayed out all night.

According to police, Yusaku Togami, 51, of Kyoto, hit his wife Katsuko, 44, a snack bar hostess, in the head and face several times at his home Sunday evening in a quarrel over her returning home in the morning that day.

In Himeji, Hyogo-ken, Hiroyoshi Kano, 66, unemployed, was arrested on charges of seriously injuring his wife Tsutako, 59. He stabbed her with a kitchen knife at his home early Monday morning after the wife refused to make breakfast for him because the husband was on diet.

Kano also injured Yasuhiko, 33, eldest son, who had attempted to stop him, according to police.

Now This Is the Real Me

Japanese society is both renowned and notorious for one of its many paradoxes. Drunkenness is rife, but alcoholism is minimal. Similarly, the drunk, if he is male, is almost honored; yet the drunken driver, if he is caught, might as well climb the 1,100-foot Tokyo Tower and dive into the arms of his ancestors.

Alcohol is fundamental and inextricable in Japanese society. Sake is not only a staple in recreational drinking but an ingredient in ritual. Whiskey and beer are consumed in huge quantities, and Johnnie Walker Black, the Scotch, stood for many decades in Japan as the prestige drink and gift, as do many foreign whiskeys still today. With street drugs rare, difficult to obtain, and users severely punished, alcohol is the universal drug-of-choice in Japan. Whatever else men might do after work, they definitely drink, and usually drink lots.

Not as openly acknowledged is the fact that their wives, bored and lonely as a class, "drink down our cooking sake," as one Japanese wife put it. In fact there have been several TV commercials flagrantly targeting these women and proselytizing converts to embibed bliss. Invariably they depict a solitary female drinker, usually aswoon and gyring in some blue spiral of the soaked senses, fingers obliviously anchored to the eternally half-full/half-empty glass. Almost anywhere else such commercials could run as *anti*-alcohol spots. In Japan it's a testament to the pervasiveness of this female escape and the Japanese advertising that these commercials have at least the visual panache to lift them hypnotically above their message, which after all is nothing more than "Be Drunk."

Because drinking is inextricably a part of the culture and the drunk such a familiar homey figure, drinking has acquired the status of a socially sanctioned release from the vacuum pack of Japanese society. *Bonenkai*, the traditional and endless year-end party, besides being the last act of group bonding for the year, is also a sanctioned opportunity to tell your boss or colleagues the thing-or-two social formula required you up till now to swallow live and cage in your belly. Understandably *bonenkai* is also famous for the occasional fistfight.

It's understandable, then, that by a series of single steps drinking has even come to be an informally recognized means of tearing off the social persona and scaling the wall:

Train Kills Two Men Fighting On Tracks

KAWASAKI, Kanagawa—Two men, apparently intoxicated, were killed by a train at Japanese National Railways' Kawasaki Station at around 10:55 p.m. Monday after they fell from the platform onto the tracks during a fight, police said.

They were identified as Shoichi Fukumoto, 43, a company employee, of Yokohama, and Kazujiro Ishii, 38, a company employee, of Zushi, Kanagawa-ken, the Kawasaki Police Station said.

According to police, witnesses said the two started fighting after Fukumoto woke up Ishii, who was sleeping on a bench. Ishii and Fukumoto did not know each other, police added.

When they fell onto the tracks, an approaching train was about 200 meters from the station. Although station officials and a train engineer warned them of the danger, they simply continued their fight. The train attempted to stop but could not, running over and killing the two men, said police.

According to police, about 100 people on the platform could do nothing but shout warnings to the two because the train was so close, witnesses said.

Truly Bad Manners

Obviously the West is at least as plagued by alcohol as is Japan, and certainly more addicted to it, and many of our crimes, too, frolic or fume in the train of drink-bought liberation. What strikes one as different, though, is the great disparity between the peaceful social psyche of the Japanese and the faceless anarch that leaps out when this persona breaks. On the one hand there is a civil, obliging, tolerant citizen; on the other the typhoon's howl. The gulf is too wide, too startling the single leap across it, too trivial the stimulus. It, too, bespeaks not a layered psyche, or a descent by stages through the different strata of conscious and unconscious, but a thin, tough integument stretched over naught . . . then bursting.

Then, too, there are the deeds themselves, their "quality" more than their kind, really—since murders, rapes, and thefts are universal to our species—as well as the causes and catalysts for them. The murder that began our tale, Nobuko's alleged crime, it's bizarre features and wretched excess, is not a sole anomaly in the Japanese mural, as we have seen repeatedly. On the contrary, violence, murder, rape . . . they find cartoonish life in the ubiquitous *manga* comics, and in daily life are the walking ghost of what the Japanese have abandoned to become "perfect," whether conjured by alcohol or simple desperation.

Pair Nabbed In Strangling Case

CHIBA—The body of a man, with bandage around his neck and both hands bound with bandages, was found by a neighbor under the eaves of an apartment here Thursday afternoon.

Police identified the man as Tadaichi Fujishiro, 45, resident of the apartment.

He died of suffocation, police said.

Toshihisa Yamada, 38, unemployed, and an 18-year-old Chiba youth, were arrested on suspicion of murder Thursday at about 11 p.m. They had been drinking with

Fujishiro at his apartment from Thursday morning, police said.

Police said Yamada and the youth confessed that they were upset at Fujishiro's bad habit of drinking. When Fujishiro fell asleep, police said they bound Fujishiro's hands with bandages, and choked him with another bandage. Then, hanging Fujishiro, who was still alive but unconscious, from the frame of a second floor window with more bandages, the two fled, according to police.

The weight of Fujishiro's body broke the bandage and his body fell to the ground under the window, police added.

Sorry

These crimes are all the more rending to the fabric of Japanese society the less they conform to the formulas that mold the Japanese social psyche and knit society together. Worse than crazy, they are very bad form and let the side down. In spades.

Things are held together in a formulaic society the only way they can be, not by internal logic but by conformity, obedience, hierarchy, unanimity, civility, and the regular anxiety about whether or not you know the variables (like the status of someone you meet), to which you can apply all the rules you've memorized. So when things come apart, as they do in crimes or violence, it's no small matter, because it is only right action that holds things together. And crime and violence are not right at all.

Yet, inevitably, they happen. And we've seen that they can happen pretty exotically in Japan. So, having no way to prevent them—human beings being the fallible creatures they are, the Japanese included—it's necessary to have some means of rectifying them, some way of putting the genie back in the bottle. In Japanese society this is absolutely vital. With only conformity and not rational principles to appeal to, reestablishing that conformity is indispensable. The tear in the fabric must be mended, everyone must hold hands again—especially the offender whose act breached the social conformity.

In the West, with its adherence to and dependence on principles, a criminal's motives, his attitude *before* the crime, weigh considerably in the balance by which we judge him. In Japan, where there are no firm or consistent principles by which to judge "reasons," where "reasons" are never trusted as much as conformity to produce the correct behavior, it is much more important what the offender's attitude is *after* he commits the crime. For what is really at issue in Japanese society is not the individual or the "reasons" for his behavior but the social skin and restoring its uniformity. In the United States we invariably plead innocent. In Japan they always plead guilty. The social uniformity is restored in Japan by the criminal confessing his crime and saying he is sorry for having committed it. A crime and its consequences cannot be undone, in any case, but the unanimity, the collective dream, can be revived. For this resuscitation the criminal must acknowledge his wrongdoing by confessing the crime (as proof that he knows the Wanted from the Unwanted), and denounce his departure from the social formula by saying he is sorry (proof that he is contrite for the harm he did and a voucher for his future conformity). Thus is the water sponged up and the bubble restored.

So almost invariably in Japan do criminals publicly and immediately confess and repent, usually even before they are officially arrested—a fact that accounts for the 99 percent conviction rate for individuals arrested. Of course, we are talking about ordinary people who commit crimes. *Yakuza* are pros, rarely cop to anything, and sometimes actually die in shoot-outs with the police—an unfathomable prospect to ordinary Japanese. Judges, for their part, often reward contrition with lighter sentences, for they, like Japanese society as a whole, implicitly understand the importance to them all of *domo sumimasen* (*very* sorry).

I Love It, L.A.!

In many ways illustrative of the chaotic Japanese murder and its crazy fallout is the Miura case.

In 1981 Kazuyoshi Miura, thirty-four, a tall, good-looking small-time importer of goods and wearer of hip shirts, designer jeans, gold chains, and lizard-leather cowboy boots, took his third wife, Kazumi, to Los Angeles on a business trip, where they both were shot, he superficially, she fatally (after some months of coma).

Initially the story played itself out in Japan along predictable lines: Innocent, peaceful Japanese couple fall victim to whacked-out *gaijin* mean-street. Miura himself denounced America itself as violent and wept during his interviews.

Then in 1984 the Japanese media began to report on other features of Miura's life. In 1979 something similar had happened to another woman he had been involved with, Chizuko Shiraishi, whose body was found outside Los Angeles but not identified until five years later. Miura was said also to have taken out huge sums of insurance on Kazumi. Hundreds of articles were published about him, some claiming him to have been a child arsonist and robber. Charts and spider graphs detailing his many romantic affairs were published.

Then it was discovered that a sex-flick actress, Michiko Yazawa, had come forward to confess that she had tried, at Miura's request, to kill his wife Kazumi (also in L.A., which apparently had the rep by now) three months before Kazumi had been fatally shot. Yazawa claimed that Miura had given her something like a hammer and promised to marry her if she killed Kazumi. She had dutifully but futilely beaten Kazumi on the head, until the latter escaped.

Undaunted, Miura had remarried a fourth time, opened a genteel coffeehouse, written a book, bought a flashy *Fair Lady Z* car, and become a media darling. Even when, finally, he and his ex-sex-pic queen were indicted for the first "attempted" murder, Miura was ready with a pre-prepared statement of his innocence, read on TV by his fourth wife.

Despite all the entertainment Miura had provided them, many Japanese still expected Miura to fold his hand finally and play by the basic social formulas necessary to them all. Thousands upon thousands signed petitions demanding truth and justice. Not only was it murder, it was scandalous! They wanted him to confess. They wanted him to say he was sorry.

But it seems his many trips to the city of Angels had not failed to leave their mark on him.

Incidentally the left in Japan is still waiting (and will wait forever now) for Hirohito to say he is sorry for World War II.

False Note

At noon in the spring of 1986 Yukiko Okada, one of the more adored of Japan's legion of female pop singers, slipped the leash of her manager, scrambled to the roof of the seven-story building housing her agent's offices, Sun Music, and sailed off into both the next world and pop's mini-immortality. She had tried to slash her wrist and oven-gas herself that same morning, but was caught at it by a neighbor. She had been taken to a hospital, where her injuries had been pronounced minor, and then released to her manager, who had taken her to the agency to get her back on line.

The life of pop singers in Japan is not the bowl of cherries it is for their Western counterparts, anarchic fun and managed millions. Not even for quite successful Japanese pop stars. They're more manufactured product than incandescent talent, tightly controlled by their agencies and managers, earning often less than do most *sarari-men*. They have not been chosen for fame because of their voices, which are often pale wraiths incarnated only by electronic hype, but usually because they emanate some special aura of *kawaii* (cuteness). They have countless competitors of the same ilk flogged forward by other agencies and managers, and if they do manage to cut a hit song, they will sing it ever after in precisely the same way, imitating the same accompanying gestures, wearing the same exact clothes—the latter of which are almost always expensive samples from the safe world of designer fashions. For these pop singers there is no youthful rebellion in their performance and, one suspects, none in their lives.

And yet . . . if it's not all freedom and fire, it's still leagues better than the life ordinary Japanese girls lead as office ladies, schoolgirls, hardly rich and with a single looming prospect, marriage. Was it that bad, Yukiko?

Of course the answer's no, not even from her point of view, one might safely guess. The objective circumstances of their lives are not usually the cause of suicide among young Japanese, if one means that those circumstances were infinitely far from being so horrible as to require suicide.

There are two types of suicide in Japan: Okada's (and that of the two dozen or so schoolgirls who imitated her in the ensuing days), and that of Mishima, the eminent Japanese novelist and nationalist who commited ritual suicide, *seppuku*. The one is a terminal tantrum, the other—as repellant as it might be to us—a personal agony and a public testament to the depth and sincerity of his feelings about Japan having lost its spiritual way. The latter is a fierce act of personal will. The former is a surrender of that will and everything else personal—the kind of suicide that is prevalent in contemporary Japan. And it is the elderly, always the first casualties in the modern, urban disintegration of the extended family, even more than the young who hasten it, who increasingly resort to this deliverance.

Aging Professor Strangles Wife, Takes Cyanide

KUMAMOTO—A professor of the medical department of Kumamoto University, Mizuho Kanda, 61, aparently killed himself and his wife, Chieko, 59. They were found dead on a futon in the living room of their house here by a visitor Wednesday at about 11:50 p.m., police said.

After Kanda apparently strangled his wife, he killed himself by drinking potassium cyanide. Suicide notes directed to relatives, police and university staff were left in his living room, according to police.

Police quoted from the death note, "I did it to make my wife comfortable, as she asked. I am sorry for giving you so much trouble."

According to people concerned, Chieko had been growing frail, and Kanda was also in bad physical health recently, and had been absent from the university.

Police believe Kanda killed her right after he had made a telephone call to a friend at about 11 p.m. that night.

Kanda had been the chief of the medical department since 1975. He was a councillor and also a member of the university's Ethics Committee, which judges the propriety of heart transplants and other issues. He was also the one who identified the cause in the Morinaga milk poisoning case of 1955.

Exit

Seneca, a first-century Roman philosopher and writer, and a suicide himself, wrote that there is no need to endure an unwanted life, that the exits to death are everywhere: "A thousand doors open upon it." Though the general suicide rate in Japan is comparatively modest (not much higher than that of the United States, for instance), suicides among the contemporary Japanese are remarkable, as are their violent crimes, for

the often trivial circumstances that launch them and, unlike
their violent crimes, for the contained, almost casual manner
in which they're undertaken. Okada's maniacal determination
to end it right this moment is more the exception than the rule.
Usually it seems to be a matter either of quietly accumulating
enough dreamy *Liebestod* to vanish contentedly through the
veil, or suddenly getting the idea—like just realizing you can
sell the car and fly to Florida. In the sense of the latter, the
Japanese seem to have an intuitive understanding of Seneca's
insight: You don't really have to wait for things to get downright horrible; you can leave anytime you want!

To most Westerners death is a permanent disintegration in
the void. Or worse, eternal tenure in a black pit with dirt in
your mouth. Even most Western Christians don't really seem
anxious to leave the green pastures for the Valley of the
Shadow. To the Japanese, on the contrary, death is very much
alive: animate, near, familiar, personal. Many Japanese families maintain *butsudan* in their homes, a family Buddhist altar
on which are kept pictures of ancestors and deceased relatives,
whose spirits are felt to be present and to whom the living
members occasionally address themselves. Flowers, food, and
ko (incense) placed on the altar, moreover, give an animate
sense of life to the dead.

The dead themselves have their days. *Bon-odori*, the summer folk festival, celebrates the return of visiting souls, who
must be treated and comforted by the living. *Meinichi*, or the
death-day of a deceased relative, is celebrated by the entire
family each year, and the *kanji* comprising the word itself actually mean "life-day." The dead even receive new christen-
ings, so to speak, upon dying. *Kaimyo*, a posthumous name
bestowed upon the deceased spirit by Buddhist priests (and paid
for by the family in a contribution by no means petty), also
carries with it a specified rank, commensurate with donation
apparently. So it seems that even in death the Japanese cannot
escape the pox of status.

To the Japanese, thus, is death quite alive, and their voluntary passing from this to that life is more a change than an

annihilation. Perhaps in part because of this, there really isn't any stigma attached to suicide in Japan. By rights (doctrinal ones) there should be, of course, since Buddhism condemns suicide. Yet in Japan "principle," or contradictions thereof, we note again, are less important than the social formulas.

Together

A Japanese *sarari-man* "is" his job, and a Japanese wife, still more often than not, "is" her family. Group identity is personal identity in Japan, and that can lead not only to the team play responsible for company success and national economic hegemony but to the family disaster. Willy Loman, in Arthur Miller's famous play *Death of a Salesman*, kills himself hoping to leave at least some insurance money to his children. The thinking is despairing and skewed, but understandable to Western audiences, emotionally moving to them in fact.

Yet how would these audiences react if Willy, feeling the same hopelessness, instead of driving off to crack up his *gaijin* jalopy alone, invited his sons Biff and Happy along for the crash? Or say he stoically strangled them on stage? Or gave them cyanide and glumly watched them thrash till the end, when he could take his dose?

Woman Drives Into Lake Biwa Killing Self, 2 Sons

NAGAHAMA, Shiga—A 33-year-old woman, apparently despondent over her weak health, committed suicide by driving her car into Lake Biwa Sunday morning. The woman's two sons were in the car with her and were also killed in the incident, police reported.

A local angler said he witnessed the car drive off the dock at Nagahama Port at around 12:10 a.m. and called police.

Police located and salvaged the car from a depth of about four meters.

According to police, the dead were identified as Kayoko Nagasao, wife of Tadashi Nagasao, 36, of Notogawa-cho, Shiga-ken, and their two sons, Takahiro, 10, and Kenji, 7.

A note by Kayoko addressed to her husband was found in the car. It said she had lost the will to live because of her weak health, "although I feel very sorry for taking our two innocent children with me on this trip to the other world," police said.

She had been suffering from back pains over the past few years.

In January 1985 Fumiko Kimura, a native of Japan but living in Santa Monica with her husband, Itsuroku, an artist-manqué and partner in a restaurant, took her two children, one four years old and the other six months, to McDonald's (which is as much a familiar landmark on the urban Japanese terrain as it is on the American), and walked with them into the Pacific toward her homeland.

Fumiko managed only to kill her children. She herself was rescued. Itsuroku, her husband, who à la Japanese tradition had reportedly been keeping a mistress in an apartment for the previous two years, when told at the hospital of his children's deaths, wept, then expressed some small envy for the strength of the bond between his wife and their children.

"Family suicide" (*oya-ko shinju*) is all too common in Japan. Though it is illegal, few judges will actually sentence a parent who has the bad luck to survive. If suicide is not without its small honor, failure at suicide is shame enough. Even worse, a mother who kills herself and leaves her young children behind is often reviled as an *oni*, a "fiend."

The ironic twist, of course, is that the epithet if not the act may be understandable, given the marginal domestic virtues of the "stranger" to whose care the children might well revert.

CHAPTER 8

*Learning on
the Chain Gang:
Nightmare in
Japanese Schools*

Karate Club Inflicts Deadly Punishment

One Takushoku University student is dead, another seriously injured—the result of physical punishment inflicted Tuesday night by other club members for a minor infraction.

The students, both freshmen, were beaten and kicked in a dormitory room in Tokyo's Kodaira for failing to return the uniform of a senior member of the club after washing it for him.

Fatally injured was Tetsuya Mori, 19, of Gifu-ken. In critical condition after two hours of surgery to repair internal organs is Sadayuki Ichihara, also 19.

Police arrested six students, five of them 19 years old. The sixth is Takehiko Ogata, 20, a student in the private university's political science department. They were charged with inflicting bodily injuries and inflicting injuries resulting in death.

In previous incidents at the school, the death of a freshman member of a cheerleading club led to the club's dissolution by the university and the arrest of seven juniors. Fourteen members of

a now-defunct karate society were expelled following the death of a student in "a practice" in 1970. Two students were arrested in the case, including the club's vice-president.

The latest incident was not expected, according to Raizaboro Kato, the director of the university's student counseling department. The university will again act to disband the club, however, after professors meet to discuss the case, he said.

According to police, a sophomore agreed to wash the uniform of a senior, then ordered a freshman to wash it. The freshman did so, but asked another freshman to deliver it. The second freshman forgot to return the uniform on Tuesday.

At 11 p.m. Tuesday, the sophomores summoned all nine freshman members to a dormitory room, told them they were collectively responsible for the gaffe, ordered

them to sit at attention and kicked and beat their heads and bodies for about 20 minutes.

After Mori and Ichihara groaned and fell unconscious to the tatami, one of the sophomores telephoned for an ambulance.

Club captain Tatsuo Suzuki, 21, said the incident was unexpected, as punishment should be administered only during the practice period, and not in the way it was inflicted in this case.

Police said, however, that sophomores had been inflicting violence on freshmen from time to time as a way of "putting spirit" into them.

The surviving, non-hospitalized students are being questioned by police. The students are hesitant to speak on the matter because they fear reprisals, according to police.

The club won the East Japan University Karate Tournament in May.

Jack-in-the-Box

In the *bento* box of incongruous social formulas that capture and rule the Japanese social psyche, none seem more at
odds than *enryo* and *gaman*. Often charmed by the former and
aghast at the latter, the Western traveler may fail to perceive
the prodigious but exhaustible self-control gritting its teeth behind both.

Enryo is that famous Japanese penchant for (or "show"
of) diffidence and restraint that makes the Japanese so endear-
ing so quickly to Westerners, whom the Japanese often consider forward and presumptuous. Offered a drink, a Japanese
parched near death may well deny the slightest thirst, or
drowning in drink already may well risk death getting it down.
Such obligingness can't help but conquer the suspicions of the
uninitiated and self-centered.

Gaman, on the other hand, is that attitude of the Japanese before goals and obstacles to martial their energies, to endure hardships and persevere till success or the bitter end.
Gaman may have reached its giddiest glory and gore in Bushido
("way of the warrior"), the spiritual and ethical code of the
samurai, the feudal warrior caste, beginning informally as early
as 1100. In the Tokugawa period (1603–1868) Confucianism bent
Bushido to the responsibilities of bureaucracy, and Zen ethe-
realized its frigid love affair with death. Bushido, ever enam-
ored with the sublime, self-consciously equated its samurai
devotees with the cherry blossom, whose glory is to fall at its
loveliest without regret. In practice it was more id-riddled, permitting samurai to have several legal bedmates and to Cuisinart
passersby (or delinquent karate students) for deficient defer-
ence. Its more touted virtues were loyalty, honor, courage, pi-
ety, self-denial, and resolve.

The Meiji Restoration, in 1868, assimilated not only many
of the samurai into the merchant and bureaucratic classes but
also much of Bushido, or at least the aspects that survive today
as the high-octane fuel for Japanese success: *gaman*, group fe-

alty, sexism, and *doryoku* (effort), the latter as exponential
monomania.

Because of its association with the failed glories of World
War II, Bushido is not as acknowledged as a living force in Japanese life as are the virtues and formulas it has bequeathed the
modern Japanese. Over one-half of the young Japanese men of
high school and college age train in at least one of the martial
arts, in tens of thousands of *dojo* spread all over Japan. Perhaps
Bushido lives on most self-dramatically in *misogi*, the practice
of near-naked and immobile meditation under and amid the
freezing torrent of a winter waterfall. Such resoluteness is most
familiar to the West in a Japanese icon and artifact: the *hachimaki*, a colored headband worn to show an unbreakable determination before great tasks and monumental missions—or of
late just group affiliation during any to-do. With typical Japanese disregard for Western notions of congruity, the *hachimaki*
has been grimly tied on by everybody from samurai to sushi
chefs, from kamikaze to runners in the All Japan Businessman's Long-Distance Relay Race.

But let there be no doubt, however different their station
or goal: Each of them has an undeniable, uniquely Japanese
resolve. It is powerful, implacable, and narrowly focused like a
cold laser light. It tries to absorb all the other psychic energy
and harness much of the instinct. Freighted as it is with otherwise anarchic and conflicting impulses, it inevitably leaps out,
when sparked, with a mad, bright fire.

Such resolve outside the *dojo* and the thundering cataracts
is even more ubiquitous if usually less dramatic. It is resolve
and only resolve, after all, that holds the colliding impulses and
conflicting formulas of Japanese society together. It is at the
core of the Japanese approach to life and at the root of their
education system.

The successes of that education system are legendary:
99.99 percent attendance rate, virtually 100 percent literacy,
number-one in the world on achievement tests in science and
math, 94 percent rate of students making it to high school, of

whom over 94 percent of those will graduate. The American school system, in comparison, leaves over 20 percent of its citizens functionally illiterate, drags American students farther behind Japanese students every year in math and science, compulsorily passes even the hopeless from junior high into high school, so that only 70 percent of students who start high school finish. Moreover, once the Japanese students bound directly for industrial jobs graduate from high school, they give Japan the very asset most American managers say they themselves lack: an educated, capable, and committed work force.

What's less well known in the West are the Draconian means by which the Japanese achieve these successes, and the mortal price they pay for them.

Until he is about five, the Japanese boy is Id-as-Emperor in his home. He gets what he wants when he wants it, and thereby learns to see his mother as the archetype for women: servants to his desires. Even outside the protection of his home other women will oblige his wants, and he regularly expects to have some woman rise to give him her seat on the bus.

He rarely sees his father. One study showed that more than half the college-age sons didn't communicate with their fathers at all. Eighty percent of these sons, on the other hand, said they talked with their mothers. As such the image of the father is played out in popular culture either as silent and remote, or as an ineffectual figure of ridicule.

At around five years, though, the noose of social formulas begins to tighten about the boy's neck—and these days it's starting to tighten even sooner for some Japanese tikes. *Seito* (school kids) can still be in diapers when they begin rudimentary drills like raising arms, and toddlers master marching along routes mapped out on the floor. Four-year-olds can attend special strength and endurance classes. There are athletic institutes for infants, where tots leap to the beat en masse like frogs, each dressed in his and her official warm-ups.

But for those little *shoguns* who manage to evade such pre-school training and the compromises to their deified desires that contact with other little *shoguns* inevitably exact, emerging restrictions can come as a shock:

I'm Bad!

Yoshi's big day of the week is at hand again. He puffs himself up like a *fugu* fish and pounds about on short bow legs like a samurai. And so he is, of sorts. Yoshi is four, and woe to those three or two or one. Or girls. One is coming to his home today. Good. He will punch her.

Otherwise blessed, Yoshi is deprived in his lack of sisters. Punching practice is not what it could be. There's always *Okasan* (Mom), but he already suspects her yelps are theatrical and strictly for his benefit. There's no terror galloping in her eyes. And where's the fun without that?

But today the injustice is redressed. Mom's women's group meets today, and little Hiromi will come with her mother. Hiromi is three. Ha-ha, three is nothing! He will punch her.

Yet first there is this looming indignity of good clothes. Mom scoops him up, and though he screams and twists and spits and pinches, she stuffs him into his new Mickey Mouse shirt and pants. He screeches at her that she is an ugly old sack of *he* (fart), and she looks hurt. Yoshi feels a little guilty and worried that maybe he has flushed his promised (if he is good) trip to *Makudonarudosu* (McDonald's) down the toilet. But Mom kisses him, so all is well.

The doorbell chimes and Yoshi makes fists expectantly. Hiromi enters clinging to her mother, wild-eyed with terror. Yoshi beams with pride at his power to awe. Hiromi's mother sets her over in the corner of the room with some origami folding paper. Yoshi swaggers over and stands with hands on hips above the little girl. He snatches the piece of red origami from her and pronounces the color a bad one. Hiromi folds her hands in her lap and looks at them. Such insolence is unbrookable to Yoshi, who whacks her on top of the head. Now there's a real scream.

Hiromi's mother comes over to cheer Hiromi up and give

her some more paper, and smiles at Yoshi. Yoshi's mom chides him gently. It all feels so terribly invigorating, he administers several more bracing slaps while the ladies talk excitedly to one another, for some reason in a strange new language today.

Then something unexpected. Everyone is adjourning early. He and Hiromi are being carted along. Outside, down the block . . . ah, to the park.

But what's this? A blond *gaijin* lady and a little blond girl. The girl is small. She must be no more than two. Two is nothing! He will introduce himself. Whack!

So, they make the same sound as little Japanese girls when punched!

Yoshi's world suddenly turns to nightmare. The sun is eclipsed by a giant shadow stooping toward him, his ears are scoured by a shrill human braying, his vision filled by the angry blue eyes of a grown *gaijin* female-fiend. Eeiiii! She has actually struck his bottom.

Yoshi's mother drags him wailing and limp over to the little *gaijin* girl, pushes his head down to make him bow, shakes his arm till he blubbers *sumimasen*. It is a miserable fate for a once proud samurai, and surely Yoshi will grow up like many of his male contemporaries, nostalgic for the good ole days when men were men and women weren't.

It is unknown if Yoshi gets to *Makudonarudosu* for a consolation burger.

Education-Mother

The devoted and gentle martinet behind all the educational activity and ambition is none other than *ofukuro* (or *okasan*)—Mom. She is devoted entirely to the education of her children, so much so that she has engendered a new phrase in Japanese dictionaries: *kyoiku-mama*, "education mother." She rises at five or six in the morning before the other family members, and wouldn't think of going to bed before her children have finished studying and eaten their ramen (noodle) snack,

at midnight or later. She spends patient hours filling out stacks
of applications and waiting in sign-up lines for special schools
for her little scholars. She transports her apprentice academic
stars to classes in strength, agility, rhythm, music, calligraphy,
sports and martial arts, and waits doggedly outside for them
while they're there. The exotic *bento* meal she packs for them
each day is universally accepted as an index of her love, and
of the child's pride or shame.

To monitor the progress of her children and the particulars
of their courses, the *kyoiku-mama* makes sure she attends
every school meeting and takes every opportunity to speak with
her children's teachers. Where it's permitted (in private, extra-
school classes) she will sit in the back of the classroom with
other *kyoiku-mamas* auditing the activities. She will also research the background of the teachers and compute the success
ratio of their former students. And in order to better prepare
herself for this monumental, lifetime task, she will attend
kyoiku-mama classes, which teach her how to tutor her children in their weaker subjects. Insofar as their education is concerned, she is her children's incentive, their conscience, their
ambition, and their will itself.

It is common for a Japanese mother to sleep in a room with her
children, not with her husband.

After School, After Life

As if all this were not sufficient devotion, the *kyoiku-
mama* will take a part-time job so that she can afford to send
her children to the private cram and prep schools Japanese students attend. Though the man in Japanese society is the principal yen winner, in fact over 40 percent of the work force is
composed of women. At the same time, women's wages are
only about 55 percent of what men's are, and women occupy
only 4 percent of the decision-making positions in the business
and employment world. That women work to the considerable

extent they do, and for the modest wages they get, is due in no small part to their desire when they become wives, not to be independent or to have a separate discretionary income but to give their children "more" education.

In a formulaic society the absence of clearly defined and consistent rational principles tends to confuse or even eliminate logical criteria for assessing actual value and practical contribution. *Oyabun* will promote incompetent but faithful *kobun*, Japanese baseball teams will go on hiring sometimes mediocre *gaijin* players for astronomical salaries just because *gaijin* players are by formula said to be better than Japanese players, and in general formulas tend to be reinforced in the face of opposition rather than appraised. Quality tends to become an amorphous, indeterminate aspect and is often replaced with quantity. In the same way, *kyoiku-mamas* believe that "more" education is intrinsically good, lots is better, and most is ideal.

But to pay for more-lots-most education, much-more-most money has to be accumulated by the *kyoiku-mama*, forcing her to take whatever work at whatever wages she can get. Strength classes for kindergartners can alone cost $400 a month.

The biggest expense, though, comes from attending *juku*, the private "cram" schools, also called *yobigo*, or "preparation schools." There are *juku* from preschool level through high school, well over half of whose students also attend *juku*. Going to *juku* three afternoons a week following regular school can easily cost over $250 a month, and $5,000 a year is not an unheard-of sum for a family to spend on one child's *juku*. In fact, so popular with *kyoiku-mamas* are the *juku* that there are from 35,000 to 50,000 at any given time, representing a growth industry worth $5 billion to $6 billion a year. As a result, more than a third of the space in Japanese bookstores is devoted to cram books.

In Japan, where anything can still be co-opted into formula, education is not so much process as it is packaged product, and values as well as purpose can get lost in the packaging:

19-Year-Old Jumps To Death In Koshigaya

KOSHIGAYA, Saitama— A college student jumped from a eight-story condominium here to her death Friday night, apparently worried about her wish to become a nurse, police said.

Police identified the young woman as Yukari Kawamura, 19, a second-year student at Tokyo Seitoku Junior College and the eldest daughter of Kazuo Kawamura, 45.

Yukari was found lying in the parking lot of Park Heights, a Koshigaya condominium, at about 11:45 p.m. and was taken to hospital but died soon afterwards.

Police learned that her wish was to become a nurse but she had been worried about not being able to master the piano, one of the college's courses.

However much purpose or pride such a system might provide the *kyoiku-mama*, what it presents her children with is not only opportunity but nightmare.

For the first three years of elementary school the main pedagogic task is inculcating basic social formulas rather than instilling the angst of ambition. But after this short, halcyon introduction to schooling, things suddenly get quite serious. Even young children can leave home for school (schools) as early as 6:30 A.M. and not return until 9:00 P.M., after which time they will put in another three hours of individual study. And they can do this six days a week and then attend practice testing at the *juku* again on Sunday morning. *Seito* (students) attend public school eleven months a year and do special "homework" the remaining summer "vacation" month—if they're not attending all-day summer *juku*. Compared with the

180 days a year American students attend school, the Japanese face 240.

In secondary school there is a strict dress code that prescribes not only uniforms (*seifuku*) but exact hair- and skirt-lengths, for which there are often regular, individual, morning inspections, with rulers for precise measurements. The students serve one another their class meals and clean up their schools (they are their own janitors). Moreover, through ninth grade it is the brighter students who are expected to help the dimmer as an afterschool activity, since children of all ability levels jointly attend the same classes and virtually no one is set back a grade. This egalitarianism, however, has its counterweight in the seating chart, which organizes the desks in an overt ranking by ability. Hence the pressure is applied not only for individual achievement but for group success and honor. In the same way their parents are expected to master if not reconcile the incongruous porridge of social formulas, the children are supposed to juggle the often incompatible goals of competition and cooperation, of self and selflessness. Consequently winning in such a system is no more sure a way of saving oneself than losing is of dooming oneself:

14-Year-Old 'Good Scholar' Hangs Self

NAGOYA—In the latest of the recent spate of suicides involving schoolchildren, a 14-year-old middle schoolboy, whose school records were excellent, hanged himself near his home in Aichi-ken sometime Saturday or early Sunday.

Shigehiko Ono, a second-year student of Tokai, Aichi-ken, was found dead in a barn about 100 meters from his home by a member of his family at about 7:20 a.m. Sunday, the police reported.

His death came less than two weeks after Koji Sakai, also 14 and a second-year middle school student, hanged himself in Suzuka, Mie-ken, on March 6, apparently after being bullied at school.

Shigehiko, eldest son of Yuji Ono, 48, an office worker, had been missing since Saturday morning when he left home for school.

The boy left no suicide note, the police said.

They added that Shigehiko had been chosen to speak on behalf of the students at a graduation ceremony held on March 8, although he was not good at public speaking, and had apparently had a great deal of difficulty in preparing the text he read at the ceremony.

A Japanese saying: "Sleep five hours, pass. Sleep six hours, fail."

Another Japanese saying: "Sleep four hours, pass. Sleep five hours, fail."

If Japanese students lead the world in achievement, they also make a good run at the laurels for both bullying one another and killing themselves.

The cruel, obsessive grind they often endure from mid-elementary school through high school is devoted exclusively to the aim of gaining entrance to one of the better-reputed colleges or, ideally, of attaining one of the few prized places in a prestigious national university, the zenith of which is Todai (Tokyo University). Graduate from one of these first-rank schools and your career is made—or, if you are a Japanese female, your career is "married." But so competitive is the struggle for entrance to one of these schools that it takes the whole first twenty years of one's life, spent in maniacal studying for the "examination hell" that precedes it, just to have an average-to-slim chance at it. On a national basis, a third of all aspirants to college discover they have failed their entrance exams.

Yet long before one sits trembling with that final exam before him or her, the effects of the struggle have taken their toll. Even among the winners there are the usual casualties: scholars with whole continents of their personality unexplored and undeveloped, students so disoriented in values they can't tell piano from life itself, and kids so burned out they can't reanimate their purpose or summon the energy to go on—with school or even with life.

How much worse for the losers. Quite early on they, and those around them, have recognized them as failures in the great academic spawning race. If they are introverted or weak, they are likely targets of bullying—the endemic *ijime* in Japanese middle schools—by both their more successful fellows and their angrier fellow failures. And even for those simple, ordinary, sad laggers who are not bullied but who cannot excel however much they try or are driven to try, suicide can seem a serene alternative to a no-win, humiliating game:

Despair Drives Boy To Suicide

KISARAZU—Poor school grades and illness apparently drove a third-year middle school boy to hang himself on Dec. 13, Futtsu police disclosed Tuesday.

Local fishermen found the 15-year-old boy hanging by the neck in woods close to his home. He had left a note at home, saying: "I am sick and tired. I don't feel good."

The boy had been suffering from a glandular disorder, police learned.

Just at the time—in middle school—when the personal restrictions on adolescents have reached a stranglehold, the blood and brains of these young people are deep-frying in a hormone bath. With anarchy running riot in the veins, a corresponding and equally ferocious institutional tyranny tries to regiment their social behavior. The consequences of such antagonistic pressures—especially for the tougher, more extroverted among the lagging, to whom suicide is neither attractive nor understandable—are all too often violent rage and revenge:

8 Angry Students Hurt 10 Teachers

KAKOGAWA, Hyogo—Ten teachers were injured when they were kicked and beaten up by eight students in the teachers' room of a Kakogawa middle school and one of them was made to grovel on the floor on Feb. 10.

The violence occurred at Yamate Middle School after a homeroom teacher, 25, in charge of a second-year class told his students on Feb. 10 that they would be ostracized unless they went straight.

On hearing that, five third-year students thought that the teacher had spoken ill of them, and went to the teachers' room with three second-year students during the lunch break. They demanded

Sensei

that the teacher squat on the floor and apologize.

When the teacher refused, the students hit him while yelling abuse.

More than 10 other teachers who happened to be present tried to intervene, but the students hit them too.

When the first teacher knelt on the floor, the students shouted that he should lower his forehead to the floor.

When the teacher prostrated himself on the floor, they hit him again.

Parents came following emergency phone calls and the turmoil subsided after about 30 minutes, but the first teacher suffered an injury which required three weeks' medical treatment and nine other teachers, including two women, were injured in varying degrees.

The teachers whose responsibility it is to guide these junior and senior high school students toward their respective terminals in the social schematic obviously have their own dilemma. As successful products of the same educational and social system for which they're training their students, they are much more likely to be forceful advocates of this system than they are to be its critics. The virtues of compliance, self-subordination, conformity to the social formulas, study, and more study are eminently apparent to them in their own career achievements. Japanese teachers make from $30,000 to $50,000 a year, and the profession of *sensei* (teacher) is an honored one. Even the word *sensei* still conveys to most Japanese a status, a prestige, a dignity that the English word *teacher* misses by miles. Literally *sensei* means "firstborn"—the highest status.

By and large Japanese teachers take their responsibilities as seriously as they do their dignity. They know in detail the strengths and weaknesses of each of their students, and they take profound and active interest in the welfare of their charges, including that part of their lives Westerners deem "personal." But for the Japanese student there is virtually no "personal life." Japanese teachers not only inspect their students for deviations in dress and grooming before school, they patrol the neighborhood looking for waywardness after school. And in the evening they visit the students in their homes in order to confer with the ultimate mentor and guide, *ofukuro*.

Hence the Japanese teacher's virtue is also his defect. Concern can become officiousness; guidance, prescription; teaching, training; authority, despotism. The word of the *sensei* is traditionally unquestioned, so that the position is sometimes more admired and admirable than the person. With the role honored, there is often too little incentive for the teacher himself to extend his intellectual range or pedagogic ability, just as there is little tendency among his students to challenge and test the teacher's knowledge in class. In fact, because the teacher is so used to going unquestioned by his pupils, he is likely to see any divergence from his authority as a personal affront and an attack on the whole system of authority—and authority, we recall, is the sanction for what is Wanted and Unwanted, and still the foundation and source for many social forumlas.

And to defend that authority, the Japanese teacher has the weapon and shield of corporal punishment:

Teacher Beats Boy With Pipe

TOKOROZAWA, Saitama —A middle school boy, beaten with a vinyl chloride pipe by his social studies teacher, has suffered a serious injury and has been hospitalized, police said Monday.

According to the Hanno Police Station, Yukio Aoki, 28, a teacher at Hanno Nishi Middle School in Saitama-ken, beat two second-grade male students, including the injured 13-year-old boy, in a classroom at the school at about 2 p.m. last Wednesday because they had forgotten to bring textbooks for the social studies class.

Aoki hit each of them once on the head with the pipe, about 50 centimeters in length and one centimeter in diameter, which he had frequently used to beat errant students with.

The injured boy resumed his seat in the class and went for athletic training afterwards. But shortly after he returned home around 6 p.m. he got a severe headache and had to be taken to a nearby hospital by ambulance.

Doctors at the hospital found that he was suffering from a brain hemorrhage caused by an external shock.

Statistics are notoriously manipulable and unrevealing. Japan, for instance, is well known to have a violent-crime rate among the lowest, if not the lowest, in the world. But such rankings, of course, depend upon one's definition of crime. Noting the ''crime'' and the sentence for it below, one has to wonder about the definition given by Japanese statisticians for such occurrences as family ''suicide,'' bullying, punishment, and ''discipline.''

Teacher Gets 3 Yrs For Killing Student

TSUCHIURA, Ibaraki (Kyodo)—High school teacher Kazunori Amamori was sentenced to three years' imprisonment Tuesday for causing the death of a student by beating him unconscious.

Amamori, 39, was found guilty by the Tsuchiura branch of the Mito District Court of involuntary manslaughter in the May 1985 death of Toshinao Takahashi, 16, a second-year student at the Gifu prefectural Giyo High School where he was a teacher.

Passing the sentence, the presiding judge said Amamori's "serious act" was apparently not motivated by educational or disciplinary purposes, but rather by the criticism of his fellow teachers, who accused him of failing to use corporal punishment on students.

The guilty verdict comes at a time when public attention is focusing on the issue of corporal punishment of students.

Moreover, critics charge that the problem is complicated by excessive school rules which many students are required to abide by even after school is over.

Amamori claimed that he resorted to physical force to "discipline" Takahashi, who broke a school regulation and then refused to apologize. The boy died from head and stomach injuries, and from shock resulting from the beating, according to hospital officials.

The incident occurred on May 9 last year during a school trip to the Tsukuba Expo '85 in Ibaraki-ken. Amamori summoned Takahashi and several other students to his room at an inn in Yatabemachi, near the exposition site, to question them about breaking school rules.

According to police reports, Takahashi took a defiant attitude toward the teacher and refused to apologize for using a hair dryer in violation of the rules.

Amamori kicked and punched Takahashi, who was kneeling in front of him. He claimed at the time of his arrest that he had intended only to discipline the student.

Corporal punishment for offenses such as recalcitrance, disobedience, and defiance of the "rules" is supposedly in regular though not universal use in Japanese middle schools, where such "offenses" are to be expected. Globally, the ages of twelve to fifteen are a miserable time for adolescents and a trying one for parents. In Japan this period of maturing is all the more difficult, given the restraints and impetuses imposed by the social formulas. But not only is it difficult because the students are exploding at the same time the teachers are screwing the lids tight. Teachers have a somewhat ambiguous relationship with their students, especially in the rapidly changing milieu of urban Japan. On the one hand the *sensei* is a traditionally remote figure, unassailable or even incomprehensible. On the other hand, he is a very familiar figure often involved in the personal lives of young adolescents ever more influenced by Western notions of informality, self-expression, and irony. The formulas governing the first, more aloof role are firm and traditionally well known. But, for the second, more personal role, by which an uncertain teacher tries to catch up with increasingly hip and skeptical students on the big new wave into the future, such a role is probably intrinsically equivocal, by nature without firm rules—anywhere—and the more so in Japan, where outside the rules can mean lost in limbo, and indeed "under the influence of an evil spirit":

Bullying Incident Teachers Punished

The Tokyo Metropolitan Board of Education Thursday announced actions taken against the principal and five teachers of Nakano Fujimi Middle School in Nakano-ku, Tokyo, for their involvement in a case of bullying, over which a 13-year-old student of the school killed himself in February.

The board handed down the punishments after summoning the teachers to its office Thursday afternoon. They were punished for actions, resulting in the loss of public confidence, which the board said violated the Local Officials Law.

The severest punishment was given to Namio Fujisaki, 57, the homeroom teacher of Hirofumi Shikagawa who hung himself in a toilet of the Japanese National Railways'

Morioka Station on Feb. 1. The punishment calls for his resignation and does not entitle him to retirement allowance. This is tantamount to a dismissal.

Fujisaki was punished for his involvement in a mock funeral bullies staged for Shikagawa last November. He signed a collection of prank eulogies.

Furthermore, on Feb. 6, five days after Shikagawa's suicide, Fujisaki asked the students of his class to keep quiet about his contribution to the prank eulogies.

Fujisaki was also punished for working part-time for about 25 years for a company which makes tests.

The salaries of two other teachers, who also contributed to the prank eulogies, were cut, as was that of Isao Nishi-

kawa, 57, the school's principal.

The other teacher, also involved in the mock funeral,
and Kaoru Serizawa, head
teacher of the school, were
reprimanded.

In connection with the
bullying incident on Feb. 12
in the class of Manabu Saito,
29, the board ordered Saito
and Serizawa to undergo a
one-year training period outside the school. Saito was one
of the two teachers whose salaries were cut for their involvement in the mock
funeral.

The board accepted the
resignations of the principal
and two other teachers involved in the prank funeral.

At a press conference after
the punishments were an-
nounced, Nishikawa said that
he had thought a lot about
the dignity of human life and
human rights since the death
of Shikagawa.

Fujisaki said that he felt he
lacked ability as a school
teacher. "I might have come
under the influence of an evil
spirit when I signed the collection of prank eulogies . . .
I am now sorry I did."

Most of the school's teaching staff remained in their
rooms after a graduation ceremony, waiting for the an-
nouncement of the punish-
ments of their colleagues.

Masahiro Shikagawa, 42,
the father of the victim, refused to comment on the
punishments but said, "I
hope school authorities will
strive to eliminate bullying in
schools. That's what Hirofumi wanted."

Abrupt Resignation

It's another of those frequent paradoxes one encounters
in the Japanese that their cultural sensibility can be so much
at odds with their social psyche. In much of their art as well as
their aesthetic expression in daily life, the Japanese prize the
subtle, the indirect, the suggested, the ambiguous. They give
more value to feeling than to precise exposition, and in fact
regard wordiness as a vice. The best of what passes between
two people is inexpressible. *Haragei* (gut language), a special
rapport by which truly simpatico people communicate without
words, and *yoin* (reverberation), that inchoate emotional resonance that is more profound than the particular image that
evoked it, are both eminent cultural expressions of this value.

Much of formal Japanese arts also embodies the virtue of
suggestion and ambiguity. The Western philosopher Spinoza said
that a thing is defined not so much by what it is but by what

and "where" it's not, and the Japanese have a special acumen for expressing this. *Ma* (the vacant intervals between the filled spaces) is a matter of palpable and profound reality to them, and is emphasized in conversation as well as in art. The blank areas in certain kinds of Japanese painting are themselves given a name, *yohaku*, because their contribution to the Japanese preference for disparate rather than symmetical proportion is as indispensable as the shapes and "things" they separate. The preference for asymmetry, incidentally, finds expression in something as banal as the windows in Japanese homes: There are no standards for their size or placement.

However, the Japanese social psyche, with its dependence on and allegiance to formulas, is by definition hostile to ambiguity in relationships, personal or institutional. One simply has to know whom one is speaking to, his status, his corporate affiliation, his community, and eventually his family background. Indeed that's what a good proportion of the Japanese social formulas exist for: to elicit and respond to this information and to accommodate it to the rest of the formulas in the social grid. Hence, ambiguity, especially for the teacher, can be an intolerable anxiety:

Female Teacher Commits Suicide

YAMAGATA—A 46-year-old primary school teacher of Yamagata, Yamagata-ken, leaped to death from the roof of her three-story school, leaving behind a note saying that she had lost confidence in her teaching, it was learned Tuesday.

According to reports from Yamagata municipal No. 10 Primary School, the teacher, Noriko Ito, who was working overtime alone on the night of Dec. 14, jumped from the roof of the building to the ground 20 meters below.

One of the school's security guards found the dying teacher on the concrete ground shortiy after 9 p.m. and rushed her to a nearby hospital, where she was declared dead an hour later.

The sixth-grade teacher left behind a note in which she said that she had lost her ability to run her class.

A ladder was found extended from the third floor to a water tank on the roof, leading police to believe that the teacher had committed suicide by jumping from the roof.

Just as Japanese students probably top the international list of students throwing in the towel—not on their studies, but on their lives—Japanese teachers probably do the same. With fifty students in a class, and working hours that start at dawn and end late at night, the circumstances faced by these teachers are already difficult and demanding. Add to that responsibilities that go way beyond the pedagogical and into the personal, with conflicting needs for strict discipline and humane pedagogy, intellectual unassailability and familiar relationships, with competing expectations for individual and class achievements, for genuine learning and the gross memorization of the trillion facts the students will need to regurgitate during "examination hell" if they're to get into a decent university—with all these contradictory demands, impossible missions, exhausting and inexhaustible efforts, *sensei*s too, bid terminal adieu.

These conflicts can reach critical mass when a Japanese teacher finds himself caught between both students and superiors, and losing face with both. A situation bad enough for Westerners, it is often unresolvable for Japanese:

Teacher Kills Self After Reprimand

AGEO, Saitama—A middle school teacher committed suicide Friday afternoon by hurling himself from the top of a five-story school building in Ageo after being warned by the principal for inflicting corporal punishment on a student.

Toru Honda, 30, an art teacher of Kamihira Middle School, made a second-year female student sit on the concrete floor of an outside verandah for several minutes Thursday morning because the girl wore black stockings in violation of the school rules which require white stockings.

Principal Hideo Aoki, warned Honda that such punishment, which is a sort of corporal punishment, should not be inflicted.

When Westerners look at the industriousness of Japanese students and their preeminent standing on achievement tests and then note the pervasive and accumulating successes of Japanese business and industry on the international scape, they are likely to come to certain erroneous conclusions—especially in America, where students generally spend little time on studies and prove it on achievement tests, and where trade deficits to Japan benchmark our failures. Given this panorama, we are wont to infer that the Japanese educational system is nearly ideal and certainly an appropriate model for the West. Such a thesis gets more prominence the worse we do.

There's no doubt that American students need to study more, and probably apply themselves to more exploitable studies. But there is much in the Japanese school system that suggests the West should not imitate it even if there weren't cultural obstacles to its doing so. After all, it is still rote memorization that is the main preoccupation of all these Japanese students studying all day long all of those years—and memorization aimed at one end only: mastering the exams that will permit them to enter prestigious universities. What these students learn that is of actual use to their future employers they in fact learn only *after* high school, and almost all of that on-the-job. Once in university, with the dreaded "examination hell" behind them, they give themselves over to much-earned but unproductive indolence and revelry. And regularly the companies that hire them out of college do so not because their majors are useful to the companies but in accordance with certain social formulas: the status of the graduate's university, his appearance and avidity, his amenability to group goals and obedience, his relationship to an alumnus already in the company. In fact, the company does not expect him to know much that is of use to them; they train him to do that.

So, much of the education to which we Westerners are likely to attribute Japanese success in business and industry has very little to do with the Japanese educational system in itself, but rather with the social formulas governing social behavior in general.

Most questionable, we see, though, are the consequences of an educational system that drives its students so fiercely to so artificial and so pedagogically dubious a goal as "examination hell." The human casualties are substantial, and counted among them are the winners and the losers.

Those lost souls who fail their entrance exams, who try and fail again, and wander, year after year from testing site to testing site, are called *ronin* (wave-men)—the same name given those samurai whom fate had made masterless in the wars and debris of feudal Japan and who tossed about, disconnected and bereft, on the waves of hazard.

CHAPTER 9

Foreign Gods, Foreign Freaks: *The* Gaijin *in Japan*

AMERICAN FATHERLAND
THAT IS AN ARTICLE OF MY CREED
LEADER OF THE PACIFIST MOVEMENT.

(inscription seen on a pair of jeans)

Cultural Conflict

On June 5, 1986, during the Japanese professional baseball season, the pitcher for the Kintetsu Buffaloes threw a low inside fastball to the Hankyu Braves' 250-pound American giant called "Boomer," trying to take advantage of the notorious "expanding strike zone"—that area where a pitch would otherwise be a "ball," but that Japanese umpires feel obliged, out of national solidarity, to declare a "strike" for Japanese pitchers throwing against *gaijin* mercenaries.

But the pitch was too low and inside even for the umpire to redeem, and it rocketed off the shin of Boomer. The ball ricocheted away from the huge, dark foreigner in horror, and the pitcher, Ono, quickly doffed his cap and bow-bobbed in apology. But sometimes sorry's not enough, for *gaijin* anyway, and Boomer skipped one step, then casually jogged the remaining two or three strides it took his enormous *odaiko*-drum legs

to reach the mound, where Ono said, "Oh no," and gave dignified ground as he was eclipsed by an insane, windmilling black
typhoon. Boomer dwarfed everyone on the field, and the swarm
from both teams trying to pull him off Ono looked like the Lil-
liputians tossed helplessly on the earthquake that was Gulliver.

In no situation are the conflicts between the formulaic society and the "rational" society greater or more evident than
in those having to do with the *gaijin* (foreigner) in Japan. If
Japanese living temporarily in the West have difficulty in adjusting to the absence of a guiding and comforting grid of social
formulas, how much more onerous for the Westerner in Japan
having to adapt himself to such a grid. To the Japanese the
formulas represent safety, stability, security, comfort. To most
Westerners the Japanese social formulas mean only artificiality
and restriction. And even more defeating than restricting is
the knowledge that eventually dawns upon the Westerner that
even were he to master the maze of the Japanese social psyche,
he would never be accepted as one of them by the people
born into it. The experience of even so deeply committed a
Japanophile as Lafcadio Hearn, the writer, testifies to this
predicament.

Because social cohesion itself in Japan depends not on rational principles but on agreed-upon formulas, there is no ra-
tionale at hand for the Japanese strong enough to undermine
the simple, surface distinction between "us" and "them," *ware
ware nihonjin* and *gaijin*, Wanted and Unwanted. With no firm
principles underlying that would permit a flexible surface, there
are no rules or means by which one could join the Japanese.

Consequently it is almost impossible for Westerners to
grasp the emotional connotation of Japanese words such as
tanin (stranger), *yosomono* (outsider), or even the relatively
neutral term designating the foreign outsider, *gaijin*. Such
words carry a valence of psychological segregation ranging from
mere anxiety to near revulsion, feelings that are tense enough
among the Japanese themselves—who are notorious for
neurotic-pitch shyness (*hitomishiri*)—but that can be unendur-

able around foreigners. One shouldn't be surprised, then, that
the Japanese share with the Saudis the highest rate of social
phobias in the world.

And there are foreigners enough in Japan to make the Japanese regularly uneasy, if not enough to make the foreigners
relaxed: perhaps a million (if illegal aliens are counted), though
a staggering 674,000 of these are the so-called Koreans, paradoxically indigenous to Japan. Koreans included or not, these
foreigners are subject to the exclusionary attitude of the Japanese. *Nakama*, a word meaning "pal" and "one of us," de-
marcates a Japanese social category into which Westerners
seldom truly fit, in spite of the nominal or official membership
a Westerner might have in a Japanese organization.

Besuboru (baseball), or *yakyu*, as it was called during
World War II, offers an object lesson in this reality—or "two"
realities in this case.

Besuboru, it's quite obvious, is a different game in Japan
than it is in America. True to company spirit, Japanese baseball
teams with few exceptions are named not after the cities in
which they play but after their chief corporate owner-sponsors.
The Giants are not the "Tokyo" Giants but the Yomiuri Giants,
after the newspaper giant. And the Swallows, also of Tokyo,
are not the "Tokyo" Swallows but the Yakult Swallows, after
the dairy-drink king, and thus have more to do with gulps than
flights. (Try: Rupert Murdoch Indians? Dr. Pepper Orioles?) Demure uniformed usherettes offer assistance in the stands, and
fans, if given to loud monotonous chants, are nevertheless nonviolent and civil, usually even returning foul balls to the field.

Predictably, in Japan *besuboru* is thoroughly a team sport
founded on mastered fundamentals, group compliance, and
"fighting spirit," the latter of which is demonstrated by endless
practice and a sober, often nonexistent "private" life. Moreover, except for the championship series, in Japan tie games as
happily fulfill the social formulas as do victories. In American
baseball, on the contrary, victory is essential, as are million-
dollar celebrities, free-agency, musical-chair franchises, tan-

trums, and drug rehab. Consequently when *gaijin* players join
Japanese teams, it is not only an immediate case of *tanin* and
hitomishiri, it is a general cultural collision of multi-car caliber.

At the quiet end of the continuum characterizing this clash
there are the rigorous, exhausting practice and training routines followed by Japanese teams. Reggie Smith, former San
Francisco Giant who went to Japan to play for the Yomiuri
Giants, bemoaned the fact that the sport in Japan was like real
work, even at $1 million a year. Inflated salaries, of course, are
the draw. Even if he never played in the U.S. big leagues, a
gaijin player may easily make a few hundred thousand dollars
a season, while the average Japanese baseball player earns
around $70,000—a grotesque discrepancy that can't help but
exacerbate the cultural conflict.

Then there is simply the stone boredom and airy alienation
felt by American players on the team. Undeniably members of
the team, they are also irremediably "outsiders." Each Japanese team is allowed two foreign players, but sometimes there
is only one, who, even with attached interpreter, is bound to
lead an isolated existence. Japanese television periodically does
a video-bio on this or that *gaijin* player, who, after the initial
glamour of contact with a foreign culture and the thrill of sign-
ing for a starring role and a salary many times larger than he
could dream of getting in the more competitive U.S. major
leagues, is invariably shown a bit at a loss for society, if not
downright spaced out on anomie. After one year with Tokyo's
Yakult Swallows at $2 million-plus, an existentially stressed
Bobby Horner (dubbed "Red Devil" in Japan) waived off a reported $10 million three-year Yakult contract offer to fly home
and flap bats with the Saint Louis Cardinals.

At the clamorous end of the continuum, there is the palpable cultural clash described at the beginning of this chapter:
an American batter attacking a Japanese pitcher who has just
hit him with a pitch. It is doubtful—though some doubt this—
that a Japanese pitcher would intentionally hit a batter with a
pitch, not even a *gaijin* batter. After all, not just Japanese

baseball but Japanese society is held together by compliance with the formulas, so if pitchers started deliberately throwing balls at the players, where would it all end? If a Japanese pitcher does accidentally hit a batter, though, he will apologize. Some *gaijin* players, being *gaijin*, predictably don't care about the Japanese formulas or adhering to them and are instead freer and more determined to respond to their own "justifiable anger." To the Japanese, of course, this is literally scandalous, and definably "insane"—further confirmation they are dealing with the barbarians.

Bad Barbarian

If you are a Westerner living in Japan you basically have only two choices insofar as the image you hope to project: good *gaijin* or bad *gaijin*. Neither will ever really make you *nakama* (one of the boys), nor will projecting one rather than the other necessarily have the results you'd expect.

Brad Lesley is a *gaijin* pitcher playing for the Japanese Hankyu Braves. He is insane. Or so most of the Japanese fans have decided. While Japanese ballplayers all have uniform crew cuts, Brad has bushels of chaotic curly hair escaping from his tiny uniform cap. He himself is huge, barging, anarchic. There is nothing contained or formulaic about Brad. He does not walk so much as charge and barrel. The parts of his body rush in diverse directions and seem completely unharmonized to Japanese perceptions. When he misses a pitch, gets a bad call, or otherwise suffers disappointment, Brad is promptly plunged into bastinadoes of interior torment, the tiniest of which are immediately made into manifest leaps, writhes, barks, scampers, and trills. When he strikes out a batter, wins a game, or generally feels good, Brad behaves exactly the same way, unless he is really up, in which case he slaps and punches his teammates around. Brad is a totally unpredictable creature, always slipping up and down the bank of what's Wanted and Unwanted. He is a menace, a Japanese nightmare, everything

Japan dreads, dreams, and doesn't dare. They call him "Animal." That is the name on the back of his uniform.

And the Japanese fans love Brad "Animal" Lesley. Even those who hate him love him. He epitomizes every stereotype of chaotic unrestraint and belligerent individualism the Japanese have of the untutored Western *gaijin*.

Early on in Japan Brad Lesley proved a quick study. He realized that as a foreigner he would never really be accepted into Japanese society, no matter how hard he worked at it, no matter how completely he mastered the social formulas. So, instead of trying to do so at all, Brad Lesley actually had the cheek to exaggerate, to the point of parody, all those attributes of his origin and traits of his own that are so contrary to those of the Japanese social psyche, attributes and traits the Japanese, given the precedence of formula over fact, were likely to see in him anyway. And the Japanese, far from being scandalized, loved it. Brad confirmed everything the popular mentality believed about the uncivilized *gaijin*. Look, they *are* barbarians. Hurray for the barbarians!

Good Barbarian

Randy Bass is the first-baseman for the Hanshin Tigers, a regular contender recently for the Japanese championship. Randy is not at all like Brad. Randy is a quiet family man, with short hair and, compared with the body antics of Brad Lesley, economical and graceful of movement, though he is big himself and a power-hitter. Known for his short-cropped beard, Randy shaved it off on TV a couple of years ago with a razor made by a company that reportedly paid him almost $200,000 to do so. Randy has stayed in Japan longer than most *gaijin* ballplayers, and with his unassuming manner, homey gentility, and tremendous success on the field, he is a favorite among Japanese fans. He has been able to parlay that success and popularity into a large farm in his native Oklahoma and a comfortable home in Japan. The Japanese do not seem to resent this in Randy the

same way they do many of the other patently overpaid and
underperforming *gaijin* transplants. In fact, when Randy Bass
won his league's triple crown and led his team to the pennant,
a Tigers' cheering club created a wildly laudatory chant: *"Kam-
isama! Hotokesama! Bassusama!"* ("God! Buddha! Bass!"). If
Brad "Animal" Lesley is the *gaijin* as patronized barbarian,
then Randy Bass is the *gaijin* as respectful, laconic, unassuming guest.

And yet . . .

Sadaharu Oh makes physical truth in Japan of the adage
"living legend." Son of a Chinese father and a Japanese
mother—a hybrid status that by formula would otherwise doom
him, too, in all social provinces but entertainment—Oh is the
world leader in home runs: 868 between 1958 and 1980, when
this demigod retired from playing and soon became manager of
his team, the Yomiuri Giants. Some few years later, with Oh
still at the helm, the Giants were meeting the Tigers and Randy
Bass in the last game of the 1985 season. Even for a final game
of the season it was to be a special game—and what turned out
to be an extraordinary test of the Japanese social psyche. For
Randy Bass had hit 54 home runs that season, and unexpectedly was threatening the single-season Japanese home-run rec-
ord, also held by Oh with 55, who looked on from the other
dugout. The tension, as well as the significance, radiated far
beyond the stadium that day.

In the end the same sorry cliché won out over a chance
for human fraternity—at hand in trembling immanence, reso-
nant with the potential for liberating the Japanese heart from
the Japanese cage.

God, Buddha, and talent notwithstanding, Randy Bass was
still more *gaijin* than Tiger, or player, or man, or fellow human, and all day the Yomiuri Giant pitchers never threw him a
ball he could reach, much less hit.

Goethe, the German writer and philosopher, once wrote
that in life one must be either a hammer or an anvil, the striker

or the struck. Given the rigid, formulaic nature of the Japanese social psyche, with its strict dichotomies and oversimplified surface distinctions, the Japanese often seem mesmerized by a vision of the world expressed in Goethe's adage, and doomed to swing between two psychic poles where one is everything or nothing.

The most common expression of this tendency among the Japanese is their notorious vacillation between feeling superior and feeling inferior, the most frequent touchstone for the estimate being the West and Westerners. The Japanese have had a traditional contempt for most other Asians and have conquered many of them at various times. But the West was something else again. The West has that framework of rational principles that enabled it to create science and sophisticated technology, which in turn gave it the might, first in the person of Commodore Perry last century to force open the gate into Japan, and then in the person of General MacArthur this century to vaporize it.

However, in between these two superior avatars, and since, the Japanese have had astonishing successes, militarily beating Russia (and for a while everybody else) and now economically trouncing everyone. Alternately, each of these failures and successes respectively seems to have been met by the Japanese with complete humiliation or swaggering arrogance—that is, with a wholesale revaluation by the social psyche of its innate wretchedness or natural brilliance. And not much in between, as if being Japanese can only be revealed to the world in an artificial social persona that is either perfect or pitiful.

This is one reason such opposites as Brad "Animal" Lesley and Randy Bass can both be such hits with the Japanese. Both players are arguably more skillful than many of their Japanese counterparts—a cause for some possible feelings of inferiority among the Japanese fans. Yet both men, in their contrary ways, also confirm the Japanese suspicion that the Japanese, as a people, are really superior. Brad after all is an "animal" and simply begs for superciliousness, playing even to the grandstand's approving disdain. Bass, probably because he is so unarguably superior to almost every Japanese player, is the more liked the more unassuming and humble he acts. His humility in a sense honors the Japanese "way" by suppressing or deferring his own, and thereby concedes to the Japanese their general "superiority."

It may not be logical, but it's certainly a way for everyone—Brad, Bass, and fans—to have his cake and eat it too, a formula much more important than logic in Japan.

Rocky-san

If the normal attitude of the Japanese to the *gaijin* is hopelessly ambivalent, nowhere is it more single-mindedly and unambiguously worshipful than in advertising. In TV commercials and in magazine ads Western models are probably used almost as much as Japanese models, certainly as much if one counts in the "halfs," as the Japanese call people of mixed Japanese and Western parentage. *Gaijin* model and promote clothes, makeup, exercise equipment, drinks, houses, patent medicines, gifts, furnishings, computers, records and tapes, golf and sporting equipment, bridal raiment, even some cars— everything but the most traditionally Japanese products and services, such as food and vacation spas. *Gaijin* faces— and bodies—smile or glare at one from out of the media hundreds of times a day, a visually overpowering testament not only to a Japanese sense of insecurity but to their willingness, even if unavowed, to submit themselves to the judgment of foreign standards (often only to rebel against them later).

And if anonymous *gaijin* faces have this much appeal, how much more so "famous" *gaijin* faces:

Exterior-Day-Close-Moving-On Stallone-*Interminable!*

From ground level our camera races on rails shooting up at Sly Stallone in togs, muscles and sweat eating up hunk-chunks of green yardage with each long, locomotive stride, a great *gaijin* giant from our low angle, tearing the blue veil of sky. We hear him suck wind with every alternate steed beat of hoof, and blow fume on the other. Here is a man, our lens shouts, unafraid to rip life up at the roots.

Dissolve to arty tight close-up of pale beer in glass, the sound of pouring effervescence.

We dissolve back to Sly, post-aerobic stance, and hear his voice-over in the magic of simultaneous deep resonance and nasal whine. He is musing, candid but manly, idly listing the inventory of his existence.

He skips over the mansion, doesn't mention the swimming pools or the Rolls, none of the tangible assets. He goes straight to the lighter-than-air stuff, where the character and soul float without inner tubes.

Beer fizzing on the screen, Sly's voice admits that in his life there is love . . . courage . . . and . . .

Long pause for humility, then fade out to void, and in on interminable pastiche of southern California leisure culture: jogging, eating, swimming, kissing, driving, good kids and friendly cops, all irradiated in seamless sun and sprinkled liberally with KIRIN CANNED BEER props and inserts—this chic montage to be the visual backdrop for Sly's broodings till final fade.

But miles to go before we sleep . . .

Next, in voice-over, we hear a chorus of airy female voices, siren dreams, beckoning the thirsty and lonely: *Together . . . together . . . together . . .*

Imperceptibly we stagger into contrapuntal voice-overs, the girl chorus alternating with Sly reciting, apparently aloof to petty matters of pitch, pace, passion, or pronunciation.

He promises we can make dreams come true.

Together . . . together . . . together . . . trill the girls.

The existential pain must be too great for Sly to bring clearly to voice, because now it sounds like he is advising "buying" courage in the heart. Surely, your own heart tells you, that must be "finding" courage in the heart. You have a bad moment there when you recall another meteoric success, Faust, and his great "buys" from Mephistopheles, but you weather it.

Sly seems to be weathering his troubles too. He assures us that love is stronger, though sorrow is half of the meaning, and swears that even long dark nights have to turn into new days, and stormy clouds go away. The reason this is so, he soliloquizes, is that Love is ours (an epiphany mysteriously edited to soundtrack first over an image of a man and his parrot, then two dogs, and—sane by contrast—finally a can of beer). Then more apostrophes to courage (yet again) and to walking hand-in-hand through life forever (*Together . . . together . . . etc.*).

Now you know why he's running—surfeit of courage notwithstanding. He's being chased by the ghosts of incredulous, outraged poets.

Final fade as Burbank sun sets on can of Kirin beer and the longest TV commercial (over five minutes) in this world or the next.

Ham

Japan, Tokyo especially, is an exorbitantly expensive place to live, or even visit. Rent, dinner and drinks, cabaret—all can cause fibrillation in the wallet if not in the breast. But the kind of money that can be made there outpaces even such adrenaline expenses. Baseball players infinitely less talented than Randy Bass, who after all was hardly a household name when he played in the U.S. big leagues, make salaries in Japan that must require the Heimlich maneuver to spend. So it shouldn't be a surprise that movie and media stars would slip quietly in and out of the yen-stream to make ads endorsing various products.

Yet, however financially logical such a move, it hardly mitigates as much as a degree the jarring effect for a Westerner catching their culturally impacted act in full color. Karen Grassle, who played Ma Ingalls on *Little House on the Prairie*, seems a suitable choice, decked out in rural apron and the same hairdo she had as America's anima-mom, to promote *Country Ma'am* cookies. But John Travolta, though he does seem to conjure carbonation in his endorsement of a soft drink, also seems forever petrified by Japanese TV in a Saturday-night forest of frantic dancing.

Gaijin seem linked almost alchemically in the Japanese psyche with oral gratification. This or that drink, alcoholic and not, has attracted the keen business sense and photographic acquiescence, at least, of people like Mickey Rourke, Ringo Starr, Gene Hackman, Mike Tyson, Marcello Mastroianni, and Mel Gibson (mentioned earlier in a downright sybaritic-looking chug-a-lug and postpleasure stupor).

James Coburn, an American film star of stylish menace, carries over some of his usual screen persona into his spot for Japanese *Lark* cigarettes, if rather incongruously. The plot in the minidrama driving the commercial revolves around Coburn's deft moves and insider know-how enabling him to escape an assortment of rather pitiful villains. Their final comeuppance arrives invariably when Coburn is asked by some hidden contact, "What you speak?" Coburn seems to know what this means, because he looks confidently through the camera at us and says, "Speak Lark"—which, one guesses, is a sort of password to safety if not eventual lung disease.

Perhaps the most thought-provoking of *gaijin* commercials, however, is one involving Sean Connery, who among other guises is the immortal James Bond. In this incarnation, though, he is . . . well, Sean Connery perhaps . . . standing in warm tweeds and wood paneling, and what seems to be quiet reverie. Dignified, slightly melancholy music anoints his reflective mood, a small nostalgic smile plays upon those famous long, cold lips, which have thrilled heroines and melted the iciest of female adversaries. Seeming to have retrieved some precious memory from the vault of a life balanced evenly in conquest and loss, Sean looks at us and muses poignantly, "My heart, and Ito ham." Fade to a big pink ham and silence.

After all, what more is there to say?

The *Gaijin* Who Came to Dinner

Besides internationally celebrated faces willing to spout a
bit of rubbish for a lot of yen, there are international carpet-
bagger faces willing to dress up, stay mute and stand still, and
be the repository for Japanese fantasies of *gaijin* fame. Usually
self-promoted as "look-alikes," they blow into town in the train
and dust of the real celebrities they look like, do their effigy
gig at hotels, supermarkets, expos, and on TV, where they are
interviewed for their opinions, no less, opinions that the inter-
viewer seems to think have been anointed as fortunately as
their faces. This charade is all the more inexplicable as one
realizes these breathing house-of-waxers look nothing like the

luminaries they imitate. When Prince Charles and Lady Di came
to Japan in 1986, two aping shadows suddenly appeared on the
actual and video landscape. They had the hair colors right, and
the little-*p* prince even wore a uniform cum medals from props.
They only had to stand together, like nuclear fusion, to pull
squeals (small modest Japanese ones) from a willingly conned
throng.

And yet it seems that in Japan not even similarity (however remote or willed) to famous looks is required for some
gaijin "success." Longevity alone seems all that's asked for
sometimes. There are many resident *gaijin* celebrities in Japan
who appear regularly on talk shows, game shows, TV ads, who,
from all appearances and by the most generous standards, have
achieved a sizable fortune and a small fame that far outstrides
their modest talents. In fact, their abilities seem often to consist
of garrulity, fluency in Japanese, usually blond hair, and a Job-
like patience for being gaped at. Though they would deny it,
their real virtue is to dramatize, in the magnified and public
arena of television, the same function all *gaijin* perform for
the collective Japanese psyche: to be a touchstone for the complex feelings of inferiority and superiority the Japanese have
vis-à-vis the West. Whatever the talents or mediocrities of these
house-broken *gaijin*, they are valuable because they are barbarians who have been tamed, prized not because they are
gifted but because Japan is gifted enough to have made them
worthy of sitting at her table.

Harro!

It's not only gifted or (the justly or unjustly) celebrated
gaijin who are the object of a Japanese mixture of admiration
and contempt. Ordinary *gaijin* receive their share of each, as
well as much of something too ambivalent to be defined by
either. As a *gaijin* in Japan one is still a freak, whether he be
a god one moment or a barbarian the next. Only recently have
large enough numbers of Japanese begun to live and work
abroad to begin eroding the physical and psychological insular-

ity that has kept Japan safe but parochial for centuries. So, to many Japanese a *gaijin* is still a thing of wonderment and occasional hilarity. Japanese children, even adolescents, still light up at the mere approach of a *gaijin* on the streets, as if a beast had suddenly raised itself upon hind legs and took to raiment. These same kids will dog the heels of *gaijin* not quite out of earshot, crooning a repetitive, endless song of *harro*s, hoping, one supposes, that this will act like salt on a bird's tail. This nagging, if harmless, patronage has been known to torment otherwise peaceful *gaijin* beyond their endurance, provoking them to chase and even sock one of the astonished, voluntary Japanese retinue.

Then, too, there is the zoo experience, probably notched on the belt of every *gaijin* who has ever lived in Japan. Sunday, that one day of the week when Dad might even possibly make a whistle-stop at family life, seems to be not only the day when the whole family gets together but the day they are freed to behave as they will. And nothing seems to bring out the will to behave that way so much as *gaijin*, as if during that one day a week the cohesion of the family is restored and cemented by its common arrayal against the spectacle of the foreigner. Consequently, a *gaijin* finding himself or herself at the local zoo on that day is likely also to find that everyone else has forsaken the prosaic charms of the lion and the koala to aim their excited Minoltas, Nikons, and Canons zooming and shuddering at the long white animal in human drag.

Let You Entertain Me

If you are a *gaijin* in Japan as a tourist or visitor, you aren't likely to be the object of such discrimination (or able to recognize it as such), since you have been identified as a "temporary" oddity and therefore essentially placed outside the normally fixed distinctions prescribed by formula. As such you're free pretty much to crash around the store breaking the social crystal with impunity, simply because your status gives you a dispensation from knowing what the crystal is and how

to treat it. In this instance the Japanese are freed also to respond individually to you as either Wanted or Unwanted: Some
will see you as a Wanted tourist or treasured curiosity; others,
more rarely, as an Unwanted foreigner or ill-mannered ignora-
mus, that is, someone who doesn't know what to do and what
not to do. Most Japanese even today still try to avoid contact
with foreigners just because it is so anxious-making dealing with
someone who doesn't know what's right and wrong, especially
in a culture where knowing that is everything and not knowing
it is doom.

If, though, you are a *gaijin* resident in Japan, you are fair
game as that which the social formulas define you to be: a crazy
ride at the carnival.

You, your wife and two-year-old daughter have escaped
from "The Incredible Shrinking Hutch" seconds before family
suicide might have appeared a quite reasonable alternative. On
the whitecaps of stifled rage and claustrophobic breathlessness
you wash up on the serene shores of Mem-Mem-Do, your *kissaten* of choice when amok is only a motion away. *Kissaten*,
Japan's unique brand of coffee shops, are the real refuge from
the free-fire zones of urban ambition. There are hundreds upon
hundreds of them in every city, each, believe it or not, with its
own atmosphere, and many decorated according to a theme.
When you are in a European mood, you go listen to jazz at the
Left Bank, but today you are nostalgic for things such as a back-
yard, crummy cars, and failed rebellions, so you come to Mem-
Mem-Do for the opiate of rough pine paneling, American rustic,
and sixties slush by Cat Stevens, Leonard Cohen, Melanie. Here
you can weep it all out.

Your daughter preoccupied with a rice cake—an artifact
you try to ignore as an intrusion on your dream of perfect past/
perfect place—you are just sinking into the right-on, peace-Man,
far-out mellow anachronism of Donovan, when . . .

"*Ano . . . sumimasen, sensei.*" ("Ah, excuse me, es-
teemed teacher.")

You open your eyes. There is a Japanese man right here

in the middle of mellow Donovan's trying to catch the wind. This is profanation, not to mention schizoid. And there are two little Japanese boys smiling with him. What is happening?

Haltingly the man tells you his sons . . . "want you to speak."

They all look on expectantly.

Any other day you would oblige them. But today you need to be with . . . yes, you hear her in the background . . . Joan Baez, wrapped in the sad comfort of her voice. So you speak to them in German.

They look stunned, almost cheated, as if the machine has eaten their coin. Dad gives it a game try, though. *"Mein Auto,"* he announces cryptically.

Gads, it must be contagious, you gasp to yourself, seeing another Japanese fellow rise hypnotically from his chair to approach your table. He is a short fellow with a mustache, the latter a rarity in Japan. For several seconds he stares mutely at your wife, who has closed her eyes in a valiant effort at repression, then he pulls out a thick cigar in wrapper and ring and holds it out to her. "So nice to be you," he mutters, drops the cigar in her lap and flees. You remember it's Sunday. The carny's in town. Donovan has been crushed by an elephant and Joan is screaming.

On the way out of the coffee shop and failed time-tunnel, you run into a Japanese man who wants just a "little" (*"sukoshi,"* he promises) of your daughter's blond hair.

> *NATIVE OPINION: A female student from Australia stayed at our home recently. As she was walking along the street with my sister, a grown-up man happened to pass by near them. The man was apparently not intoxicated. However, as he passed them he said with a dirty smile on his face, "This is a pen," without any reason. I heard that the Australian girl got very angry with him.*

Due to the nature of my job, I have many opportunities to meet foreigners. One of them told me that a Japanese man once said to him, without any reason: "This is a dog." He was upset because he thought that the man was insulting him by calling him a dog.

I am really ashamed of such childishness on the part of some Japanese people. Douglas MacArthur, the U.S. commander-in-chief in Japan after the war, said as he was leaving here that the Japanese people were mentally only twelve years old. Are we Japanese still only twelve years old in an international sense?

Tokyo is becoming an international city. I can only think that those who use such nonsensical English to foreigners are doing nothing but insulting others.

(O.T., company employee)

Eigo

English (*Eigo*) has a special status in Japan. It manages to be everywhere and nowhere. By the time a Japanese student graduates from high school, he has had six or seven years of it, and will get another two to four years of it if he goes to university. Yet it will be very unlikely after this, say, decade of English, that he will be able to converse intelligibly on even a beginner's level.

Such prodigious incompetence, though, is not really his fault. Except for some diplomats and company men whose work will take them to English-speaking countries or put them into regular contact with English speakers in Japan, there is little need actually to learn English. Students, who prepare from middle school on for the English part of the "examination hell" tests, and specialists (such as medical doctors and scientists, who must learn English to keep up in their fields) often learn to *read* and sometimes *write* it well but may not be able to vocalize so much as a single coherent sentence. Beyond these cases, English is more of a minimal social insignia—like our wearing at least thongs and a T-shirt to enter a restaurant— than a practical tool.

In fact *Eigo* in Japan is now much more an indigenous social formula than a foreign language. It is often more important to be seen taking English than either to learn or fail to learn it. An enormous burgeoning industry of private language schools and "colleges" has sprung up to exploit this national compulsion—and dignify a deathless fad—in which even untrained native speakers of English can easily earn $50 to $100 an hour conversing aimlessly with earnest if aimless students. Even in university, students will often have only a single practical English class, called "Conversation," though almost anything but conversation occurs there. There are usually about fifty students in each class, far too many for anything but bedlam or boredom. And even if there were fewer, the formula that condemns standing out from the group mocks the course title and terminates their will to speak in class. Hence it is both further mockery and a saving grace that the class meets only once a week (an interval that exterminates any memory of the previous lesson), and at that meets for only about an hour. Nominally the classes are ninety minutes in length, but professors at Japanese universities—as per formula—come to class ten minutes late and leave ten minutes early. To come "on time" is to let the side down.

If the students of English are for the most part unperturbed dilettantes, many Japanese teachers of English are oblivious masters. Often prodigies of English grammar (that is, the formulas of the language structure), they suffer unawares from an inbred system in which errors have been blithely passed on from mentor *sensei* to obedient protégé *sensei*, and for which there is little "real" English to test and correct it. So Japanese textbooks of English faithfully repeat the prescribed English errors of generations past, and few if any who use them know to blink an eye.

Nor, for that matter, does anyone really care. English, however much it may be the international language of commerce and science, is for the normal urban Japanese only the language of play. One fixture of morning Japanese TV is Riki, an adored darker-skinned gentleman of perhaps subcontinental roots, who enacts a *gaijin* freak-figure of the sort that flatters by contrast the Japanese viewer's sense of himself vis-à-vis foreigners. The Japanese have a formulaic condescension to darker-colored peoples and openly ape primitive tribal antics to evoke their stereotypical image of them. Riki, who speaks both Japanese and English, is sent out by his producer to literally chase down aghast *sarari-men* on their way to work, in order to confront them not only with his unique appearance but with English questions of the primer sort meant to exact public (and televised!) torment from them: "What did you have for breakfast?" and "Where is your wife?"

English words speckle the lyrics of Japanese pop songs, popping out unexpectedly and with a mind of their own, like pimples. In advertisements, too, they appear with sudden willfulness: an entire page in a magazine can be filled with *kanji* squiggles from the midst of which will leap *Love*, *Member*, *Golden Bullworker*, *Action Lady* and boldly *Sold Out*, confusingly meant to mean For Sale.

Mad Muse

There is even more play in product names. For example, that now famous soft drink, the name of which sounds wrung from a postworkout athletic supporter, *Pocari Sweat*. Quite the marketing coup that, hmm? And that other drink, the one that sounds like something West Coast cows do and you wouldn't drink, *Calpis*. What whiz in the ad agency's creative-concepts department fathered that on an English dictionary? And yet despite this affront to marketing logic and linguistic manners, both these products have long, long legs with Japanese consumers. Newer entrants into the marketplace, and still of unproven longevity, are the hair-care products *Joy-Jack*, and *Ultra Hard*, names perhaps unconsciously inspired by a visit to the adult video store.

More frolicsome still are the English names given Japanese automobiles, many of which are targeted strictly at the Japanese consumer and never get off the islands. If you've got *oyabun* clout you might drive Nissan's *President* or their *Cedric*, Toyota's *Crown*, or—watch out, girls, here he comes—an old goat's dream: Mitsubishi's *Debonair Executive*. A step down, and you can have a whiff of immortality with an *Eterna*, comic interlude with a *Laurel*, or *sarari-man*'s after-hours confirmation with a *Chaser*. For "new adult sports," as one Japanese automaker puts it, you can muscle up to a *Silvia* or a *Fair Lady Z*. But if you're solid bourgeoisie and eschew all reflected flash, you can settle for *Accord*, hope it's just a *Prelude*, hint at hidden *Vigor*, or admit it's a *Charade*, throw it all away for a *Starlet* or, Zen-like, dismiss all of it as *Mirage*.

As a kid anywhere else in the world might don a shirt painted with the indecipherable but lovely calligraphy of *kanji*, the Japanese, and not just the kids, "wear English." Sometimes it's just a mute message, like HANDS, sometimes a cracked maxim, like BE A FRANKIE PERSON; and sometimes it is a disheveled invitation to madness, such as these tidings on a sweatshirt:

> Unity wake the phone
> my Home trying not
> to be on Sunday, Pal

Or an obliging mirror for callow narcissism, as the desperate assurance on a notebook:

> Mine.
> Mine is my file note that enhances my
> sense and personality. All my
> friends pay attention to me.

Or the incongruous, salacious promise on a plasic linen-storage case:

> Tasty tool makes your Life Fragrant,
> also your mind.

Or a furtive mania, paradoxically proclaimed to the world on a hood's jacket:

> Here, we are alone at last—Identity

Or the simple poetry of a simple observation, as the one on a photo album:

> A seven-year-old girl. Her mind is like
> a marble. It rolls and wanders
> everywhere. Under the table and
> into the farthest corner.

Other times "Japlish," as the hybrid is dubbed, comes near to the strength and eloquence of *memento mori*, as in the script printed on a girl's autumn scarf: THINK ABOUT YOUR LIFE AGAIN. And even expresses—printed on the price tag for a coat—the poignance in an otherwise unspoken elegy for the Japanese themselves:

> WE ARE CHERRY OF THE SAME PERIOD.
> GLAD, SAD, AND FALLED TOGETHER.

English is all about the Japanese and rattling around in the hollow doll that is the collective psyche like so many mismatched puzzle pieces. Not really language, but word-chimes, even "poetry" when fortune's winds hoist it above doggerel. Hamburgers can be had not only from "Macudonarudosu" but from "God-o." And what otherwise would be mere mortal smokes transubstantiate to visions of *Tender* and *Peace*, or the mystery of *Misty Midnight Tiny*. English is an ambience for the ordinary Japanese, part of the formula for aural aesthetics and emotional music rather than a currency for ideas and facts. And as visual terrain it has the same effect: a familiar physical and psychic landscape, devoid of practical information, but electric with intimate melodies for the senses. Neon signs burn cold light into the soul, singing "Passion," "Sand," "California," ringing them off the wet streets, blind glass, and crowded concrete sheets. It's their siren song for an America of the imagination, their own Atlantis beneath the grid of group and gain, another shimmering kingdom of desire.

CHAPTER 10

The Dying Doll:
Mortal Shocks

NATIVE OPINION: My grandfather, who was born in the Meiji era, is now ninety-two years old and healthy. He likes to tell me stories about the old days. His tales always surprise me. For instance, there were even people in his day who were wearing chonmage, *or topknots.*

I will be a grandmother in sixty or seventy years. When I do, what should I tell my granddaughters about the Showa *era?*

Should I say, "The Showa *era was a good era, and Japan was the strongest economic power. However, there were the extortion cases and the disastrous crash of a Japan Air Lines' jumbo jet. Oh, yes, there was a social problem of school bullying and many primary and middle school students committed suicide. Women advanced into every corner of society in the* Showa *era. Oh, yes, and aerobics were quite popular." (I.S., high school student)*

It is not only the Japanese who are uncertain about what is happening to Japan and anxious about its direction. Already Japan has outgrown its small archipelago fortress and leaped across the seas that once isolated and protected it. Japan has penetrated virtually every market economy in the free world to become the number-one world creditor, at plus $240 billion; with the United States now the world's number-one debtor, at minus $370 billion. If Japan did not have to import 99.6 percent of its oil, its $79 billion trade surplus would be even higher. In fact, foreign oil accounts for nearly half of Japan's total import costs. Nor does Japan's new strength and wealth depend on manufacturing alone. Only 34 percent of Japan's total output comes from manufacturing. Thirty-seven percent comes from its service, insurance, financial, and real-estate sectors, which themselves have worldwide effects. The world's ten largest banks are Japanese; the biggest insurance companies and securities firms are all Japanese, as is the world's largest stock exchange. And beyond these figures there are the growing number of private banks, factories, and companies in the United States owned by the Japanese, whose investments in U.S. Treasury bonds (as much as $150 billion) literally underwrite nearly 40 percent of our gargantuan trade and budget deficits. Were the Japanese suddenly to withdraw these investments, a financial crisis would ensue in the West. This from a people who forty years ago lived in rubble, a people who still have no natural resources, who inhabit islands collectively no bigger than California, of which only 15 percent can be cultivated, a people who depend in some measure upon the rest of the world for almost everything essential but rice, fruits, vegetables, dairy products, and sheer human effort.

The Japanese economic miracle has occurred in so short a time that no one can be certain what ultimate changes it will create in Japanese society itself or in the West. However, some effects are already apparent, repercussions that are prescribing changes or dictating the few real options.

As their burgeoning commercial and financial power has spread throughout the world in the last decade, it has, of necessity, taken the Japanese with it. The Japanese have always loved to travel; famous for their group tours, it's also one of the formulas in the social schema that young women take at least one group tour abroad before they get married, perhaps never to leave their pumpkin again. But such tourism hasn't ever really promoted a broadening of the Japanese perspective; rather, foreign places become mere hanging charms on a fixed Japanese view of the world. The Japanese have usually traveled not to discover something new but to confirm their viewpoint—not to grow but to stay the same.

Now, however, the Japanese are coming not just to see Disneyland or the Grand Canyon or Westminster Abbey but to live and work in the West, often for years. And they are coming in ever-increasing numbers: about 200,000 in North America, 148,000 in South America, 81,000 in Western Europe, as well as 63,000 in Asia. And when they leave their islands to come to these continents, they bring along that Japanese social psyche that has served them generally well in Japan, but which may be useless or even counterproductive in the cultures of their new residence. It's not a wine that travels well.

As we've seen, one of the formulas knitting together the skin of that social psyche involves the sharp distinctions the Japanese draw between the sexes, and also between the Japanese (*ware ware nihonjin*) and everybody else. In more than one Japanese business or factory transplanted to the West, the initial local euphoria at the prospect of increased employment has soured. Employees have complained about Japanese indifference to their personal rights, women and minority employees have filed job-discrimination suits, and local governments have complained about the lack of community spirit and corporate donations from Japanese companies (who even at home have no tradition of PR or civic service).

From the parochial viewpoint of the Japanese social psyche, of course, the angry response of these groups is surprising and unwarranted. The "deal" from the Japanese point of view is strictly money-for-services. The local workers or executives get jobs, good salaries (often more than the Japanese working beside and even *above* them), benefits, company status, and an open channel for their ideas about improving productivity. The Japanese, of course, get finally to make the big decisions—and no part of the deal provides for the *gaijin* to become Japanese. Fair enough, but the *gaijin* work force is also often expected to accommodate itself not only to work standards but often to unexportable Japanese social formulas.

The same sharp division the Japanese make between themselves and "others" has also helped lead them into numerous incidents of apparent copyright infringement. Rather than giving these "appropriations" a tired nod, as Western companies once did in the face of Japanese "imitation," these companies have begun to take legal steps to disabuse the Japanese of their notion that "what's ours is ours, and so is what's yours." Over this issue, just for example, IBM in a 1988 arbitration gained a settlement with Fujitsu for the use of IBM material in its software that in the end will likely bring IBM an estimated $833 million.

Thus, as the Japanese are forced by their new economic power into more direct contact with Westerners, the insular prejudices and inadequacies of their social psyche will encounter more obstacles and incite more Western criticism. Prime ministers have even had to suffer these hard lessons: Tanaka terminally in the Lockheed bribe scandal, and Nakasone embarrassingly in the fallout from his formulaic remarks about the low intelligence of American minorities.

How the Japanese ultimately respond to these Western obstacles and criticism will depend on a whole complex of forces. But the struggle for the mind of the Japanese people has already begun, a struggle fought not mainly by the Japanese against Western advocates of the Western point of view but among the Japanese themselves.

Samsara

In a translated article, "The 'Japan Problem' is of America's Making" (*Japan Echo*, Autumn 1987) Osamu Shimomura, who is also author of the Japanese book *Japan Is Not to Blame*, argues that the so-called "Japan Problem" is strictly a fabrication of the West, in particular the United States, where Reaganomics has caused a huge budget deficit through its disastrous policies of reduced taxes, increased military spending, and supply-side fantasies. Hardly anyone would dispute the argument that these policies contributed substantially to the U.S. budget shortfall. But that they are to blame for the American trade deficit with Japan, and exclusively at that, is eminently disputable. Fortunately there are as many advocates in Japan as in the West for a balanced, evenhanded critique of the problems and failings besetting the relations between Japan and the West. It is the advocates for an image of national innocence—of which there are many in Japan (as in America)—that pose the danger.

Shimomura's piece is a polemic, one has to understand, aimed at the Japanese themselves. As such it is of interest to us here first for *how* it argues its thesis. In pleading its case for Japanese guiltlessness, it ignores those facts that would compromise its extreme view: Japanese policy and practice that effectively bars much foreign competition or cripples it by making it too costly, the "dumping" of Japanese manufactured goods in the West at prices lower than their manufacturing costs (or at least the magic disparity between the high price of Japanese goods sold in Japan and the lower price of the same Japanese goods sold abroad), not to mention the parasitically swollen prices the Japanese consumer has to pay for most things. Moreover, even the article's expressed arguments, some of which have intrinsic merit and would otherwise be cogent, get generally lost in exaggeration and sophistry: for instance the argument that swallows its tail to aver that "free trade" means "free" even to permit (Japanese) policies restricting "free" trade.

This method of argument is typical of a social psyche composed of formulas. Being based on literal formulas, it is much like any religious fundamentalism: It can brook no middle ground. The formulas are either all right, or all wrong. Unlike

rational principles, which can be manipulated to permit a plu-
ralistic and flexible social skin, formulas *are* the social skin, and
hence cannot be manipulated without threatening the integrity
of the skin itself. Japan is either good, or bad—there is nothing
in-between for the formulaic mind, and all criticisms are potentially life-threatening.

In fact the most common question foreigners are asked by
the Japanese must be, "Do you like Japan?" As if that said it
all: liking it or not liking it. Or as if Japan were that simple and
monolithic that you could affix one emotional valence to it. But
to the Japanese social psyche the question is not only apt but
exclusive. Its aim is to elicit an answer that validates only the
Wanted aspects of Japan and magically make invisible the Unwanted aspects. Principles permit distinctions and shadings in
judgment; formulas are just right or wrong.

At the heart of the argument in the Shimomura essay is
the lament that the Japanese themselves have begun to believe
the West's criticisms of Japan for its invidious trade policies.
And here the writer reveals the real anxiety: the fear among
some in the ruling Japanese elite that the ordinary Japanese
will abandon that narrow vision of themselves and the world
imposed on them in the formulas of their social psyche—
formulas promoted by an elite who exploit them to their own
profit—and will lift shoulders from the collective Japanese
wheel to go their individual ways.

And there is legitimate reason for this fear. A mid-1988
CBS poll showed that 46 percent of Japanese believed the
strained trade relations between Japan and the United States
were due to Japanese restrictions and not, for example, to poor
quality U.S. goods (34 percent). We've noted also that in Japan
many of the postwar incentives motivating the ordinary Japanese to identify his interests with authority and with the forces
that generally conserve the social formulas are being threatened: assured jobs, lifetime employment, available overtime,
steady promotions, and ever-increasing wages and bonuses.
Furthermore, the standard of living in Japan, while dramati-

cally rising since the war, has nevertheless not produced some of the rewards for the urban middle class that usually attend such economic achievement, such as comfortable and affordable housing, or even very affordable food or consumer goods. The Organization for Economic Cooperation estimates that Japanese consumers must pay almost three-quarters more for standard consumption items than do Americans. The Japanese save more (18 percent) than Americans (5 percent), but then they have to: the average wedding costs $60,000, the average funeral and grave maintenance $30,000 to $40,000; in between these two ceremonies food and housing are twice as expensive as they are in the United States, and gasoline four times dearer. For though wholesale prices in Japan have declined sharply since 1985 (the year *endaka*, the yen revaluation, began), retail prices have continued to climb, costing Japanese consumers, says the Japanese government, over $140 billion in overcharges.

An oft-claimed index of contentment in Japan is the huge percentage of Japanese counting themselves among the middle class. But this "middle class" is so broadly conceived as to be almost meaningless. In any case, this percentage has shown a drop from 88 percent in 1986, to 75 percent in late 1988. The poll by the Economic Planning Agency also found that those dissatisfied with their standard of living rose from 20 percent in 1987 to 27.5 percent in 1988. Given the growing dissatisfaction of many Japanese with these and other conditions, the potential for change in Japanese society is, if not immediate, still quite real.

Moreover, when this class is polled these days, as it is regularly, it shows if not an entire shift in values, nevertheless a shift in the trend. Only about half the Japanese say they are still willing to forgo more consumer goods to keep Japan dominant. And among the younger adults, for whom the list of personal goals was once led by concerns for company success, career advancement, and income, the list now often shows a preference for leisure time, family life, housing, clothes, and diet. And though the government has responded to the wid-

ening popularity and social wisdom of this wish list and legis-
lated a selective, phased-in cut from the six- to a five-day work
week, these are not necessarily the mantras the economic shoguns, with one worried eye on Korea and Co. and another on
domestic social shifts that threaten their wealth and power,
want their *sarari-men* and workers chanting in their hearts.
Indeed, a 1989 study by the Japan Productivity Center showed
that while 75 percent of the unions wanted shorter working
hours, only 41 percent of the companies said they planned in
fact to shorten them.

Traditionally Japan watchers have stressed the continuity
of the Japanese mentality and Japanese society throughout the
various historical epochs and upheavals. Stressed, too, is the
Japanese ability to pour imported notions into existing Japanese molds. Rock music, baseball, foreign cuisine, and democ-
racy have all been examined from this point of view. Almost
invariably the conclusion or implication is that such continuity
will persist.

But the present situation is unique in some ways. Japan's
wealth and economic power must perforce pull it ever more
out into the world, and the world ever more into Japan. So
must its reliance on exports of goods, services, and investments
for that wealth, not to mention the government's annual dilemma of a budget deficit (yes, Japan has one too). Moreover,
new Asian competitors for this wealth are necessitating Japan's
shift from conformist to creative thinking, a shift exemplified
in its establishment of techno-science cities, such as Tsukuba
and Kumamoto. And in general, international business, satellite
communication, rapid air travel, tourism, foreign television and
goods, even universally popular rock music, have all come to
Japan and made it part of Marshall McLuhan's "global village."

Japanese women, who make up 40 percent of the work
force yet only 4 percent of decision makers, are increasingly
aware of their options and rights. The *California Management
Review* published a 1988 study of business opportunities for
women in Japan, where 75 percent of women are college graduates yet only 25 percent work after graduation. The study

found that though fewer than half the Japanese companies offered any hope of advancement for women employees, American companies operating in Japan, in hiring and promoting
more Japanese women, are establishing new egalitarian standards of employment that can't help but erode the old Japanese
formulaic notions of a woman's place. Indeed, for four years in
a row the Japanese female student's first or second choice of
employer has been IBM. In 1985 women helped pass new leg-
islation mandating equality in employment. Traditionally they
already have most of the power in the household, and when
they get the birth-control pill, an inevitability, they will have
control of their own bodies, a cornerstone to control of their
own lives.

Many men, too, a lot of them young entrants into the work
force, are growing tired of being parodies of work and play and
want a fuller life that neither can give them. Even baseball
players, those stanchions of team spirit and selfless effort, have
formed their own union to get more money. And Japanese companies, invariably seen in the West as a single, unified, conspiring adversary, are being forced by the stronger yen to
compete more fiercely with one another for the diminishing
Western market and a poorer Western consumer. Still more
astonishing, major Japanese corporations, always felt to be
hand-in-glove with Japanese banks to assure Japanese continuity under the invisible letterhead "Japan, Inc.," seem increasingly to be more contiguous than continuous. Nissan, for
example, recently abandoned its financier partner and principal stockholder of the last half century, Fuji Bank, in favor of
Citibank, to swing a complex bond-debt-cash deal that brought
the automaker an assembly plant in Mexico.

Moreover, these and other changes in contemporary Japanese life will have a unique effect on that special ability of
the Japanese to transform themselves dramatically and en
masse. We've noted that a social psyche made up of memorized
formulas rather than rational "principles" is but an unsupported surface. Having no structure beneath it, the entirety of
it is more easily and dramatically changed in some ways than

is its Western counterpart, which is nailed to "reasons." Many of the wholesale shifts in Japanese social history have been first the brainchildren of a small ruling group and only then the goal of the ordinary Japanese mass, many of whom were either dragooned or indoctrinated into unanimity. Not many Westerners realize, for that matter, how different Japan might be today had the occupying Western administration following World War II not changed its mind in the late forties about the democratic reforms it had introduced. The political and social contention in immediate postwar Japan permitted by such reforms led to a Socialist-led government in 1947, and by 1949 many labor unions (which included teachers, white-collar government *sarari-men*, and nationalized-industry employees such as railroad workers) were led by Japanese Communists. In that year, with the assistance of the occupation, Japanese conservatives and industrialists mounted the Red Purge, in which activists of the left were fired from their jobs, removed from their offices and leadership positions, and—some—arrested. To whatever degree, Japan would likely not be as conservative today had this imposition not taken place.

Today, however, the ordinary Japanese are more affluent and knowledgeable, and hence in a better position both to resist social shifts dictated from above and to institute their own. Thus it is hardly certain that the continuity the West insists on seeing as an expression of eternal Japanese character should persist. Certainly it will be increasingly difficult for the segment of the ruling elite who have such aims, to dictate this so-called "continuity" to the ever-more cosmopolitan *urban* Japanese, who make up 80 percent of the population and for whom space and cost considerations mean smaller families (3.3 average members), more utilitarian and individualistic values, and less contact with the village mentality that enforces collective effort, formulaic thinking, and conformity in general. Given their rapidly expanding knowledge of the world and their growing preeminence, the middle class are more likely to respond to naturally evolving conditions (such as increasing affluence and personally appealing foreign influences, including cheaper products beginning to flood Japan from the newly industrialized countries) than obediently to inflate dictated formulas into mass movements and massive change. And as they become more confident of their power and prerogatives in economic ways, they are likely to grasp their potential power politically. Certainly Noboru Takeshita's (and later Sousuke Uno's) resignation as prime minister was strongly driven by general popular opinion, a force in Japan usually dismissed as permanently embryonic and habitually ignored by prime ministers. Henceforth politicians may ignore it at their peril.

A formulaic society survives as such only so long as most of its members continue to abide by the formulas. Some obedience can be constrained by laws, but the most productive means toward compliance with social formulas are those arising necessarily from social circumstance (as when an exorbitant cost of living compels a demanding work ethic and an anxious obsequiousness to authority), or voluntarily from uniform, collective opinion (as in the formulas first memorized and practiced in the Japanese school system). But as the social circumstances in Japan change, and as ordinary Japanese come more to resent the inequitable apportionment of rewards for the sacrifices required of them by the collective ethic, and as individual Japanese assessments undermine the authority of their a priori social formulas, Japanese society itself will increasingly become less monolithic and conformist.

Right now the Japanese of Shimomura's persuasion want it both ways. They've galloped into the stream but still long for the safety of the shore. They want Japan to have the influence and acumen to exercise its economic power on a global scale and still keep the fixed-formula vision of the Japanese village and feudal society. That, of course, is impossible. The rest of the world, being unversed in (and in fact excluded by) Japanese formula, will not have it. And the ordinary Japanese—especially the younger ones—perceiving now the limits of the social formulas to give them the benefits of their country's wealth, will have less and less of it.

What some of the privileged elite fear, and try subtly to

convince the ordinary Japanese to fear, is not really, as they claim, the importation of foreign goods but the intrusion of a new and different vision: specifically, an *individualism*—a concept often disparagingly associated with "egoism" in Japanese (*kojinshugi*). True individualism would shatter the hollow doll that is the Japanese social psyche and put in its stead a skeleton of rational principles and standards of personal judgment that is always the source of genuine democratic equality—a very disruptive, inharmonious, disunifying prospect for Japanese society as it is. Yet one for which there seems no alternative but the old recourse of a designated external enemy, in this case, predictably, America. Today one-third of Japanese say they feel some unfriendliness toward America, and there are those in Japan who see in these feelings the nostrum to end internal Japanese dissension.

Like the Tokugawa, they dream of closing and sealing the lid. However much some powerful and some ordinary Japanese both might like to do this, it's probably not feasible. Even today Japan keeps a tight rein on immigration, and the number of foreigners living in Japan are proportionally much lower than the number of Japanese living abroad. For instance, about 33,000 Americans live in Japan (not counting the 60,000 rotating military personnel), or only about one-fifth the number of Japanese living in the United States. Yet neither these relatively smaller numbers nor the Japanese barriers of language and culture have saved Japanese society from the changes wrought by foreign influence. Even if that weren't the case, it's doubtful the Japanese could run an international economic empire while ensconced in castles in Japan. Nor are they likely even to try it and risk losing all they've sweated for to the "Four Tigers" (Korea, Hong Kong, Taiwan, and Singapore). Only about 23 percent of Japan's exports go to all the rest of Asia. Twenty percent goes to Western Europe, and a whopping 39 percent goes to North America. Indeed, U.S.–Japan joint trade amounts to 20 percent of the Free World's total commerce. There is simply no other market both large and rich enough to replace it. At least not until the Chinese and the Soviets achieve yuppie status.

There are other emerging factors in Japanese society which, however much they may seem like a loss to the "culture" of Japan, militate against the susceptibility of ordinary Japanese to dictated, collective formulas.

Following other German thinkers, the aesthetician Friedrich Schiller made an important distinction between what he called "simple" and "sentimental." "Simple" described features of art and culture in their indigenous appearance, when they are still natural, vital, and unselfconscious. "Sentimental" defined the later imitations of those features, which, however identical they may appear to the originals, are merely superficial copies, petrified as self-conscious ritual, mere aesthtic decorations for societies void of the forces that had first created them. A number of the traditional Japanese ceremonies that themselves supply some of the formulas in the social psyche, such as the tea ceremony and cherry-blossom viewing as they are popularly practiced, have become "sentimental" ornaments, self-conscious social reflexes. And while this is melancholy for culture, it is a natural process and salutary for the growth of the individual—Japanese or otherwise—for whom it is easier to free himself from forces manipulating him through mere surface routine than through deep mythic ritual still psychically binding.

Such liberation is often the more necessary for the individual Japanese, whose social psyche has been so highly and intricately developed at the expense of his individual personality, whose inchoateness can erupt into shockingly anarchic, violent behavior—directed at the self or others—outside the guidance of the social psyche's formulas. As we've seen, the Japanese social psyche is largely a creature of memorized formulas, as is memorization itself the main instrument of learning in Japanese education and of much social intercourse in Japanese society. However successful this faculty—memory—has

been in bringing the Japanese to this point in their economic
and social success story, it cannot get them much if any further.
Memorization, and its creation, the Japanese social psyche, under duress has only endurance, stoicism, and what the West
calls "suppression" to respond with—until it exhausts itself and
Jack jumps out of the box. There is nothing in the hollow doll,
no alchemy of self, by which to transmute the maddening and
otherwise finally intolerable slings and arrows of our human
fortune. Both personally and professionally, the hollow doll is
inadequate to meet the Japanese future, not just on a few islands but in our joint world, and the Japanese, faced with their
current choices, and in order to become what we all must finally—more our individual selves than any national mario-
nette—can only let this doll die to dwell immortally in the
"sentimental" world of ceremony.

Nor in every case should this passing be cause for any regret. "Culture " is one of those numinous notions, like "family," "love," "God," and "country," that gain our uninspected
admiration as much for what they fail to acknowledge as for
what they try to advertise. America is not only the land of
"free" people; it is the land of millions of hungry, homeless,
illiterate, unemployed, and often untreated ill people. The concept of "culture," like these other cozy ideas, should not in
itself be sacrosanct, sheltering, as we've seen it do, not only
legitimate legacies that vivify the soul and life of a people but
ceremonial excuses for attitudes and behavior that are often
exploitative, discriminatory, insensitive, and destructive, not
to mention suicidal.

It should not be overlooked, however, that there is also
the potential for some gain, if not in any particular face or
avatar the Japanese social psyche might temporarily assume,
then for its disposition to be superficial, for the doll to be "hollow." Japan is often belittled these days for having no "foreign
policy." What such a perception may actually indicate is that
Japan has no foreign policy that is "ideological"—that is, no
principles of the idea-driven sort which the "rational" superpowers have always fenced into narrow, exclusive orthodoxies

and for which they have seemed willing to destroy themselves if not the world.

A century and a half ago John Keats said that what had been unique about Shakespeare was that he had "negative capability." Being unbound by any single dominating humor or personality, Shakespeare was free to create the myriad characters he set and strutted upon the stage. Likewise, Japan, being not only bereft but freed by its social psyche from the necessity of ideological attachment, could exploit this facet, but unlike Shakespeare on his stage or the West on its, portrays no extreme personas or espouses any ideology. After all, to be aloof to doctrine, unaddicted to ideas, does not prevent a culture from having ideas or from being intelligent, strong, cooperative, generous, successful, or even wise—all of which Japan is increasingly showing itself to be.

Indeed Japan's foreign policy recently has begun to emphasize such lineaments. At the Paris Economic Summit of 1989 Japan made proposals to relieve Third World debt and attack environmental pollution, allocating $40 billion of its own toward these ends (with fewer commercial strings attached), making it the world's largest donor. In 1988 Japan had also moved to mediate the Vietnamese withdrawal from Kampuchea, to contribute $5 million and an observer to the U.N. peace-keeping efforts in Afghanistan, and even volunteered to send men to help ensure the truce in Namibia. Already Japan is the second highest contributor (behind the United States) to the United Nations. Japan also has its own version of the Peace Corps, JOCV. Moreover, Japan has done as much as any country recently to maintain currency stability and to be responsible and sensitive in its U.S. stock and bond holdings. As for statesmanship with risk, in mid-1988 Japan sent its foreign minister, Sousuke Uno (later prime minister), to Israel, the beginning of contacts that may eventually lead to Japan's ending its compliance with the Arab economic boycott of that country. This visit may seem inconsequential to some, but to Japan it has real dangers: Seventy percent of its oil comes from Israel's Arab antagonists.

All of this, by most definitions, is successful and productive foreign policy, yet none of it came with ideological homilies or provisos. If Japan continues to nurture and practice such a "Zen foreign policy," in which her international statecraft would resist the temptation to promulgate her older, fulsome fantasies of herself, as well as transcend the West's often outmoded, even illusory and perhaps fatal doctrinal obsessions, she will have transformed a cultural curiosity into a national character and an international virtue rare in human affairs. Both Japan and the world could well do with such a mediating and benign influence. All of us can well do without another superpower transfixed by ideology.

For much of the first half of the twentieth century, of course, Japan did try its hand at grand foreign policy tied to ideology, like its Co-Prosperity Sphere, brought to the rest of Asia on a sword. The harvest of such a belligerent fancy with its own ideas, of course, was a Japan gone up in smoke. Having handed the power to create foreign policy over to its military once already and seen the horrific results, it would seem unlikely that the Japanese people would soon do it again. More than 80 percent of the Japanese support that article of their constitution that renounces Japan's right to go to war *ever*, and 71 percent oppose more increases in Japanese military spending. Whether they would *politically* oppose any Japanese government bent on (gradually) building a world military power—given the long-standing propensity of the Japanese social personality to acquiesce before authority—is another question.

It is such past popular acquiescence among the Japanese and the recent increases in Japanese military spending that gives some observers pause. Japan now has the world's third highest annual military expenditures, at $48 billion, behind only the United States and the Soviet Union. Japan has more than three times the number of destroyers as does the U.S. Seventh Fleet in the western Pacific, as well as five times the U.S. number of antisubmarine airplanes, 180,000 troops, over 1,200 tanks, and 160 F-15 fighter planes. It's obvious, too, that Japan could produce nuclear bombs if and when she cared to.

But in today's world (as opposed, say, to that of nineteenth-century Britain—another island power), military muscle is not the pillar of international success it was. Contemporary Japan, until recently without a military, demonstrated this, just as the superpowers, with their unusable nuclear bombs and their economic woes, have demonstrated it conversely. Now, too, even puny countries can immediately jeopardize great powers and potentially devastate an island kingdom with a single acquired nuclear bomb, offsetting military might in ways an earlier Britain's might couldn't be offset. The concern, thus, is not that Japan's Self-Defense Forces are growing (Japan still spends only a bit over 1 percent of its GNP on defense; the United States spends 6 percent), but that Japan might acquire an ideology that would skew its aims from its flexible, utilitarian commercialism and launch its military beyond its defensive, local posture. If it is revenge, face, disdain, or mad ambition that hatches a new national persona with a self-proclaimed messianism, the Japanese will have joined our nightmare rather than helped awaken us.

Climbing No Mountain

Whichever direction Japan takes, it will be influenced markedly by the Japanese vision of themselves vis-à-vis the West. In Zen there is a koan that goes, "First there is a mountain, then no mountain, then a mountain." This little Japanese catalyst for personal liberation obviously has its implications for enlightenment, and even its explanations in epistemology. But it also has its practical insights about our habits of misunderstanding. Zen, brought from India via China, took root and has endured in Japan not only because it suited the skewed appreciation of Bushido, the austere ethic and aesthetic of the samurai, but, quite the opposite, because it was just the cure for the rigid, ritual-bound, stratified society and formulized personality of the Japanese. Like any method or instrument for enlightenment Zen starts at the point where the unenlightened student himself is—in this case wrapped in the Japanese social persona, with its Veg-O-Matic vision of life as a slice-'n'-diced mind's meal of formulas, and the adamant will the student uses, unknowingly, to sustain it. Then Zen lets the student exhaust them all—the machine, the formulas, the mind, the will, and the student himself, until they vanish like the smoky wisps they are, leaving just the simple truth.

The mountain koan is one such catalyst, and one suited to the Japanese, among others. Probably ever since the Portuguese arrived in the sixteenth century with their firearms and big ships, and certainly since Perry arrived with his black ships and big guns, the Japanese psyche has been compelled to be preoccupied with the West and with Westerners. With its science, its weapons, its irresistible, conquering courtship, the West necessarily became a touchstone for the Japanese sense of themselves. World War II, and its cataclysmic conclusion and defeat for the Japanese at the hands of the very Westerners they felt they had come so near to conquering and thus exorcising from their souls, only served to confirm and deepen the distorted role Westerners seem doomed to play in an obsessive drama staged both inside the Japanese and out upon the world. In his state visit to Washington in early 1988, the new Japanese prime minister, Noboru Takeshita, seemed deliberately to turn to a TV camera to make an exaggerated yawn, as if to show the Japanese back home how unimpressed he was with the West— revealing instead how greatly the West still figures in his and the Japanese mind.

To the Japanese, the West has always, and alternatively, been only one of two mountains. Now . . . yawn . . . just more landscape against the sky . . . then . . . a volcano on fire in the eye. We—like they to us—have never actually been real to them. Just shadows that dance in their dreamscape, sometimes mere fluttering leaves the sun dapples in their eyes, and then suddenly a blaze that blanks the sun itself. We have figured too mightily, too antipodally, too quickly to be both less and more than myth to them right now—to be that third mountain, just itself.

But someday. Both of us, all of us, more simply human.

■ ■ ■

Sayonara

On January 7, 1989, Hirohito, 124th Japanese emperor in a 2,649-year-old line of succession, died—like his emperor grandfather Meiji and his prince brother Takamatsu before him—of the malady no one has in Japan until he is dead of it. And like Takamatsu, who died in February 1987 of cancer without ever having been told the nature of his illness, Hirohito almost assuredly was never whispered the name of his body's secret assassin.

In the agonizing weeks leading to his death the collective psyche of the Japanese people underwent a remarkable alchemy. Until his illness (a harbinger of which had occurred a year before) Hirohito had come to exist for his subjects much as a minor household deity: a remote, seldom considered, and apparently irrelevant presence. In an *Asahi Shimbun* poll in the spring of 1986, only 22 percent of the Japanese said they felt any affection for him, and though another 33 percent said they felt reverence, 40 percent said they felt "nothing." Then in late 1988 the emperor grew gravely ill and was obviously approaching death. To their surprise many Japanese felt an awareness gather beneath the edifice of thought, an inchoate understanding that somehow this diminutive familiar was, after disappearing into the wallpaper for decades, again about to become luminous, blindingly if but for a moment, and at the very moment of his eternal disappearance. A god was going to die and take a world with him.

For years before his death Hirohito only rarely appeared outside the sanctum of his palace—on his birthday and on New Year's Day, or at his beloved sumo tournaments—preferring instead to putter in his private laboratory amid the marine flora and fauna that was his life's true passion. Thus, as was so often the case throughout his life, without his physical presence to give flesh and limit to his reality, it was left to imagination and myth to spin an image in place of the man: for the left an effigy to burn, for the right an icon to worship, but for the majority scarcely there at all.

From his adolescence on, Hirohito lived a comparatively confined existence, dominated by routine, remote from his subjects, and for a time attending an institution of learning created solely for his benefit and in which he alone comprised the entire student body. Later, as emperor, it would be the struggle between an ascendant military and an eclipsing constitutional government that would conceal the real emperor and manipulate his public image. Afraid of issuing orders the constitution theoretically entitled him to but the military might disregard—a disobedience that would disclose the illusion of his power and undermine the small but real authority invested in the imperial system—Hirohito as emperor became something of a hollow doll himself, the army's samurai doll, photographed after 1931 only in uniform, a doll the glimpse of which, after 1936, was not permitted to common eyes—all in all a mere ceremony of celestial authority for the military's great expectations and the nationalist's fantasy of a divine jingoism.

Because of the remoteness fate and politics consigned him to, and because he kept no diaries we are likely to see, there will always be those who debate Hirohito's role in the Japanese decisions launching the Pacific War. That he did not use his authority to prevent the war we know for fact. That he could have brought himself as emperor to oppose it, with so many about him for it is questionable. After all, as a real individual expressing his autonomous will, Hirohito had scant existence, probably only a little more to himself than to his subjects. His personal preferences were largely confined to the tiny ambit of the palace grounds, and even his expressed preference for Nagako over all other candidates to be his empress-wife was not the cause of her selection over strong court opposition (she came from outside the Five Families, from which consorts were usually chosen); the cause, rather, was his father, Taisho, finally brushing the objections aside. His rare acts of willful intrusion into politics (the Tanaka affair in 1929 and the Young Officer's Revolt in 1936) were strictly defenses of the integrity and existence respectively of his national government.

On the contrary, Hirohito's real existence was the symbolic one dramatized stereotypically in the roles of crown prince, then regent, then emperor. And these roles, we know, had, since the Meiji Restoration if not since the shogunate, been ceremonial abstractions, more formulaic mystery plays for Japanese values than existential dramas of individual lives. In his role as emperor it was the duty of the man to make manifest not his transient personality but some immortal virtue. For Hirohito, it was *Showa*, Harmony Made Manifest, his divine task being to bring the realities of his human community into accord with the emerging and current patterns of heaven.

These are fundamental and well-understood notions in the East which find spiritual expression in Buddhism, Confucianism, Taoism, and Shinto. In the West we say "God is on our side" and argue about His wishes. In Japan there are eight million gods and they are on nobody's side but their own—hence the daily rituals and superstitions to curry their capricious favor. But the royal and genuinely religious means to peace and harmony in the East is to discern the present arrangement of the cosmos (which, being impersonal, has no "wishes") and conform to it.

As *tenno heika*, god-king, this was Hirohito's self-proclaimed mission on behalf of his people. But living gods, be they Eastern or Western, have a terrible time of it, stuck as they are halfway between heaven and earth. In a couplet-poem to God, William Blake demanded in exasperation of the deity:

> If you have form'd a Circle to go into,
> Go into it yourself & see how you would do.

Be it Bodhidharma, Buddha, (God-)Jesus or Bando VIII, Randy Bass or Oh, Elvis or Yukiko, or Hirohito himself, being a god in the sticky muck of matter's circle seems to be as problematical as it is for confessed mortals like our poor Nobuko. The prism of corporeal existence seems to fracture the light of the eternal and make it excruciatingly hard to read its truths. Confusing celestial harmony and the more mundane political kind, Hirohito, like other emperors before him, acquiesced to

be the divine excuse for the ambitions of the merely powerful and woefully mortal. That in his role as emperor it would
occur to him that he should do otherwise is probably a Western chimera. All logical options are not necessarily available
psychologically.

Yet we do know that for all of his imperial silence, his
manipulated public imagery, his demure governance, it was in
the last days of the Pacific War and the first years after it that
Hirohito was able to assert himself—to the deliverance of his
people—and engender a harmony between them and, if not the
arrangement of heaven, at least the conditions of their time
and place.

Opposing his generals, whose bottomless reserve of hubris
even following Hiroshima and Nagasaki kept awful faith with
the formula of certain (now "eventual") victory and disposed
them to sacrificing the remaining Japanese to save Japan, Hirohito spoke against "the annihilation of the Japanese people
and a prolongation of the suffering of all humanity." He declared the nation no longer able to wage war or likely to defend
itself against invasion. It was time to "bear the unbearable."
On August 15, 1945 Hirohito's subjects heard his voice (the royal
voice of the Crane) for the first time on radio. The stiff, formal
cadence and antiquated diction of the ossified Kyoto court language made parts of the emperor's broadcast incomprehensible
to many in his audience, robbing it of some of the profundity it
has in retrospect, including history's perhaps most famous under-
statement: that the war had not necessarily gone to Japan's advantage. The emperor ordered the nation's acceptance of the
provisions of the Joint Declaration of the Powers, the same demanded in perfect love and hate: unconditional surrender.

A few months later, on New Year's Day, 1946, Hirohito,
in his role as god, issued his last divine decree, the imperial
rescript that renounced both his own divinity and his race's
sacred preeminence. Hirohito himself apparently conceived and
volunteered this act of demythicizing. After his decision to surrender, it was his next move to bring the condition and consciousness of his people in accord with history's arrangement

of the moment. Superficially it was a deprivation: God was dead, Japan was just another country, and the Japanese merely people. At a deeper level it was a redemption: His people had been freed from a constricting if comforting illusion and from the authority behind it, by which the powerful had manipulated and almost annihilated them.

But lo and behold, if god were dead, Hirohito wasn't. Nor yet was the myth of the Father and the pageant of filial obedience and devotion the people enacted before him. In the years immediately following the war the man-king made manifest the ordinary harmony for which he'd had to settle and went out frequently and widely among his people, most of whom in turn showed the fascination and liberated affection appropriate now to one who had transformed himself from an unapproachable shrine to everyone's father.

Then, in the years before his death, Hirohito began gradually to vanish from the public arena, etherealizing in the inconspicuous pace of his own mortal seasons. He was outliving his contemporaries, both those on the left who blamed him for the war, and those on the right who still revered him. His skein unwound imperceptibly into the invisible. More and more he was to exist for his kingdom as an eidetic afterimage, a familiar phantom radiant on the surface of the mind's eye. For the ordinary Japanese, his corporeal being came to exist less in his own frail entropy than in associated emanations, such as the much-reported annual parade of the mother duck who led her ducklings through traffic and into the emperor's moat, an incarnation provoking more national adoration than did the serenely vanishing emperor behind the moat.

At the end he existed for his people most palpably, if agonizingly, in the middle-earth and meta-reality where technology and religion, matter and spirit, have become indistinguishable, where flesh and blood themselves were distilled into neon numbers marching across a thousand public marquees, digital light ticking his temperature, pulse, blood pressure, and respiration, until they and he had reached absolute zero.

The man who was god then not was dead. The Japanese clock stopped, and the New Year's calendar closed only seven days—but eighty-seven years—into its subtractions from life. Another was printed on the eighth day to commence a new Year One, a pristine page for our ephemeral, histrionic scrawl.

At the second he vanished, Hirohito obliviously played his final part to liberate his people from the momentum of the past: He discarded his name, exchanging it for his epoch's, and thus his life for frozen history. He disappeared utterly into the sentimental world of ceremony. With him went the myth of celestial breath and light, the last divine afflatus to exalt and animate the hollow doll. Dying, if not dead, was a people's dream of an eternal Father and their own perpetual, sanctified dependency. Hirohito himself had become *Showa* in the only realm where Harmony may perhaps prevail, leaving his human name to decay and his race to make what of Harmony's fallible variety they can with other mortals.

Bai-Bai (Bye-Bye)

Lying alone on the pale green *tatami* mats, smelling their musky aroma of one distant dried-and-pressed summer, dead and deathless, you watch the light retreat gracefully from your vacant apartment to allow the night to close this small drama. The reflected glory of a huge Toyota sign lends an eerie incandescence to the few tiny rooms, now emptied of furniture, silent. It seems too small ever to have held life, and yet it did, if sometimes like a vise then sometimes, too, like a piano for the small melodies of family.

A music comes to its last chord, passing through the looking glass for memory to whistle and march its phantoms by.

Whistling yourself, you stroll out into your last night in Nippon, a million blazing worlds in the sky too unachievable to shed much light, cool salt air drifting off the sea, tall bamboo shadows whispering with their leaves.

Looking up, you find your aimlessness has brought you to a bistro you had seen only by day, called Jamming Sugar. In-

side, just a few patrons, who sit quietly sipping beer in near
darkness, listening to a man seated on a stool in a small pool of
light playing clarinet. He is wearing an old wide-brimmed felt
hat pulled down over his eyes and a white shirt with green
sleeve garters and open collar. His music is a tough, mournful
blues, wavering, like Sidney Bechet's, with a melancholy just
barely saved from sadness by strength.

You get a table and order a beer. He plays for almost an
hour, and the single poignant sound holds his audience silent
and absorbed throughout his set. His listeners seem reluctant
even to whisper. There is just the sound of the bartender shuffling glasses, and the breathy crying of the man's playing.

When he breaks, you make your way to the toilet at the
end of the bar. There is already a fellow in there, relieving
himself in the wall trough next to yours. Neither of you speak,
your shoulders almost touching, listening to each other's breath,
smelling the acrid aroma of your common beer-piss. Without
thinking, you start whistling again, as you did during your walk
and, catching yourself, embarrassed—since Japanese themselves rarely whistle—stop. Suddenly the fellow startles you by
whistling himself. You look up to find him smiling at you. A
wry but authentic smile. *"Biru,"* he says conspiratorially,
pointing at the beer-of-the-past in your troughs and inadver-
tently pronouncing your name the Japanese way. *"Hai"*
("Yes"), you say, and gazing into his amiable face, you abruptly
realize that for some time now the Japanese have ceased to
appear Japanese to you. Subtly, gradually, somewhere along
the way, they stopped looking like a people and began looking
like people, just people. So much for your own hollow doll.

There must be something odd about your gaze, because he
does something rare among Japanese: He reaches up a solici-
tous hand and pats you on the shoulder. *"Bai-bai"* ("Bye-
bye"), he says.

Finished, you stand at your trough still, looking vacantly
at the wall. Indecipherable *kanji* graffiti swim murkily on the
surface. Then some words laboriously penned in an alien English catch your attention, pulling your eyes and your heart into

focus. The words of another wanderer, this one a lone *ronin* riding atop the waves outside the strict geography of his nation and race, feet intact if over the edge, the onion peeled, if not to nothing then at least down a few layers to this short public shout, a scrawled testament to his small, solitary victory:

Thank god I am surfer

You leave whistling.

■   ■

■   ■

Aftershocks

It was that famous Greek Zen-master of 500 B.C., Heraclitus, who said, "You can't step twice into the same river," and, less metaphorically, "Everything flows, nothing stays." Well, that's easy for Heraclitus to say; he was a philosopher whose toys of choice were the eternals (though one suspects he wasn't nearly so sententious upon getting day-old bread).

For the nonfiction writer, especially when he is shuffling in the gutter of Truth's littered detritus and breathing the daily flatulence from the Zeitgeist's oblivious engines—and for whom day-old bread is a miracle come one day sooner than he dared hope—for him change is hell. He writes in sand who writes about the present.

One temporary dike such writers erect against the re-arranging surf of Change is the "postscript" (aka "epilogue," "afterword"). It is a pitiful barrier tossed up by the desperate and certainly mocked by the gods. But since the reader has had enough time anyway to spot me for the former who only imagines himself at times to be the latter, there seems little point in foregoing such a gratifying—if self-deluding—device. Thus, case-by-case, if not by chaos, the following:

Taken together Japanese men and women still present a formidable unit. As workers they have only half the absentee-ism of Americans and one and a half times our productivity. They have only one-third our divorce rate and they live longer.

■

And though the average Japanese family spends twice what we do on the mortgage and food, that family has about $80,000 in personal savings.

Taken separately, though, they portray realities that are as personally revealing as they are statistically informative. The average *sarari-man* is still taking only 60 percent of his paid vacation time and is seeing his family one-sixth the amount of time his American counterpart sees his. A recent poll shows his favorite recreation on Sunday to be "sleeping." In an effort to wean the *sarari-man* away from his addiction to work, the Japanese government has not only encouraged a five-day work week, but (partly through a nationally televised cartoon showing *sarari-men* killing themselves with overwork) propagandized in general for *reja* (leisure)—beyond the sedentary pachinko and the elitist golf—going so far as to fabricate new holidays like *ii fufu!* (Good Married Couple!).

The Japanese woman has been making real but painfully slow progress toward equality. Unfortunately she still earns only 60 percent of what a man does, holds only 5 percent of the management positions, and must use the same name as her husband. As yet she does not have access to birth-control pills. Worse, she seems to be surrendering to the ersatz liberation of smoking more cigarettes. On the brighter side, however, a baby-sitting industry has begun to emerge as more women enter careers, and authentic Japanese feminism has recently begun to blossom—into a Venus's-flytrap, some old-guard male politicians must feel. It was women who voted many of them out of office in 1989, and women who in many cases were voted in in their stead. In an irreverent and well-aimed jab at male political domination and its wrongheaded priorities, nineteen women leaders formed a mock shadow cabinet shortly before the 1989 elections. Dressed in bright colors, the "ministers" derided the gray suits of the real (male) cabinet as "rat" colored. The women "ministers" suggested there be a "global" housekeeping and moved that golf courses be turned into cattle pastures. They also promoted the credible theory that women are superior to men because they don't spit on the ground or urinate in public.

The best hope for change in the gender roles lies with the young Japanese, the *shinjinrui* ("new humans"). An international study by Japan's Management and Coordination Agency found that 43.7 percent of young Japanese (eighteen to twenty-four years old) disagreed with traditional marriage roles, the first time ever that negative responses predominated (30.6 percent said that men should work and women stay at home). The direction in which they would change their society is more uncertain and problematical. The same study showed that though the young in all countries ranked "living as I like" first, Japanese youth were first in wanting to get rich. More horrifying to the Japanese power elite, though, must be the finding that while a majority of American youth professed a willingness to sacrifice their own interests for the sake of society, only 5.5 percent (the lowest of any country polled) of young Japanese said they would.

In a broader study of Japanese society in general, Japan's Economic Planning Agency found a growing awareness among Japanese of the disparity between their income and their quality of life. Compared with the United States and selected Western European countries, Japan ranked first in economic stability and in health, but below average in opportunities for living space, social activities, learning, and culture. In a special subcategory, only 39 percent of the Japanese were found to have modern sewers as opposed to 82 percent of residents in the other countries. A national Japanese women's organization found that 70 percent of Japanese women were dissatisfied with their residences. As for air pollution, Japan's Environmental Protection Agency reports some big cities, such as Tokyo, continue to exceed auto-exhaust limits.

In politics some irony (and some bad and good news) for Noboru Takeshita, the disgraced ex-prime minister who was forced to resign following the disclosure that he had received over a million dollars in contributions from the Recruit Company, namesake of the influence-peddling scandal. It was Takeshita who had wrested away another ex-prime minister's (Tanaka's) faction at the end of the latter's demise—and apparently wrested some of his doom too: Tanaka had also been forced from office by a money scandal (Lockheed's), the inquiry into which had been led by no less than Yusuke Yoshinaga, Tokyo public prosecutor, who was now investigating the Recruit scandal, Takeshita's undoing. That was the irony and the bad news. The good news was that this time Yoshinaga didn't pinch any of the leading *daimyo* politicians reportedly involved—a grace not forgotten or forgiven by voters later on.

In one of the tremors immediately following Takeshita's fall (one day after it, in fact), Ihei Aoki, who had managed Takeshita's campaign finances, by way of atonement slit his wrists and hung himself with his necktie.

Sousuke Uno, Takeshita's successor of mayfly evanescence (two months), must wish at times he'd done the same. Originally dubbed the LDP's "Mr. Clean" because of his apparent uninvolvement in the Recruit scandal, he no sooner took office than he found himself fingered by one "Madam A" as an inveterate if unpolished philanderer. In a Japanese first, "Madam A," acting more as a wronged and exploited modern woman than as the silence-bound "geisha" the old social formulas would have had her be, publicly blew the whistle on Uno to the *Sunday Mainichi* magazine, which itself defied the old formula of silence about politicians' private lives. Uno, "Madam A" told the world, was pompous, coarse, conceited, and a cheapskate to boot. On their very first date (in a private dining room at a swank eatery), Uno, she announced, had brutishly brushed aside her feminine protestations, plopped down a ten-grand deposit, and taken her, so to speak, right there on the floor. His cavalier treatment of her, she suggested, might now extend to the polity in general. She did hurt the altruism of her cause a bit, though, by sulking publicly about Sousuke's failure to give her the required consolation gift when he dumped her.

Besides embarrassment at his public humiliation, Uno, for

his part, must have felt some secret bewilderment. Had he not simply done what Japanese males had been doing for centuries—and what politicians had been doing in spades? How had he, between strokes, as it were, gone from being a stud to a reviled whoreson? Under the old formulas he had merely been affirming his privileged masculinity. Under the new he had patently been screwing around.

It was in light of the new formulas that the electorate judged him and his party. In mid-1989 elections for the Tokyo Municipal Assembly, the LDP lost twenty of its sixty-three seats. Stunned and confused, Uno and his defenders clumsily tried to turn the great antiquated ship of male prerogatives into the wind of reasons. Referring to the unpopular new consumption tax his party had inaugurated, Uno elliptically explained that women take such things "emotionally"—running himself instead onto the reef of male condescension. His agriculture minister, Hisao Horinouchi, rushing to Uno's defense, proclaimed woman's place to be in the home and made the public judgment that Socialist Party Chairwoman Takako Doi was unfit to be prime minister because she wasn't married. Brave words, and hopelessly out of touch. In the subsequent July 1989 elections for the upper House of Councilors, the LDP was crushed, and Sousuke Uno resigned his brief public tenure to go home and face his wife privately. The old-boys' ship was breaking up; the LDP's thirty-five-year monopoly on power was coming to an end. It seemed a good time to be bullish on necktie stocks.

As for Toshiki Kaifu, the LDP's second try at a "Mr. Clean," his main claim to this honorific seems to be that his "gifts" and donations from the Recruit empire were apparently legal. His chief cabinet secretary, Tokuo Yamashita, however, had to resign after it was reported that he, Yamashita, had kept a young mistress. Kaifu, though he had never before held a top party or cabinet post, can tell which way the wind blows, and immediately appointed a woman in Yamashita's place.

Along with Uno's affairs and the Recruit scandal, it was Japan's new 3-percent consumption tax that scuttled the LDP and is now lifting up the rock of Japan's consensus myth. First rammed through the Diet by the ruling LDP against opposition, its widespread unpopularity helped undo both Takeshita and Uno, who along with other politicians were seen to be lining their own pockets at the same time that they were dipping into the ordinary guy's. Now the tax is finding a hilariously disunified response among the Japanese people. Some businesses are adding it to their prices, others are afraid to, and others simply refuse to. The cities of Nagoya and Yokohama, for example, have both decided not to add the tax to bus and subway fares and simply to pay it instead themselves. The tax is proving to be one of those mere legalities that haven't the intrinsic power to assume the authority of social formulas but can only flounder about in the catch-as-catch-can spaces between them. The tax itself may yet prove to be one of the casualties of the LDP debacle.

Prices in Japan continue to hold the power to boggle the minds of both Japanese and Westerners alike. Researchers from the Union Bank of Switzerland purchased thirty-nine grocery items in each of fifty-two cities around the world. The items cost $260 in London, $340 in New York, $570 in Helsinki, and in the most expensive city, Tokyo, $890. Land prices are equally ruinous. Retail space in Tokyo's Ginza shopping district now goes for $650 a square meter monthly. Australia actually went from a debtor nation to a creditor nation principally by selling off 40 percent of its Tokyo embassy grounds: 6,000 square meters for $800 million.

Such costs, of course, bespeak a corresponding wealth—if not for the ordinary Japanese, then for the ever-increasing numbers of extraordinary Japanese. A select if not inconsiderable number of Japanese wives now have few chores to do after they drop the kids off at school, making their once sacrosanct identification with duties and chores more sentimental self-image than reality. This hollow doll may well persist for some time in popular myth after it has long since vanished as a real exemplar inside the house.

Wealth can distort perspective in wackier ways, too, naturally. A current Japanese obsession arising from a dangerous error in analogy is causing gold to be employed rather zanily: Some Japanese are massaging one another with it, ingesting it medicinally, and using it as a condiment ("Do you think the broccoli needs more gold dust?").

Japanese affluence is giving some household pets a better shake, though, not to mention a whole new perspective on life. In the spirit of the wretched excess popularized by Hojo Takatoki, the fourteenth shogun regent of the Kamakura shogunate (fourteenth century), who housed his numberless dogs like opulent princes (and who himself became so dissipated he had to become a monk for a while), trendy Japanese are toting their dogs and cats off to spas like Kinagawa Hot Springs, where the pampered dears go through millions of yen dressing up, promenading, dining at tables, and sleeping in Western beds, hottubbing it, even tying the knot in a formal ceremony when, one gathers, their baser natures have made it necessary.

Gaijin, loath to miss a financial feeding-frenzy, continue to rush centripidally to the center of the yen pie. Pat Boone, public Christian and *puer aeternus*, has started appearing in Japanese magazines to flog *Artnature*, something the ad claims is "The Worldwide Hair Technology." Pat smiles confidently out from two photos and you really can't tell, but maybe the body is at long last lagging (starting at the top) behind the unflagging spirit. Even the Great Communicator himself, our fortieth president, Ronald Reagan, is not immune and has traded 40 minutes of great jawing for $2 million (plus $5 million more in expenses) at the Fujisankei Communications Group's 1989 shindig in Hankone, the mountain resort outside Tokyo. No mere man of words, the ex-president made a brief appearance on the mound at a baseball game and hurled two parabolic wonders for his money. In our hearts we know this great patriot and champion of the balanced budget will donate that shamefully obese gratuity to our defunct treasury.

In education the realities have only grown more demanding. With ever more high school graduates competing for a lagging number of university places, competition has grown stiffer still. Almost half of the half-million-yearly applicants for admission to universities are now *ronin*, those who have failed to qualify previously. Over 70 percent of college students are now enrolled in "private" rather than "public" or "national" universities.

Japanese middle school continues to offer object lessons in pressure-cooking. In one notorious incident, a fourteen-year-old boy whose parents cut off his eight-dollar-a-month allowance because of his poor grades hacked his parents and one grandmother to death. Japan's Economic Planning Agency ranks Japan number one in home life (a ludicrous extrapolation from low divorce rates, themselves arguably due to cultural factors such as female dependency and a pragmatic marriage "Deal"), but another international study shows Japanese teenagers ranking lowest in their satisfaction with family life and their family relationships.

In another well-publicized incident, a middle-school teacher at wit's end tethered the more fractious of his charges to a center pole to keep control of them. The parents of his students were reported to be fairly evenly divided on the appropriateness of this pedagogy.

In business and economics, the Japanese continue to clean house—certainly American house. In 1988 Japan for the first time exceeded Britain and Holland to become the year's biggest foreign investor in the United States. The Japanese are even buying American cattle ranches and feedlots, impudently challenging, it seems, the cancer extra intestines make for. And speaking of cancer, a Nagoya court recently ruled, in effect, that doctors in Japan have the right to withhold knowledge of that diagnosis from their patients.

After seeing some abatement in the trade imbalance between Japan and the United States, economists are again projecting increasing net surpluses for Japan, for though Japanese exports have dropped, imports into Japan have declined even more. The Japanese have done away with their protection for domestic citrus and beef, but they are adamant in their refusal to consider the same free-trade approach to rice, citing rice's spiritual and cultural values for the Japanese. Certainly Amer-

ica twenty or thirty years ago could have forbidden imported
Japanese autos by claiming the same about "the car's" spiritual
and cultural values for Americans.

As for *Endaka*, the revaluation that virtually doubled the
yen's value against the dollar, it has not proved the panacea
for America's trade deficit with Japan that politicians and
economists had hoped. A 1989 study by Japan's Economic Planning Agency found that Japanese exporters can maintain their
strong competitive advantage even at 130 yen to the dollar,
even lower than the current exchange rate and a rate the Japanese claimed two years ago would be ruinous to Japanese
exporters.

It does look as if the United States will pick up some
needed cash (an estimated $440 million) on the joint Japanese-
American deal to build the FSX jet fighter plane, but as usual
the United States must trade some U.S. creativity—in the form
of F-16 advanced technology (some say $5 billion to $7 billion
worth)—to "earn" it. A similar exhange took place at the end
of IBM's lengthy claims case against Fujitsu for appropriation
of IBM material in Fujitsu's software. IBM will eventually get
an estimated $800 million-plus in cash, but Fujitsu will get ac-
cess to and use of the software.

Mitsubishi, General Dynamics' Japanese partner in the FSX
deal, and one of the great original *zaibatsu* (family-held industrial conglomerates), maker of current and former military aircraft like the famous Zero fighters of World War II, has not
stood idle, it should be said. It has recently branched out into
investment banking, and from its auto division now comes a
breakthrough before which the Western imagination trembles—
an item sold only at supermarkets and aimed brazenly at the
female shopper: a tiny subcompact car called *Lettuce*. Pun on
female dependency noted. No word on its shelf life after it's
out of the bag.

With Hirohito locked forever in the amber of *Showa*, imperial divinity seems to have been consigned to the cryonics
freezer. Akihito, his son, and emperor now, has already pledged
his obedience to the Japanese constitution and hinted he'd like

to be thought of the way the British royal family is—a move in the right direction, though he is probably unaware of Fleet Street's irreverent lacerations of England's royal family. Japan's far right and *yakuza* groups seem terribly dashed by Akihito's flaunted mortality, but there seems little they can do anyway to coronate the public's fixed image of Akihito. His schoolboy nickname was Brown Pig, he had a female American tutor, he personally chose and married a commoner, he raised his own children, and he likes to dance and play tennis. It is a large leap of faith indeed to watch Brown Pig fallibly slap one into the net and tell yourself this is god. If not actually as beloved and accessible as, say, that natural aristocrat, Willie Mays (the "Say-Hey kid"), Akihito might still fairly be considered a regular guy, and even dubbed the "*Heisei* kid"—after his era's name. *Heisei*, by the way, is usually translated as "achieving peace," but might make more (Western) sense rendered as "peaceful achievement."

Hirohito, if not really a god either, at least has come nominally close to Zen's version of immortality: never born, never dead. The Imperial Household Agency does not include royal births and deaths in ordinary earthly statistics, so when Hirohito died physically, he did not do so statistically. As far as the census is concerned, he kept right on going. But, then, according to the census, he was never there at all.

The notorious and flamboyant Kazuyoshi Miura was found guilty of the August 1981 "attempted" murder of his wife, Kazumi, and is serving a six-year sentence in prison. Along with Yoshikuni Okubu, the alleged hit man and Miura's former business associate, Miura is currently standing trial in Japan for Kazumi's November 1981 murder in Los Angeles. Miura is both appealing his conviction and pleading innocent to the current charges. Everyone is still waiting for him to say he is sorry.

Randy Bass left the Hanshin Tigers in the spring of 1988 to be with his ill son in the United States and was fired in June when he did not return to the team, which always comes first in Japan's corporate and sports values. Shingo Furuya, Hanshin Tigers' general manager (in Japan a job with full responsibility but no authority) watched his team collapse without Bass into last place in the Central League, twelve games behind the Yomiuri Giants. Furuya flew to the United States to try to negotiate a solution to the dilemma with Bass, but apparently failed to find one to satisfy the different views of both cultures. On July 19, 1988, Shingo Furuya cut the Gordian knot in the traditional manner of his race and leaped from the eighth-floor balcony of Tokyo's New Otani Hotel.

Brad Lesley, Japanese baseball's wild-man-of-barbaria, has realized that even his considerable fame as a pitcher pales before his notoriety as an archetype of antic *gaijin*-hood. He has given up the ball for a celebrity shtick on Japanese TV.

American baseball players, in fact, have suffered a general devaluation in Japanese baseball, and they are being replaced—not by Japanese players but by Taiwanese talent. Not only are they cheaper, more reliable, and often arguably better, they allow their names to be Japanicized, to the joy, no doubt, of certain xenophobic fans.

Sadaharu Oh, half-Taiwanese, world home-run king and longtime (sports)god himself, has been fired as manager of the Yomiuri Giants, proving again that all paths of glory lead but to the grave or the front office. Now that he's available, maybe he can rescue the LDP by becoming their candidate for prime minister.

In a victory for consciousness-raising, a picture book that has been a children's best-seller for three and a half decades in Japan is being dropped by its last Japanese publisher. Iwanami Shoten will no longer reprint *Little Black Sambo*, first written by Helen Bannerman in 1899. Li'l Black Sambo dolls are also disappearing from department-store shelves.

In a defeat for consciousness-raising, Japanese television, which like American TV is as much a hazardous landfill as a garden of good sense, recently launched a new game show rivaling the good taste of our own *Gong Show*. In this particular show celebrities move around a Goliath-size game board in accordance with the throw of huge dice heaved about by kimono-clad women. Some of the spaces on which the celebrities can land are water-filled pools, including the last, winning one, in which swim giggling, bare-breasted young women. Other pools contain, respectively, half-clothed porn stars, and two old ladies.

And speaking of inventiveness and the newfound Japanese aspiration for it, this writer recently saw the following fractured panegyric to creativity embossed in fuzzy letters on the back of a Japanese tourist in the United States:

> We staffs always support creation
> And imagine the playing spirit,
> Projects of the great creators.
> Won't you join us?
> We want to do what they do!

Sure we'll join you. But are you sure you want to do what we do?

Maybe there's hope for the West yet. Maybe, like us, the Japanese are quite capable of messing it all up for themselves.

Readings

Barnhart, Michael A. *Japan Prepares for Total War*. Ithaca: Cornell University Press, 1987.

Barr, Pat. *The Coming of the Barbarians*. New York: E. P. Dutton & Co., Inc., 1967.

Befu, Harumi. *Japan: An Anthropological Introduction*. San Francisco: Chandler Publishing, 1971.

Buruma, Ian. *Behind the Mask*. New York: Pantheon Books, 1984.

Chambers, Kevin. *The Travelers' Guide to Asian Customs and Manners*. Deephaven, Minn.: Meadowbrook, Inc. 1988.

Christopher, Robert C. *The Japanese Mind: The Goliath Explained*. New York: Linden Press (Simon & Schuster), 1983.

Cohen, Theodore. *Remaking Japan*. New York: The Free Press, 1987.

Courdy, Jean-Claude. *The Japanese*. New York: Harper & Row, 1984.

Dalby, Liza, et al. *All Japan: The Catalogue of Everything Japanese*. New York: Quill, 1984.

Discover Japan, Vols. 1 and 2. Tokyo: Kodansha International Ltd., 1982 and 1983.

Economic Outlook Japan 1988. Economic Planning Agency, Japanese Government, Tokyo: 1988.

Encyclopedia of Japan. Tokyo: Kodansha International Ltd., 1983.

Facts and Figures of Japan. Tokyo: Foreign Press Center, 1987.

Fields, George. *From Bonzai to Levis*. New York: Macmillan Publishing Company, 1983.

Hane, Mikiso. *Peasants, Rebels, and Outcasts: The Underside of Modern Japan*. New York: Pantheon Books, 1982.

Japan: A Country Study (Area Handbook Series). Washington, D.C.: The American University, 1982.

Japan: A Pocket Guide. Tokyo: Foreign Press Center, 1988.

Japan at War. Alexandria, Va.: Time-Life Books, 1980.

Japan 1989: An International Comparison. Tokyo: Keizai Koho Center, 1988.

Japan Statistical Yearbook. Tokyo: Statistics Bureau Management and Coordination Agency, 1987.

Kaplan, David E.; and Dubro, Alec. *Yakuza.* Reading, Mass.: Addison-Wesley Publishing Company, Inc., 1986.

Kawasaki, Ichiro. *Japan Unmasked.* Rutland, Vt.: Charles E. Tuttle Company, 1969.

Kidder, Edward. *Ancient Japan: The Making of the Past.* Oxford, Eng.: Elsevier-Phaidon, 1977.

Lansing, Paul; and Ready, Kathryn. "Hiring Women Managers in Japan: An Alternative for Foreign Employers." *California Management Review* 30, no. 3 (1988).

Lebra, Takie Sugiyama. *Japanese Patterns of Behavior.* Honolulu: University of Hawaii Press, 1976.

McClain, James L. "Mr. Ito's Dance Party." In *For Want of a Horse.* Lexington, Mass.: The Stephen Greene Press, 1985.

Manning, Paul. *Hirohito: The War Years.* New York: Dodd, Mead & Company, 1986.

Miura, Akira. *Japanese Words and Their Uses.* Tokyo: Charles E. Tuttle Company, 1983.

Mizutani, Osamu; and Mizutani, Nobuko. *How to Be Polite in Japanese.* Tokyo: The Japan Times, Ltd., 1987.

Morley, John David. *Pictures from the Water Trade.* Boston: The Atlantic Monthly Press, 1985.

Packard, Jerrold M. *Sons of Heaven.* New York: Charles Scribner's Sons, 1987.

Passin, Herbert. *Encounter with Japan.* Tokyo: Kodansha International, Ltd. 1982.

Pictorial Encyclopedia of Japan. Gakken Co. Ltd., Tokyo, 1986.

Randle, John; and Watanabe, Mariko. *Coping with Japan.* Oxford, Eng.: Blackwell Inc., 1985.

Reishauer, Edwin O. *The Japanese.* Cambridge: Belknap Press (Harvard University Press), 1977.

"Salaryman" in Japan. Tokyo: Japan Travel Bureau, Inc., 1987.

Seward, Jack. *The Japanese.* New York: William Morrow and Company, 1972.

Shimomura, Osamu. "The 'Japan Problem' Is of America's Making." *Japan Echo* 14 no. 3 (1987).

Spry-Leverton, Peter; and Kornicki, Peter. *Japan.* New York: Facts on File, Inc. 1987.

Stanlaw, James. "Englanese." *The World & I*, 3, no. 9 (Washington, D.C., 1988).

Statistical Handbook of Japan 1988. Statistics Bureau, Management and Coordination Agency, Tokyo, 1987.

Statistical Survey of Japan's Economy, 1988. Economic Affairs Bureau, Ministry of Foreign Affairs. Tokyo: Sekai-No-Ugoki-Sha, 1988.

Tasker, Peter. *The Japanese.* New York: Truman Talley Books, 1987.

Through Our Eyes: Visual Comparison of Japanese and U.S. Economies. Tokyo: The Japan Economic Journal, Nihon Keizai Shimbun, Inc., 1987.

Whiting, Robert. "It Looks Like Baseball, But It's Something Else." *Smithsonian* 17, no. 6 (Washington, D.C., 1986).

Other Periodicals and Media:

(Western:)

The Atlantic Monthly
Business Week
The Christian Science Monitor
The Economist
Far Eastern Economic Review
FDA Consumer
Forbes
Fortune
Free Inquiry
Industry Week
Jet
Los Angeles Times
The Nation
National Geographic
Newsweek
The New York Times
The New York Times Magazine
The Oregonian
The Spectator
Sporting News
Sports Illustrated
Time
U.S. News & World Report
The Wall Street Journal
The World Monitor
World Press Review

ABC (Television)
CBS (Television)
CNN News (Television)
NBC (Television)
PBS (Television)

(Japanese:)

Asahi Evening News
Business Japan
Business Tokyo

The Daily Yomiuri
The East
Focus
Friday
The Japan Economic Journal
Japan Journal
Japan Pictorial
Japan Report
The Japan Times
The Japan Times (Weekly
   Overseas Edition)
Liberal Star

Mainichi Daily News
Shukan Manga Times
Spa

Asahi (Television)
KTV (Television)
MBS (Television)
NHK (Japan Broadcasting
   Corporation, Television)
NTV (Television)
TBS (Television)